Essentials of
Health Economics

SECOND EDITION

Diane M. Dewar, PhD

Associate Professor

Department of Health Policy, Management and Behavior

Department of Economics

School of Public Health

University of Albany—State University of New York

Albany, New York

Director, Institute for Health System Evaluation

University at Albany, State University of New York

Albany, New York

JONES & BARTLETT
LEARNING

World Headquarters
Jones & Bartlett Learning
5 Wall Street
Burlington, MA 01803
978-443-5000
info@jblearning.com
www.jblearning.com

Jones & Bartlett Learning books and products are available through most bookstores and online booksellers. To contact Jones & Bartlett Learning directly, call 800-832-0034, fax 978-443-8000, or visit our website, www.jblearning.com.

08385-9

Production Credits
VP, Executive Publisher: David D. Cella
Publisher: Michael Brown
Associate Editor: Lindsey Mawhiney
Associate Editor: Nicholas Alakel
Production Manager: Tracey McCrea
Senior Marketing Manager: Sophie Fleck Teague
Manufacturing and Inventory Control Supervisor: Amy Bacus

Composition: Cenveo Publisher Services
Cover Design: Kristin E. Parker
Rights & Media Research Coordinator: Mary Flatley
Media Development Editor: Shannon Sheehan
Cover Image: © zhu difeng/Shutterstock
Printing and Binding: Edwards Brothers Malloy
Cover Printing: Edwards Brothers Malloy

Library of Congress Cataloging-in-Publication Data
Dewar, Diane M., author.
  Essentials of health economics / Diane M. Dewar.—Second edition.
      p. ; cm.
  Includes bibliographical references and index.
  ISBN 978-1-284-05462-0 (pbk.)
  I. Title.
  [DNLM: 1. Economics, Medical—United States. 2. Delivery of Health Care—economics—United States. 3. Health Care Sector—United States. 4. Insurance, Health—economics—United States. W 74 AA1]
  RA410.53
  338.4'73621—dc23
                          2015014283
6048

Printed in the United States of America
19 18 17 16 15   10 9 8 7 6 5 4 3 2 1

Dedication

*To two men in my life who supported and inspired
me during the endless revision of this text:*
Bill Eichengrun and Jack Rickert.

The *Essential Public Health* Series

Log on to **www.essentialpublichealth.com** for the most current information on the series.

CURRENT AND FORTHCOMING TITLES IN THE *ESSENTIAL PUBLIC HEALTH* SERIES:

Public Health 101: Healthy People–Healthy Populations,
Enhanced Second Edition Includes Navigate Advantage Access—Richard K. Riegelman, MD, MPH, PhD &
  Brenda Kirkwood, MPH, DrPH

Epidemiology 101—Robert H. Friis, PhD

Global Health 101, Third Edition Includes Navigate Advantage Access—Richard Skolnik, MPA

Essentials of Public Health, Third Edition Includes Navigate Advantage Access—Bernard J. Turnock, MD, MPH

Essentials of Health Policy and Law, Third Edition—Joel B. Teitelbaum, JD, LLM & Sara E. Wilensky, JD, MPP

Essentials of Environmental Health, Second Edition—Robert H. Friis, PhD

Essentials of Biostatistics in Public Health, Second Edition—Lisa M. Sullivan, PhD

Essentials of Health Behavior: Social and Behavioral Theory in Public Health, Second Edition—Mark Edberg, PhD

Essentials of Health, Culture, and Diversity: Understanding People, Reducing Disparities—Mark Edberg, PhD

Essentials of Planning and Evaluation for Public Health Programs Includes Navigate Advantage Access—Karen Marie
  Perrin, MPH, PhD

Essentials of Health Information Systems and Technology Includes Navigate Advantage Access—Jean A. Balgrosky,
  MPH, RHIA

Essentials of Public Health Communication—Claudia Parvanta, PhD; Patrick Remington, MD, MPH; Ross Brownson,
  PhD; & David E. Nelson, MD, MPH

Essentials of Public Health Ethics—Ruth Gaare Bernheim, JD, MPH; James F. Childress, PhD; Richard J. Bonnie, JD;
  & Alan L. Melnick, MD, MPH, CPH

Essentials of Management and Leadership in Public Health—Robert Burke, PhD & Leonard Friedman, PhD, MPH

Essentials of Public Health Preparedness—Rebecca Katz, PhD, MPH

Essentials of Global Community Health—Jaime Gofin, MD, MPH & Rosa Gofin, MD, MPH

ACCOMPANYING CASE BOOKS AND READINGS

Essential Case Studies in Public Health: Putting Public Health into Practice—Katherine Hunting, PhD, MPH & Brenda L.
  Gleason, MA, MPH

Essential Readings in Health Behavior: Theory and Practice—Mark Edberg, PhD

ABOUT THE EDITOR:
Richard K. Riegelman, MD, MPH, PhD, is Professor of Epidemiology-Biostatistics, Medicine, and Health Policy, and Founding Dean of The George Washington University Milken Institute School of Public Health in Washington, DC. He has taken a lead role in developing the Educated Citizen and Public Health initiative which has brought together arts and sciences and public health education associations to implement the Institute of Medicine of the National Academies' recommendation that "...all undergraduates should have access to education in public health." Dr. Riegelman also led the development of The George Washington's undergraduate major and minor and currently teaches "Public Health 101" and "Epidemiology 101" to undergraduates.

Contents

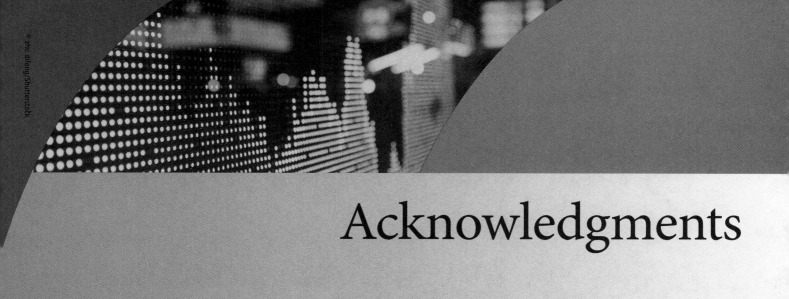

Acknowledgments

As the sole author of this book, I take full responsibility for its contents. However, a project of this size could not be completed by a single person. I am grateful to the numerous graduate and undergraduate students at the University at Albany who used sections of this book in manuscript form. Also, Shayla Golden's work on the graphics used throughout the chapters was priceless.

I could have never completed the book without the support and understanding of my family and friends. Thank you all for your patience while this *Second Edition* was developed.

Prologue

Money talks and we need to listen if we are going to improve our health system. To understand what is being said, students in public health, health administration, and clinical health professions, as well as undergraduates trying to understand these fields, must appreciate the basic principles of economics and their application to health economics.

Essentials of Health Economics provides a concise step-by-step approach to appreciating the key principles and applications of economics. It introduces readers to the principles of economics as they apply to health systems. It then relates these principles to current healthcare and public health issues. Students come away with the tools and concepts needed to understand the debates about the future of the U.S. health system.

Dr. Dewar's style is approachable and intuitive. It is accessible and appropriate for undergraduates, clinically oriented students, and those in related fields. It does not require complicated mathematical formulae and emphasizes common-sense explanations. It does not require previous courses in economics or mathematics. However, it does require an interest in understanding how the world really works and how principles of economics can be used to improve the health system. Readers will carry away an enduring understanding that will serve them well as public health professionals, healthcare administrators, clinicians, or educated and interested citizens.

This *Second Edition* includes important information on the healthcare reforms currently faced at the state, national, and international levels as well as updated system-level statistics and organizational models to allow a timely approach to the study of the public healthcare system through the lens of economics. The *Second Edition* will help students to understand the healthcare system and use that knowledge to improve it.

Health economics is not the dismal science that once described economics. It is an everyday tool that will help readers find their way through the maze of public health and healthcare issues. Give it a try—it is well worth the time.

Richard Riegelman, MD, MPH, PhD
Editor, *Essential Public Health* Series

Preface

The *Second Edition* of this book addresses the important economic and public health policy issues that serve as the background for the healthcare debate concerning access to a healthcare system dominated by increasing resource pressures.

The primary goals of this book are to enable undergraduate students and graduate-level noneconomists in related fields to:

1. Recognize the relevance of economics to health care and apply economic reasoning to better understand health care and health-related issues.
2. Understand the mechanisms of healthcare delivery in the United States and other countries within broad social and economic contexts.
3. Explore the changing nature of health care, health-related technology, and workforce planning and their implications for medical practice and public health policy.
4. Analyze public health policy issues in the healthcare sector from an economic perspective.

To accomplish these goals, the second edition's 18 chapters are organized into the following five parts.

PART I: WHAT IS HEALTH ECONOMICS?

The text begins with a basic overview of the U.S. healthcare system that emphasizes economic issues that affect healthcare delivery and finance. Chapter 1 examines the main system-level issues and the organization of the system. Chapter 2 demonstrates the usefulness of economics in understanding healthcare issues.

PART II: HEALTHCARE MARKETS

Part II examines the competitive market in Chapter 3, the "failures" of the competitive framework in an expanded Chapter 4, as well as the role of government interventions to correct for failures in the competitive market in Chapter 5.

PART III: DEMAND

Part III examines the demand side of the healthcare economy. Chapters 6 and 7 present the factors that influence the demands for health and health care. They explore the observed patterns in the quality and price of health care. Chapter 8 discusses the market for health insurance, including the private and social insurance models. Chapter 9 provides a discussion of health disparities that place increasing pressures for equity on U.S. healthcare expenditures.

PART IV: SUPPLY

Part IV discusses various aspects of the supply side of the healthcare economy. Chapter 10 describes the factors that influence the overall supply of health care, whereas Chapter 11 addresses the underlying production and costs that drive supply. Chapter 12 presents the market for healthcare personnel—namely, physicians and nurses—as well as the factors that influence the behavior of healthcare personnel. Chapter 13 explores the role of technological innovation and diffusion in the healthcare sector, the latest technological innovations used in the U.S. health economy, and the reasons why technology is a major factor in the rising costs of health care.

PART V: EVALUATING THE HEALTHCARE SYSTEM

This final part explores analytical methods of evaluation as well as the role of healthcare reform in the attempt to contain costs in the healthcare economy. Chapter 14 presents the models for economic evaluation and Chapter 15 compares the healthcare systems of the United States, Canada, Germany, and the United Kingdom. Chapter 16 discusses health system issues across various countries and their motivations for healthcare reform. Chapter 17 is an expanded chapter that presents healthcare reform motivations and initiatives at the state and national levels, including cases on Massachusetts and Vermont, as well as the rationale for implementation of the Affordable Care Act. Chapter 18 summarizes the major lessons learned from the economic approach to public health policy and makes recommendations to reform the healthcare system.

PEDAGOGICAL FEATURES AND LEVEL

There is tremendous excitement in the healthcare field, such as the transformation of organizational arrangements, medical technology advances, the development of new healthcare financing mechanisms, and the evaluation of the healthcare system policies that lend themselves to economic analysis. This *Second Edition* includes more information about healthcare reforms currently faced at the state, national, and international levels as well as updated system-level statistics to allow a timely approach to the study of the public healthcare system through the lens of economics. Students and faculty will be able to grasp the importance and relevance of health economics as well as how it relates to more general analysis of health policy issues through numerous examples and cases throughout the text. The *Second Edition* also includes notable health economists and other economists who contributed to health economics so that readers may grasp the many avenues and methods that are included in the field of economics. This book will have wide appeal among students of public health and health administration because it conveys the essence of the economic issues at hand while avoiding complicated methodological issues that would interest only students of economics.

This text is written with the nonspecialist in mind while focusing on how to conduct descriptive, explanatory, and evaluative economics in a systematic way. This book is accessible to undergraduates and those in related fields at the graduate level who do not have much prior knowledge of health economics or mathematics. It will be a useful introductory text in health economics that does not require any other economics prerequisites. The text would be appropriate for students in the following areas: in a school of public health; as an introductory course in health economics in an economics department; in a medical, nursing, or pharmacy school; or in a health administration program.

Diane M. Dewar

About the Author

Diane M. Dewar, PhD, is an associate professor in the Department of Health Policy, Management and Behavior, School of Public Health, and the Department of Economics at the University at Albany, State University of New York. She is also the university's director of the Institute for Health System Evaluation. She has more than 20 years of teaching experience that includes graduate courses in health economics and health policy and economic evaluation methods, as well as undergraduate courses in microeconomics, macroeconomics, econometrics, health economics, comparative health policy, introductory sociology, and introductory psychology.

Professor Dewar received her PhD in economics from the University at Albany, with concentrations in health economics and econometrics. She is a recipient of the William Waters Research Award from the Association of Social Economists, honorable mention for the Aetna Susan B. Anthony Award for Research on Older Women from the Gerontological Section of the American Public Health Association, and past president of the Public Health Honor Society, Delta Omega, Alpha Gamma Chapter. She has been a principal investigator or co-investigator on grants from the Agency for Healthcare Research and Quality, the Robert Wood Johnson Foundation, the Kaiser Family Foundation, and the Centers for Disease Control and Prevention. She was chair of the National Fellowship Panel of the American Association of University Women, has served on the Agency for Healthcare Research and Quality grant review study groups, and serves on the Health Economics Committee of the Medical Care Section of the American Public Health Association.

Professor Dewar has provided extensive service to the university community. For these efforts, she is the recipient of the University at Albany Excellence in Academic Service Award, as well as the State University of New York Chancellor's Award for Academic Excellence.

Professor Dewar's experience in the book development process includes serving as a reviewer of numerous economics and health policy textbook proposals and manuscripts from such publishers as John Wiley and Sons, Jossey-Bass, and Worth. She also has contributed chapters to numerous edited volumes.

Professor Dewar is also an ad-hoc reviewer for journals that include *Medical Care, Annals of Internal Medicine, CHEST,* and *Critical Care Medicine.* She has authored or coauthored many articles and book chapters regarding technology assessments for those with respiratory diseases, health insurance access, and the social economy of medical care. She is also a two-time recipient of letters of commendation from the *Annals of Internal Medicine* and *CHEST* for her service as a referee for these journals.

PART I

What Is Health Economics?

CHAPTER 1

Overview of the U.S. Healthcare System

LEARNING OBJECTIVES

By the end of this chapter, the student will be able to:

1. Describe the healthcare system.
2. Identify the reason why individuals demand health care.
3. Explain the role of insurance.
4. Distinguish between individual versus population health.

INTRODUCTION

In this chapter, the student will learn to appreciate the complexity of the market-oriented healthcare system of the United States. Many issues involving healthcare delivery, financing, and access are introduced as well as their influence on health status.

SYSTEM ISSUES

The U.S. health system is a complicated relationship among providers, consumers, and financers of care. The concerns of the system revolve around three issues: cost, quality, and access. Reform efforts have increased exponentially at the national and state levels as fewer Americans have financial access to care, with increased system-level expenditures resulting in nonoptimal health outcomes. One of the most sweeping reforms at the national level is the Affordable Care Act under the Obama administration. These reform efforts attempt to correct the issues of poor access, higher costs for technologically driven care, and variable quality in the most advanced healthcare system in the world.

American healthcare surveys have found that the majority of consumers rate their health care as "excellent" or "very

good." Those with poorer ratings had, among other indicators, no health insurance and no regular healthcare providers (Chou, Wang, Finney Rutten, Moser, & Hesse, 2010). These survey results are consistent between telephone and online surveys of Americans (Bethell, Fiorillo, Lansky, Hendryx, & Knickman, 2004). However, this high level of satisfaction can be a double-edged sword in that increased consumer satisfaction with care is associated with increased inpatient healthcare utilization and pharmaceutical expenditures, as well as increased mortality (Fenton, Jerant, Bertakis, & Franks, 2012). This implies that the perceived improvements in health care can lead to associated increased healthcare expenditures in the system at the expense of other sectors and economic needs.

On the provider side, U.S. physicians note that they are enjoying higher-quality health care and increased autonomy in many settings but lower job satisfaction due to the primarily profit-driven healthcare system (Scheurer, McKean, Miller, & Wetterneck, 2009; Tyssen, Palmer, Solberg, Voltmer, & Frank, 2013). As the system becomes more strained, providers spend more time and effort not on individual patient needs but on more organizationally driven incentives.

HEALTH CARE

Experts themselves are divided on the cause of rising healthcare expenditures. Of the several drivers of costs, many believe that the push occurs from technologically driven care, while others point to the broader role of insurance and health care in areas previously considered to be social or lifestyle problems (Blumenthal, Stremikis, & Cutler, 2013). Regardless of the causes of rising healthcare expenditures, the United States trails behind many countries in health status measures.

© Amble Design/Shutterstock

The health sector is a leading employer in the United States. As seen in 2011, 15.7% of the domestic workforce is in healthcare-related occupations, and spending passed the $2.7 trillion mark, which is more than 17.9% of the U.S. gross domestic product (Moses et al., 2013). Much of the expenditures—31% overall spending in health care—is a result of administrative waste (Evans, 2013). While spending increases have slowed since 2002 to a rate of 3% per year, the growth of this sector exceeds any other sector of the economy (Moses et al., 2013). This stabilization is due to the very slow increase in use and intensity of care since 2010 (Martin, Lassman, Washington, Cailtin, & National Health Expenditure Accounts Team, 2012).

Due to the increasing size and importance of the healthcare sector, more scrutiny is being placed on the costs, quality of, and access to health care and the resulting health outcomes than ever before.

HEALTH STATUS

In public health terms, the World Health Organization has defined health as "a complete state of physical, mental and social well-being, and not merely the absence of illness or disease" (Jacobs & Rapoport, 2004, p. 23). **Population health** is a focus of public health that has a very general connotation. Kindig and Stoddart (2003) have defined it as "the health outcomes of a group of individuals, including the distribution of such outcomes within the group" (p. 380). This is an emerging area, with some debate as to whether there is a difference between population health and public health (Kindig, 2007). Regardless of how the population health is defined or measured, the concept is essential for determining and reducing health disparities.

Individual health and population health can be viewed as independent concepts, but they are really more related than previously thought. For example, individual health status is a function of lifestyle choices, sociodemographics, environmental factors, biology, and medical care. Many of these determinants are shaped by the community and environment in which a person lives (Arah, 2009).

Individual health status can be measured by a physical examination of the person along any of several dimensions, such as the presence of illness, risk factors for mortality or morbidity, and overall health as determined through visual and biological testing. Individual health status may also be measured through individual perceptions on a variety of dimensions, such as physical disability, emotional status, pain assessment, and overall perception of wellness.

On both the population and individual perspectives, the health status of the U.S. population is mediocre, with increasing incidence and prevalence of chronic disease across the life span and relatively high infant mortality rates. These issues also drive the increased interest in reforming the American healthcare system.

© Voronin76/Shutterstock

SUMMARY

The goal of this book is to demonstrate how economics can provide insights into the study of human behavior as it is influenced by constraints and financial incentives. As concerns rise over the increasing size of the health economy relative to other sectors, as well as the relatively poor health of the population, economic analysis becomes an increasingly important tool in the study of factors that affect the health and health care of the American public.

KEY WORDS

- **Individual health**
- **Population health**

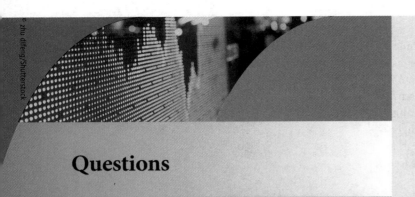

Questions

1. Specify a relationship between health care and health.

2. What is the difference between individual and population health? Which perspective would a physician use and which perspective would a public health worker use? Explain.

PROFILE: KENNETH J. ARROW

Kenneth J. Arrow was born in New York City in 1921 and pursued his undergraduate education at City College of New York. He graduated in 1940 with a BS in social science and a major in mathematics, which later led to an MA in mathematics from Columbia University in 1941. His subsequent graduate work began in economics at the same university.

Arrow's graduate studies were interrupted from 1942 through 1946 due to his service in World War II, where he was a weather officer in the United States Army Air Corps and worked on research projects. His first published paper was produced at this time, "On the Optimal Use of Winds for Flight Planning."

During the years 1946 to 1949, Arrow was a part-time graduate student at Columbia University, a research associate at the Cowles Commission for Research and Economics at the University of Chicago, and an assistant professor of economics at the University of Chicago. In these years, he focused on Pareto efficiency and social choice theory.

In 1948, Arrow was appointed acting assistant professor of economics and statistics at Stanford University and remained there until 1968, eventually becoming professor of economics, statistics, and operations research. He also held numerous posts at institutions such as the United States Council of Economic Advisors, Churchill College (Cambridge), and the Institute for Advanced Studies in Vienna.

In 1968, Arrow moved to Harvard University as a professor of economics and remained there until 1979. In 1979, he returned to Stanford University as Joan Kenney Professor of Economics and professor of operations research. In 1991, he retired as professor emeritus.

Most of his research deals with information as an economic variable related to its production and use. In 1963 and in later papers, he showed that special characteristics of health care and health insurance can be explained by differences in information perceived or obtained by providers and patients. His work, which is highly influential in health economics and beyond, has resulted in numerous awards and honors, including the John Bates Clark Medal of the American Economic Association, membership in the National Academy of Sciences, and Fellow of the Econometric Society. Arrow received the Sveriges Riksbank Prize in Economic Sciences in Memory of Alfred Nobel in 1972.

Data from Nobelprize.org. (2015). *Kenneth J. Arrow: Biographical.* Retrieved April 2, 2014, from http://www.nobelprize.org/nobel_prizes/economic-sciences/laureates/1972/arrow-bio.html.

REFERENCES

Arah, O. A. (2009). On the relationship between individual and population health. *Medical Health Care Philosophy, 12*(3), 235–244.

Bethell, C., Fiorillo, J., Lansky, D., Hendryx, M., & Knickman, J. (2004). Online consumer surveys as a methodology for assessing the quality of the United States health care system. *Journal of Medical Internet Research, 6*(1), e2.

Blumenthal, D., Stremikis, K., & Cutler, D. (2013). Health care spending—A giant slain or sleeping? *New England Journal of Medicine, 369*(26), 2551–2557.

Chou, W. Y., Wang, L. C., Finney Rutten, L. J., Moser, R. P., & Hesse, B. W. (2010). Factors associated with Americans' ratings of health care quality: What do they tell us about the raters and the health care system? *Journal of Health Communication, 15*(Suppl 3), 147–156.

Evans, R. G. (2013). Waste, economists and American healthcare. *Healthcare Policy, 9*(2), 12–20.

Fenton, J. J., Jerant, A. F., Bertakis, K. D., & Franks, P. (2012). The cost of satisfaction: A national study of patient satisfaction, health care utilization, expenditures, and mortality. *Archives of Internal Medicine, 172*(5), 405–411.

Jacobs, P., & Rapoport, J. (2004). *The economics of health and medical care* (5th ed.). Burlington, MA: Jones & Bartlett Learning.

Kindig, D. A. (2007). Understanding population health terminology. *Milbank Quarterly, 85*(1), 139–161.

Kindig, D., & Stoddart, G. (2003). What is population health? *American Journal of Public Health, 93*(3), 380–383.

Martin, A. B., Lassman, D., Washington, B., Cailtin, A., & National Health Expenditure Accounts Team. (2012). Growth in US health spending remained slow in 2010; health share of gross domestic product was unchanged from 2009. *Health Affairs, 31*(1), 208–219.

Moses, H., III, Matheson, D. H. M., Dorsey, E. R., George, B. P., Sadoff, D., & Yoshimura, S. (2013). The anatomy of health care in the United States. *Journal of the American Medical Association, 310*(18), 1947–1964.

Scheurer, D., McKean, S., Miller, J., & Wetterneck, T. (2009). U.S. physician satisfaction: A systematic review. *Journal of Hospital Medicine, 4*(9), 560–568.

Tyssen, R., Palmer, K. S., Solberg, I. B., Voltmer, E., & Frank, E. (2013). Physicians' perceptions of quality of care, professional autonomy, and job satisfaction in Canada, Norway, and the United States. *BMC Health Services Research, 13*, 516.

CHAPTER **2**

The Role of Economics

INTRODUCTION

Economics provides a framework to study the implications of individual behavior in decisions concerning efficient consumption and production given scarce resources. This chapter discusses the basic terms and ideas of economics as they apply to health care.

HEALTH ECONOMICS AS A FIELD OF ECONOMICS

Health economists examine a wide range of issues, from the nature and production of health and demand for health care, the production of health care, and the market for health care to the economic evaluation of policies and interventions. In his seminal work, Grossman (1972) developed an economic framework for the study of healthcare demand where health care is just one factor used to produce health, with others being income, wealth, biology/genetics, education, sociodemographics/environment, and lifestyle choices. These factors interact with the effectiveness of health care to improve or maintain health status.

In the United States, health economists focus on the health services market. The demand for health services includes consumption and production aspects. The consumption aspects are the perceptions of looking and feeling healthy. The production aspect is the investment in human capital. Factors affecting the demand for medical care include patient demographics, health insurance, prices of the health care in question as well as prices of substitute services or services that are complementary to the use of the good or service in question, and the role of providers in prescribing the services. The supply of health care is determined by factors such as input markets, technology, size of the healthcare market in question, and managerial effectiveness. The demand and supply functions for health care intersect with one another to establish market equilibrium, as denoted in **Figure 2-1**. Markets are able to efficiently allocate scarce resources for the healthcare services in question by establishing a market clearing price level.

Analysis of the overall goals and objectives regarding equity and efficiency of the healthcare system is the scope of macroeconomic evaluations. For example, how does the U.S. healthcare system compare with other countries in terms of cost, access, quality, and outcomes? In these evaluations, trends in healthcare expenditures and production are analyzed and compared frequently to other healthcare systems around the world. Cost, access, and quality of health care and associated population health outcomes are considered in later chapters.

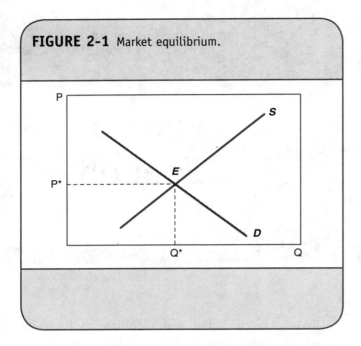

FIGURE 2-1 Market equilibrium.

THE IMPORTANCE OF HEALTH ECONOMICS

Economic analysis of the healthcare market is important due to the sheer size of the market in the overall economy (Evans, 2013; Reinhardt, Hussey, & Anderson, 2004). As Grossman posits (1972), on a micro level health care is one way of modifying the incidence and effect of ill health and disease as it interacts with other determinants of health production. Economic analysis offers ways to predict healthcare utilization and supply using a macro (system) and micro (individual) framework.

Further, healthcare provision and policy interventions are influenced by system constraints, social norms, and political–economic realities. Global, national, and local reforms and interventions are informed by economic theory. In countries ranging from the profit-driven system in the United States to centrally planned health economies as found in Britain, economic analysis is essential to understand and predict efficient levels of production and consumption of health care as well as to understand the effects of financial incentives on market outcomes.

Health economics is a field of economics that analyzes the behavior of consumers, producers, financers, and the role of government in the healthcare economy. Although health economics is based in neoclassical economic theory, it also draws on related disciplines such as epidemiology, psychology, and sociology in understanding decision making in the health economy. Like other forms of economics, it also draws on statistics and mathematics in developing and testing theories related to the markets under consideration.

KEY ECONOMIC CONCEPTS

The following basic terms are used in economics as well as health economics:

- **Scarcity**: Addresses the problem of limited resources and the need to make choices given unlimited human wants.
- **Opportunity costs**: In microeconomics, given limited resources, choices must be made among mutually exclusive alternatives. The cost associated with the choice is the value of the foregone alternative. This valuation is a crucial component of determining and ensuring efficiency in the market. For example, the opportunity cost of purchasing this text is the money that could have been spent on leisure pursuits instead.
- **Marginal analysis**: Recognizes that choices are made incrementally. In this environment, optimal decision making is based on the incremental benefits and the costs of an alternative, where, in equilibrium, the incremental benefits equal the incremental costs of the alternative.
- **Market**: The market accomplishes its pricing and exchange of goods and services through a free-price system. Prices increase when more is desired, and they decrease when less is desired. The market reaches equilibrium when the quantity supplied of a good or service equals the quantity demanded of a good or service at a given price level.
- **Supply and demand**: Serves as the foundation of price determination in microeconomic analysis. In equilibrium, price converges where the quantity demanded by the consumer equals the quantity supplied by the producer.
- **Competition**: Productive resources are allocated to highly valued and specialized uses and therefore encourage efficiency. Competition takes production out of the hands of the less competitive and places it into the hands of the more efficient—constantly promoting the efficient methods of production. This causes firms to develop new, similar products cheaply, improving the selection of products available to consumers.
- **Efficiency**: Measures how well resources are being used to maximize the production of goods and services. Economic efficiency occurs if nothing more can be achieved given limited resources.
- **Market failure**: Arises when the free market fails to promote efficient allocation of goods and services. Sources of "failures"—of the free market—include natural monopoly, oligopoly, externalities of production or consumption, public goods, and incomplete information.

THE ECONOMIC FRAMEWORK

Economics is the oldest social science that attempts to explain human behavior. It is unique among other social sciences in that it explains constrained optimization. In other words, economics explains how scarce resources are allocated among alternatives to satisfy unlimited human wants. This analysis stems from the concept of scarcity, implying that using resources in one alternative has the trade-off of not being able to use the same resources in a competing activity or alternative. For example, if more resources are applied to the health economy they cannot be simultaneously applied to another sector of the economy due to competing demands.

The key assumption of economics that makes this discipline different from other social sciences is that decisions to choose an alternative given scarcity are determined rationally. The implication of rationality is that the choices made are optimal for achieving the intended goals of the producer or consumer. Here, choices are made to maximize profits or utility/satisfaction, for example. Often, particularly in the healthcare market, decision makers formulate choices based on incomplete information that can yield nonoptimal results compared to when information is freely available.

THE ECONOMIC MODEL

As in any model building, it is necessary to simplify the behaviors of market participants into their essential parts and to tease out extraneous factors. Simplification is accomplished through the construction of models.

Microeconomic models examine the behavior of individual decision makers, such as consumers, producers, and government agents. For example, microeconomic models are used to study how consumer demand for health care can be determined by changes in insurance copayments or how hospitals provide services if faced with a nursing shortage.

Economic Optimization

Optimization is the determination of the best action given the decision maker's goals and objectives. For example, producers are faced with maximization of output or minimization of cost, and consumers are faced with maximization of utility/satisfaction. Constrained optimization takes into account scarcity of resources. For example, how much medical care should a consumer purchase given that the price of the service has changed and that there are other goods and services that the person would need to purchase with a limited income at a given time period?

The traditional framework in economic optimization is the neoclassical model with its assumption of rational decision making. Firms maximize output given technology and the prices of the resources; consumers maximize utility or satisfaction from consuming various amounts of goods and services given limited income and the prices of goods and services considered in a given period. This relatively independent behavior on the part of economic actors leads to equilibrium in the market considered, which is the intersection of the supply and demand curves.

Within this framework, the optimal consumption of goods and services is where the **marginal benefit** from consumption (i.e., the additional benefit received from consuming the next unit of the good or service) equals the **marginal cost** of consumption (i.e., the additional cost of consuming the next unit of a good or service). Individuals will continue to purchase goods or services as long as MB > MC (see **Figure 2-2**). The consumption increases to the point where the additional benefit equals the additional cost of consuming the next unit of a good or service, or the point of break even.

SUMMARY

Several important economic concepts are introduced in this chapter. First, health economics is growing in importance due to the sheer size and scope of the healthcare economy relative to other sectors of the economy. Second, resources are scarce related to relatively unlimited wants. In today's world, trade-offs are inevitable because consumers cannot

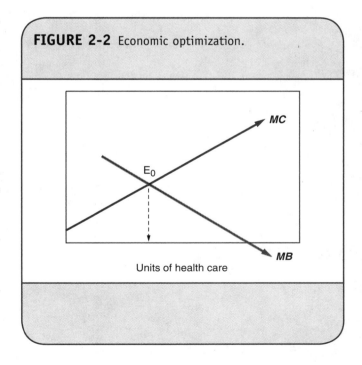

FIGURE 2-2 Economic optimization.

always get what they want. Third, medical decisions involve costs and benefits. Rational decision making results in optimal choices where MB = MC in equilibrium. Fourth, it is important to strike a balance between choices based on opportunity costs. For example, if more is spent on genetic counseling, then less will need to be spent on other services given scarce resources.

KEY WORDS

- **Competition**
- **Efficiency**
- **Equilibrium**
- **Marginal analysis**
- **Marginal benefit**
- **Marginal cost**
- **Market**
- **Market failure**
- **Opportunity costs**
- **Scarcity**
- **Supply and demand**

Questions

1. How does health economics analysis aid in the study of the healthcare economy?

2. One way to choose among alternative treatments of care delivery models is through economic optimization. Discuss this concept.

3. Why is marginal analysis important in economics?

PROFILE: JAMES J. HECKMAN

James J. Heckman was born in Chicago in 1944 and spent his early and high school years in the South and Colorado, respectively. While in high school, he worked under the guidance of physicist Frank Oppenheimer, brother of J. Robert Oppenheimer, who was the scientific director of the Manhattan Project that developed the atomic bomb in World War II. During this time, Heckman learned to appreciate the scientific method and evidence-based theories.

Heckman was an undergraduate at the Colorado College in Colorado Springs, where he majored in mathematics and studied the works of noted economists Adam Smith and Paul Samuelson. He graduated with a BA in mathematics in 1965 and then briefly attended graduate school at the University of Chicago to study economics.

Heckman transferred to Princeton University to study development economics under Arthur Lewis. However, with the growth of microdata in labor statistics, he moved on to study labor economics and econometrics. The econometrics group was very lively at this university and encouraged the application of econometrics to policy problems.

After earning a PhD in economics in 1971, Heckman was offered a position at Columbia University, which was intellectually open and encouraging. Here, he studied the empirical issues of the demand for new, good, and dynamic labor market problems and learned how to write for professional economists.

In 1973, Heckman returned to the University of Chicago and benefitted from numerous intellectual gatherings and the encouragement of colleagues and top-rate students. He also has enjoyed support from the American Bar Foundation, the National Science Foundation, and the National Institutes of Health. Currently, he is the Henry Schultz Distinguished Service Professor of Economics at the University of Chicago, where he also serves as professor in the University of Chicago's Law School and Harris School of Public Policy. He is also a professor at the University College Dublin and a senior research fellow in the American Bar Foundation. In 2000, Heckman won the Sveriges Riksbank Prize in Economic Sciences in Memory of Alfred Nobel.

Data from Nobelprize.org. (2015). James J. Heckman: Biographical. Retrieved May 6, 2014, from http://www.nobelprize.org/nobel_prizes/economic-sciences/laureates/2000/heckman-bio.html.

REFERENCES

Evans, R. G. (2013). Waste, economists and American healthcare. *Healthcare Policy, 9*(2), 12–20.

Grossman, M. (1972). On the concept of health capital and the demand for health. *Journal of Political Economy, 80*(2), 223–255.

Reinhardt, U. E., Hussey, P. S., & Anderson, G. F. (2004). U.S. health care spending in an international context. *Health Affairs, 23*(3), 10–25.

PART II

Healthcare Markets

The Competitive Market

LEARNING OBJECTIVES

By the end of this chapter, the student will be able to:

1. Describe perfect competition and how it relates to the health-care market.
2. Explain the concept of supply and demand and provide an example related to health care.
3. Show how shocks in exogenous factors underlying supply and demand can change equilibrium price and quantity.
4. Use comparative statics to analyze changes in supply pricing of goods in the healthcare market.

INTRODUCTION

In this chapter, the student will come to understand the role of the market in analyzing economic phenomena. The role of suppliers and consumers in the healthcare market will also be examined. In doing so, the concepts of perfect competition, supply and demand, and comparative statics will be covered.

PERFECT COMPETITION

The history of perfect competition has its roots in Adam Smith's *An Inquiry into the Nature and Causes of the Wealth of Nations* (McNulty, 1967). In this type of market, no one individual has the power to set the price of a good or service in question. The four characteristics of perfect competition are as follows:

1. Many sellers possessing tiny market shares
2. A homogeneous product
3. No barriers to entry
4. Perfect consumer information

An example of free-market entry is that a single supplier of alcohol swabs may be reluctant to increase the price if the resulting higher profits entice new firms offering alcohol swabs to enter the market. The high degree of competition in a perfectly competitive market means that one firm's production decision has no meaningful effect on the overall performance of the industry. Therefore, the individual producer or consumer has no market power.

Perfect Competition and Its Relevance to Health Care

Perfect competition is an abstract model and gold standard that encompasses the four assumptions previously noted. It also involves the assumptions of utility and profit maximization that underlie conventional neoclassical microeconomic analysis. **Utility maximization** is when a consumer strives to get the greatest satisfaction or value from the bundle purchased using the least amount of budgeted money. The objective from the consumer's viewpoint is to get the most total satisfaction or value from the least amount of money spent given the prices of the goods or services faced and the income level of the consumer. **Profit maximization** is a process that firms use to determine the most output given price levels that will yield the most return after production costs and the total cost outlay are taken into account. If either of the assumptions is violated, firms and consumers are unlikely to behave as the perfectly competitive market model predicts and a market failure exists.

When applied to healthcare industries, many of the assumptions of microeconomic analysis and characteristics of perfect competition often do not fit well (Gaynor & Town,

2011). Several conditions exist in the healthcare market that lead to failures of the perfectly competitive model. First, licensure reduces the number of providers in the market because it creates a barrier to entry and decreases potential competition. Second, consumers typically lack perfect information about prices and the technical aspects of medical services, which may lead to physicians practicing opportunistically rather than in the best interests of the patient, often overprescribing or under-prescribing care depending on payment incentives. Third, regulations for health and safety can lead to barriers to entry in the marketplace, where only certain types of firms may be able to compete in the market due to quality or infrastructure goals in the market (Dranove & Satterthwaite, 2000).

While deviations from the characteristics of perfect competition and assumptions of microeconomic theory may make it inappropriate to use the model to evaluate the healthcare market, the perfectly competitive model fulfills an important purpose: It can serve as a gold standard to which other market models can be compared in terms of changes in prices and outputs in equilibrium.

SUPPLY AND DEMAND

To maximize utility or satisfaction, each person consumes goods or services to the point that **marginal private benefit** (MPB) equals the price of the good or service in question. MPB is the additional benefit gained from the consumption of the next unit for the individual. The profit-maximizing firm will produce up to the point where **marginal private cost** (MPC) equals price of the good or service. MPC is the additional cost of producing the next unit for the firm. The market clearing price and the quantity of the good or service occurs when the MPC equals the MPB, with price being the coordinating device (MPB = P = MPC). This can be shown graphically as in **Figure 3-1**.

Suppose that the supply and demand in Figure 3-1 represents the market for generic antidepressants. The per-unit price of the generic is shown on the vertical axis and the quantity, q, is shown on the horizontal axis. The market demand curve, D, is downward sloping, reflecting the substitution and income effects seen with a lower price for a product. The demand curve also shows the diminishing MPB of consuming additional units of the generic drug. The supply curve, S, is upward sloping, showing that the MPC is increasing with the production of additional units of the drug. MPC reflects the variable costs of producing the good or service, which includes the costs of labor and the materials needed as output is increased. MPC increases in the short run because not all inputs are fully flexible in the time period considered. In other words, inefficiencies occur as inputs that are less fully trained for the production of the good or service in question are added to the production of the good or service. Because of the higher MPC, a higher price is needed to encourage production of more of the drug. The market supply curve is derived by horizontally summing across all firms the portion of the marginal cost curve that lies above the minimum point of the average variable cost curve.

In equilibrium, or the **market clearing condition** (i.e., a price level where there are no surpluses or shortages of the good or service in the market), price and quantity of the drug are at the point where demand intersects supply, or where quantity demanded equals quantity supplied at a given price. By definition, equilibrium occurs when there is no tendency to change. At P_0, consumers are willing and able to

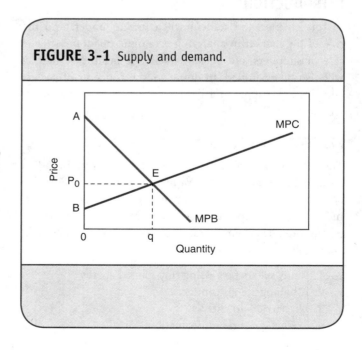

FIGURE 3-1 Supply and demand.

purchase q_0 units of the drug because that represents the utility-maximizing amount. In addition, producers of the drug provide q_0 units on the market at this price because that is the profit-maximizing amount. Therefore, both consumers and producers are satisfied with the exchange because both can purchase or sell their desired quantities at a price of P_0 and will have no incentive to change. The area under the demand curve above price, P_0, (P_0AE_0) measures consumer surplus, which reflects the net benefit to consumers from engaging in the free exchange. **Consumer surplus** is the difference between what a consumer is willing to pay and what the consumer actually pays for some level of output. Analogously, the area below price but above the supply curve (BP_0E_0) represents the **producer surplus**, which is the net benefit to producers from the free-market exchange. Producer surplus measures the difference between the actual price received by the seller and the required price as reflected by the MPC for each additional unit produced. The sum of the consumer and producer surplus is the total net gains from free-market trade for the consumers and producers.

COMPARATIVE STATICS

The demand and supply framework can be used to examine how surpluses and shortages of goods and services can occur and to study changes in prices and quantities of goods and services in various markets. This is **comparative statics** analysis and examines how changes in market conditions influence the positions of the demand and supply curves and cause the equilibrium price and quantity to change. As the demand and supply curves shift due to changes in exogenous determinants of the supply and demand functions, the price and output effects can be charted by comparing the different equilibria. Several factors, such as the number of buyers, consumer tastes, income, and the price of substitutes and complements, affect the position of the market demand curve in a

given period and therefore cause shifts in the demand curve if one or more of these determinants change. Analogously, factors such as the input prices, technology, and number of producers change the position of the supply curve by affecting the cost of production in a given period. A change in any one of these factors shifts the corresponding supply curve and alters the price and output of goods and services in the market.

For example, suppose that the number of producers has increased for the production of generic antidepressants, so that this curve shifts to the right and it is cheaper to produce the product at every price. This is because there is more produced at every original price level. In **Figure 3-2**, note that this causes a temporary surplus of the area EF in the market as price remains constant. A surplus develops because, at the initial price, the quantity supplied on the new supply curve S_1 is greater than the quantity demanded at that price. However, price does not remain constant in a competitive market and is eventually lowered from P_0 to P_1, for example, to reduce inventory costs. The lower price creates an incentive for consumers to purchase more of the drug in the market, and quantity demanded increases from q_0 to q_1. Therefore, under normal conditions, supply and demand models predict that a lower price and higher quantity of the drug are associated with improved technology, all else constant.

Price serves three important market clearing functions. First, price provides useful information to both consumers and producers regarding the relative value of a good or

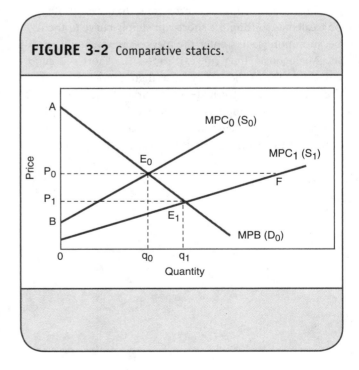

FIGURE 3-2 Comparative statics.

service in the market. For example, increases in price imply that there is an increase in the value of the good or service in question. Second, price serves as a rationing device, distributing the goods and services to consumers who value them most, denoting the willingness to pay for the good or service in question. Third, price acts as an incentive mechanism, encouraging more resources to markets with shortages through price increases and fewer resources to markets with surpluses through price decreases.

BARRIERS TO ENTRY

In competitive markets, firms may enter the industry as changes in profits occur. For example, because there are no barriers to entry in a perfectly competitive market, excess profits create an incentive for new firms to enter an industry to obtain a share of the profits, thus driving the price down and inducing more goods or services to be purchased—clearing the market. On the other hand, economic losses create an incentive for firms to leave an industry due to diminished profitability.

Normal economic profits exist when there are no excess profits or losses. When long-run normal profits exist in a perfectly competitive industry, the market is in long-run equilibrium, with firms having no incentive to enter or exit the industry. Normal economic profits result when the revenue generated just covers the opportunity costs of every input used in the production of the good or service in question. In other words, firms break even.

Entry in the long run in response to excess profits can be treated as shifting the short-run supply curve to the right because more sellers enter the market attracted by the profits. Analogously, long-run exit causes the short-run supply curve to shift to the left because there are fewer sellers in the market. For a given demand curve, these adjustments in the short-run supply curve create a change in the price of the good and eventually restore normal profits. Because of entry and exit in the market, it is expected that the typical

perfectly competitive firm earns a normal economic profit in the long run.

The importance of entry and exit in a market can be seen in the following example: Exit of firms helps to eliminate excess resources and producers from the market, creating greater efficiency. Free entry and exit of firms can occur only in perfectly competitive markets because barriers to entry and exit are nonexistent. This implies that firms will freely enter the market as profits occur to the point that profits tend to zero in the long run. Conversely, firms will freely exit the market when losses occur, leading to normal economic profits in the long run.

SUMMARY

In this chapter, perfect competition in health care was examined. Perfect competition means that individual firms are price takers and maximize profits, consumers maximize utility, no barriers to entry or exit exist, and consumers have perfect information. Based on these characteristics, it can be shown that a perfectly competitive market allocates resources efficiently when all social costs and benefits are internalized by those engaged in the market in the form of MPB and MPC. In other words, no **externalities** exist. Changes in supply and demand, as well as some noncompetitive features in the market, were also identified in comparative statics analysis.

KEY WORDS

- **Comparative statics**
- **Consumer surplus**
- **Externalities**
- **Marginal private benefit**
- **Marginal private cost**
- **Market clearing condition**
- **Normal economic profits**
- **Producer surplus**
- **Profit maximization**
- **Utility maximization**

Questions

1. Suppose that the supply curve of healthcare services is perfectly inelastic (i.e., vertical supply curve that is completely nonresponsive to price changes). Analyze the effect of an increase in consumer income on the market price and quantity of the services. Now, suppose that the demand for healthcare services is perfectly inelastic while the supply curve is upward sloping. Analyze the effect of an improvement in the technology of production on the market price of healthcare services.

2. Suppose that health insurance is nonexistent and that all medical markets are perfectly competitive. Use supply and demand analysis to explain the effects of the following changes on the price and output of physician services:
   a. An increase in the wage of clinic-based nurses
   b. The adoption of cost-savings medical technology
   c. Declining consumer income

PROFILE: ADAM SMITH

Adam Smith was born in 1723 in Kirkaldy, Scotland, and began his studies at the University of Glasgow at the age of 14 in moral studies. At this time he was profoundly influenced by the culture and thinking during the Scottish Enlightenment period. In 1740, he graduated and received the distinguished Snell Exhibition scholarship to study at Oxford University's Balliol College.

In 1746, Smith left Oxford due to the university's displeasure with his interest in David Hume's philosophical works, which the university thought were promoting atheist philosophy. Smith returned to Edinburgh and became professor of logic at Glasgow University at the age of 28 in 1751. In 1752, he was awarded professorial chair of moral philosophy at the university.

Smith was an absentminded individual who was awkward socially but had a great reputation as an engaging lecturer. In 1759, he published *The Theory of Moral Sentiments*, a major work that drew attention to other countries such as France and Germany.

In 1763, he resigned from the University of Glasgow and took on a lucrative position as a private tutor to Henry Scot,

the presumptive to the Dukedom of Buccleauch. During this time, he traveled throughout Europe, met with the intellectual elite, and embarked on his most influential work, *An Inquiry into the Nature and Causes of the Wealth of Nations*.

Upon leaving his post as tutor, Smith returned to Kirkcaldy and lived with his aging mother. During this time, *An Inquiry into the Nature and Causes of the Wealth of Nations* was published in 1776. This major work influenced the emergence of modern capitalism and made Smith one of the most influential philosophic writers of modern times.

In 1777, Smith was named lord rector of the University of Edinburgh and, in 1778, he was appointed as the commissioner of customs in Scotland. This post continued until his death in 1790 in Edinburgh.

Data from Heilbroner, R. L. (2015). Adam Smith: Scottish philosopher. Retrieved April 10, 2014, from http://www.britannica.com/EBchecked/topic/549630/Adam-Smith; Rasmussen, H. (2015). the life and works of Adam Smith--A biography of Adam Smith. Retrieved April 10, 2014, from http://economics.about.com/od/famouseconomists/a/adamsmith.htm.

REFERENCES

Dranove, D., & Satterthwaite, M. A. (2000). The industrial organization of health care markets. In A. J. Culyer & J. P. Newhouse, *Handbook of health economics* (Vol. 1A, pp. 1093–1139). New York, NY: Elsevier.

Gaynor, M., & Town, R. J. (2011). *Competition in health care markets* (NBER Working Paper No. 17208). Cambridge, MA: National Bureau of Economic Research.

McNulty, P. J. (1967). A note on the history of perfect competition. *Journal of Political Economy, 75*(4), 395–399.

CHAPTER 4

Noncompetitive Market Models and Market Failures

INTRODUCTION

Most healthcare markets rarely, if ever, achieve Pareto efficiency. **Pareto efficiency**, or Pareto optimality, is defined as a state of allocation of resources in which it is impossible to make any one individual better off without making at least one individual worse off. For example, the First Fundamental Theorem states that every competitive equilibrium is Pareto efficient. This theorem relies crucially on markets being perfectly competitive. Any breakdown in the underlying assumptions, such as freedom of market entry and exit, will lead to distortions in prices, quantities, and social efficiency. The term *market failure* is used to cover all circumstances in which Pareto efficiency is not achieved by the market. The main causes of market failure in health care are described next.

EXTERNALITIES

Externalities, or spillover effects, are costs and benefits incurred in the consumption or production of goods and services that are not borne by the individual consumer or producer. The spillover effects can be positive or negative. When other members of society are affected beneficially by a spillover effect, there is said to be external benefits. When other members of society are affected adversely, there are external costs. For example, activities that cause pollution impose health and cleanup costs on the whole society regardless of the population's lack of activities that led to the pollution, whereas the neighbors of an individual who chooses to get a flu shot may benefit from a reduced risk of a communicable illness spreading to their own houses regardless of whether they too receive a flu shot. If external costs exist, such as the case of pollution, the producer may choose to produce more of the product than would be produced if the producer were required to pay all associated environmental costs. If there are external benefits, such as preventive health care, less of the good may be produced than would be the case if the consumer were to receive payment for the external benefits to others (Laffont, 2008).

Healthcare markets will not lead to Pareto efficiency if there are externalities. In other words, the full marginal costs to society from the production or consumption of health care (SMC) is equal to the private marginal cost (PMC) plus the marginal external cost (MEC), and the marginal benefit to society (SMB) is equal to the private marginal benefit (PMB) plus the marginal external benefit (MEB). Therefore, consumption and production decisions made in the market, which are based on private marginal benefits and costs, will not equal social marginal costs and benefits if the marginal external cost or the marginal external benefit is nonzero (Morris, Devlin, & Parkin, 2007).

There are four types of externality.

1. *External costs of production* (MEC > 0; SMC > PMC). These might arise if a firm producing pharmaceuticals dumps its waste in a river, or pollutes the air. In this case, the pollution caused by the firm will impose a positive external cost on society that is not internalized by the private market price.
2. *External benefits of production* (MEB > 0; SMB > PMB). Imagine a pharmaceutical firm undertaking research to identify a new compound to bring to market. If a promising compound is discovered, this will eventually lead to the publication of scientific papers on the properties of the compound. The research undertaken by the firm may identify useful avenues of research for other firms. In this case, there may be external benefits of production arising from research and development that are not captured in the private pricing system.
3. *External costs of consumption* (MEB < 0; SMB < PMB). The consumption of cigarettes and alcohol may lead to external costs of consumption. In addition to their effects on individual health, their consumption may also have negative effects on the rest of society in terms of passive smoking and antisocial behavior, which are not compensated in the private market.
4. *External costs of consumption* (MEB > 0; SMB > PMB). Public health interventions such as vaccines may have external benefits of consumption because they can have a direct health benefit on others by reducing their chances of ill health. In addition, they are not being compensated in the private market and thus these activities should be subsidized. Given that the market transactions are not internalized by the price of the goods or services in question, when there are external benefits there will be too little consumed or

produced in the market. When there are external costs there will be too much consumed or produced in the market.

PUBLIC GOODS

Public goods are goods that may be jointly consumed by everyone simultaneously. Specifically, public goods have two characteristics. The first is nonrivalry. This means that the consumption of a good or service by one individual will not prevent the consumption of the same good or service by others. The implication is that nonrival goods tend to have large marginal external benefits, which makes them socially desirable but privately unprofitable to provide. Commonly used examples of nonrival goods include street lighting and pavements, where a large number of people can consume the good or service without creating a diminished utility on others simultaneously.

The second characteristic is nonexcludability. This means that it is not possible to provide a good or service to one individual without letting others also consume it. That is, it is not possible to exclude others from consumption. Nonexcludability means that individuals can obtain the benefits from consuming a good without paying for it. A basic example of such a good or service is national defense. Because there is no incentive for individuals to pay for nonexcludable goods, this leads to a free-rider problem in which individuals are unwilling to pay for goods and services if other people are willing to pay for them. The implication is that if everyone free rides then the good or service will not be provided at all, which may lead to a loss to society. An individual may claim to not want nor pay for the good or service but cannot be excluded from the good's or service's benefits.

When goods have these features they will not be provided in the private market due to distortions in private pricing. This is because there is no incentive for private people to pay for them. Generally, public goods are provided by the government, who then compels individuals to finance their provision via some form of taxation. Note the distinction between public goods, which are nonrival and nonexcludable goods or services, and publicly provided goods, which are goods and services that are provided by the government.

Pareto efficiency requires that the level of provision of a public good occurs where SMB = SMC. Because public goods are jointly consumed, the social marginal benefit (SMB) is obtained by summing the private marginal benefits across all individuals. Because people will free ride, the good will be provided by the government and individuals will be compelled to pay the price via taxation.

© jacomstephens/iStock.com

Most healthcare products and services are not public goods because they are both rival and excludable. The receipt of health care by one person will usually exclude another person from consuming the same health care at that time, therefore being rival in consumption. Health care can also be viewed as excludable based on ability to pay or network participation. For example, one person's admission to a hospital bed prevents another from using the same bed. However, there are some healthcare programs that do have public good properties. An example is public health interventions aimed at preventing the spread of bird flu (Morris et al., 2007).

INFORMATION IMPERFECTIONS

Market failure also arises in health care due to imperfect information, which is caused by uncertainty and imperfect knowledge.

Certainty in healthcare markets implies that buyers know exactly what health care they wish to consume, when they want to consume it, and how they can obtain it. Certainty is required for Pareto efficiency because consumers must know the quantity of health care they would like to demand, and providers must know the quantity of health care to provide. If consumers have certainty, they are able to budget their finances in order to afford their consumption. With uncertainty, a market is unable to function properly because consumers and producers do not know how much of a good to demand and supply. They are therefore unable to equate the private marginal benefits with the private marginal costs.

The assumption of certainty may hold for certain aspects of health care. For example, pregnancies may be planned, and it is possible to predict the timing of a birth and the cost of healthcare services required. Therefore, consumers of maternity services will know how much health care to demand, and providers will know how much health care to supply. Preventive services are also planned in many instances, such as annual physicals. However, the consumption of the majority of healthcare services cannot be planned in this way. This is because illness and deteriorations in health are often sudden and unexpected. Therefore, there is uncertainty in the market, and the demand for health care cannot be predicted in advance. Unless consumers and producers are well informed, they may take actions that are not in their best interests and they will be unable to equate private marginal benefits with private marginal costs; therefore, private efficiency (and so Pareto efficiency) is unlikely to be achieved.

The assumption of perfect knowledge on the part of consumers means that they are aware of their health status and all of the options open to them to maintain or improve their health. Although this may be the case for some illnesses, it is clearly not the case for the majority. Therefore, the market for health care is characterized by imperfect knowledge by both the consumers and providers of care. Providers also have imperfect knowledge of the efficacy of a particular treatment for an individual. Unfortunately, perfect knowledge is especially important in the market for health care because making the wrong decision can have much more serious consequences than the decision to, say, consume a meal or obtain preventive health care.

THE MONOPOLY MODEL

If a firm has some market power, the competitive model is not appropriate and a noncompetitive model should be used. The difference between the two models concerns how the individual firm treats market price. In a perfectly competitive market, the individual firm is a price taker. That is, due to the large number of firms in the market, price is beyond the control of a single firm, so each time a perfectly competitive firm sells an additional unit of output, market price measures the additional revenue received. Economists refer to **marginal revenue** (MR) as the additional revenue generated from selling one more unit of a good or service. Therefore, P = MR for a price taker. A noncompetitive firm with some degree of market power, in contrast, faces a downward-sloping demand curve and therefore has some ability to influence the market price. To illustrate how a noncompetitive model can be used to examine firm behavior, a pure monopoly is first considered, which is the opposite of a perfectly competitive market. A pure monopoly is a market where only one producer of a good or service is in the market.

Monopoly Compared to Perfect Competition

A monopoly is the sole provider of a good or service in a well-defined market with no close substitutes. Because it is the only seller in the market, it faces the market demand curve, which is always downward sloping due to substitution and income effects associated with a price change. Given the downward-sloping demand, the only way a monopolist can sell more of the good or service is to lower the price of the product. Assuming that price is the same for all units sold at a point in time, price must be lowered not only for the next unit but for all previous units as well. Due to this, marginal revenue will be less than price at each level of output. For a linear demand curve, it can be shown that marginal revenue has the same intercept but twice the slope of the demand curve. Suppose that the inverse demand is $P = a - bQ$. Total revenue equals $P \times Q$ or $(a - bQ)Q = aQ - bQ^2$. Taking the first derivative of this revenue function with respect to Q will result in $dTR/dQ = MR = a = 2bQ$. This MR function has the same intercept as the demand function (e.g., a) and twice the slope (e.g., 2bQ).

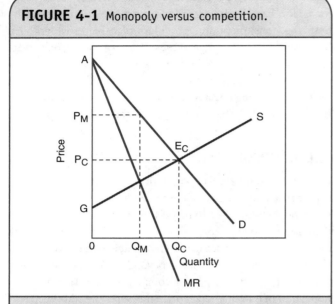

FIGURE 4-1 Monopoly versus competition.

Folland, Sherman; Goodman, Allen C.; Stano, Miron, *Economics of Health and Health Care*, 5th Edition, © 2007. Reprinted/Adapted and Electronically reproduced by permission of Pearson Education, Inc., New York, New York.

Figure 4-1 can be used to show how the equilibrium price and quantity for a monopolist compares to the market price and quantity for a perfectly competitive market. As before, the market can be examined for generic antidepressants. The market demand for the drug is AD. The supply curve is labeled GS and reflects the MPC of producing the drug. Point C represents equilibrium in a perfectly competitive market, where supply and demand curves intersect. The market price and output of the drug equal P_C and Q_C, respectively.

Now suppose that only one firm produces and sells the drug in that same market. Perhaps natural economies of scale led to a monopoly position. Further suppose that a barrier to entry caused by the economies of scale prevents other firms from entering the market. The marginal revenue curve shares the same intercept as the demand curve but has twice the slope. The monopolist chooses the price and quantity so that profits are maximized. Profit maximizing output occurs at Q_m, where MR = MC because producing and selling additional units of the drug always add to revenue than cost up to that point. Beyond Q_m, production is unprofitable because marginal cost, MC, exceeds MR. Therefore, the monopoly outcome is represented by the point M and price charged equals P_m, which is derived from the demand curve for that particular output level.

Notice that the monopolist charges a higher price for a lower quantity of the drug than under the perfectly

competitive conditions. Also note that the consumer surplus is reduced under the monopoly structure, but the producer surplus is increased. The rectangular area reflects the surplus that is transferred from consumers to producers in a market that is controlled by a monopoly. There is also deadweight loss produced by the monopoly and denoted by the triangle. Deadweight loss shows that the value of the units no longer produced is greater than the opportunity costs of the resources used to produce them. This implies that the monopoly underproduces the drug and therefore misallocates society's scarce resources. The cost of the monopoly shows up in the deadweight loss.

Barriers to Entry

For a firm to maintain its market power for an extended period of time, some types of barriers to entry must exist to prevent other firms from entering the industry. Barriers to entry make it costly for new firms to enter the market and do not exist under perfect competition. Technical, regulatory, or legal issues account for these barriers. Exclusive control over an input or economies of scale can lead to barriers because the other firms will not have the resources to make the substitute product. When production exhibits economies of scale, a firm operates on the downward portion of the **long-run average total cost** (ATC) curve, and average cost decreases as output expands. This is shown in **Figure 4-2**. An existing firm in this position has a cost advantage that results from the scale of production. Potential firms cannot effectively compete with the existing firm on a cost basis. The larger existing firm with average costs of C_1 could set its price slightly lower

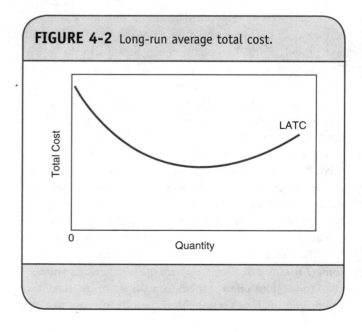

FIGURE 4-2 Long-run average total cost.

than the average cost of the potential entrant, thus discouraging the potential entrant from entering the market and also gaining excess profits. Pricing to deter entry is called *limit pricing*. Therefore, economies of scale can serve as a barrier to entry that insulates the existing firm from potential competitors. Price regulations are often put into place when a firm has a monopoly structure from this position in order to protect consumers from extraordinarily high pricing schemes and large profits to the firm.

Legal restrictions that prevent other firms from entering the market and providing goods or services similar to the existing firms are also barriers to entry. Patents on pharmaceutical products, occupational licensing, and other laws are examples of legal entry barriers in healthcare markets.

MONOPOLISTIC COMPETITION

In the monopolistically competitive structure, there are many firms with minimal barriers to entry. The main distinguishing characteristic of this market model is that firms sell differentiated products. Product differentiation is a result of advertising, real or perceived quality differences, or preferred location. Due to this differentiation, each firm faces a slightly elastic downward-sloping demand curve. Because the demand curve is downward sloping, the firm can have a limited ability to raise price without losing market share. Product differentiation leads to brand loyalty, which allows the firm to raise price and continue to sell the product. All else constant, a more differentiated product leads to a less elastic demand curve for the firm due to the consumer's perception that there are fewer substitute goods or services for the good in question, as well as increased brand loyalty.

In a profit-maximizing monopolistically competitive firm, the elasticity of the demand curve reflects the number of relatively imperfect substitutes for its product. Abilify is a good example of a branded product that faces a downward-sloping demand. Abilify, a mood stabilizer, has some generic competitors, such as the generic for Seroquel, but can charge a higher price because it has a brand name. Given the linear demand, the MR is drawn with the same intercept as the demand curve but twice its slope. The long-run ATC and MC curves all economies and diseconomies of scale.

Given the downward-sloping demand, the individual firm can earn an economic profit in the short run if the price charged is greater than the average total cost at the level of output where MR = MC. However, the limits on barriers to entry lead to the long-run normal profits for this market model. Over time, other firms are attracted to the industry by the possibility of earning economic profits. As more firms

enter the market, each firm sees its market share slowly diminish, which translates to a decreased demand for the product. The demand curve continues to shift to the left for each firm, resulting in prices declining to the point where economic profits equal zero, or price equals **average total costs** (ATC). Demand becomes more elastic and firms are no longer attracted to the industry. This results in economic profits in the long run to be zero.

Competitive Aspects of Product Differentiation

In the perfectly competitive framework, consumers are treated as being perfectly informed about the prices and quantity of all goods and services in the market. The assumption concerning perfect information implies that all firms selling identical products sell at the same lowest possible price. Otherwise, higher-priced firms lose business to lower-priced firms when consumers are perfectly informed.

However, there are costs and benefits to acquiring information. In some situations, people rationally choose to be less than perfectly informed. Positive information costs may result in consumers being reluctant to seek out all available producers of a good or service. As a result, one individual producer faces a less than perfectly elastic demand curve and is able to restrict output and raise price to some extent to attain positive economic profits in the short run. As a result, the price of a good or service in the real world is likely to be dispersed, and higher on average, than in the perfectly competitive case. Higher benefits and lower costs of acquiring information result in lower price dispersion.

Imperfect information may also affect the level of observed quality of goods and services in the market. Higher-quality goods are produced at a higher price than lower-quality goods. In a competitive market where consumers are perfectly informed, higher-quality goods sell at a higher price than lower-quality goods. In the real world with imperfect information, consumers are unsure about the exact quality of the goods and services under consideration. Therefore, if consumers base their information on the average quality in the market and pay the average price, lower-quality goods and services drive out higher-quality goods and services to the point where no products remain. This implies that, at a higher level of quality, the consumer group is better informed.

Given imperfect information about many goods and services in the real world, some economists state that product differentiation, such as advertising and branding, can lead to improved information for consumers. Some think that advertising about the quality and features of the good or service in question provides relatively cheap information about the good or service to the consumer, leading to lower prices and improved quality. Studies by Cady (1976) and Kwoka (1984) found that the prices of eyeglasses and prescription drugs were higher on average when advertising was prohibited. Even when price or quality information was not directly conveyed, a large advertisement may provide a signal to consumers that the producer has a high-quality product because the producer is confident to incur such a sizable expense. This can improve the competitive position of the firm (McCarthy & Norris, 1999). Through repeat purchases, the firm hopes to gain a sufficient return on its advertising expenses. In this case, the presence of expensive advertising generates information about the quality of the product.

Other economists such as Klein and Leffler (1981) argue that branding can serve a similar purpose as advertising for promoting competition. Because many goods and services cannot be evaluated until after purchase, branding helps to identify firms that are confident enough to invest in establishing a reputation. The argument is that firms will not invest significant sums in branding their products only to have shoddy workmanship and a resulting tarnished reputation. This would result in a significant reduction in return on investment.

Some economists believe that advertising and branding can lead to anticompetitive behavior through habit purchases rather than informed purchases, created through brand loyalty. Advertising in this argument is considered to be persuasive, creating a barrier to entry, rather than informative. Advertising can point out real differences between products, but it is most often used to create perceived differences across goods or services. For example, Centrum and the generic brand of the vitamin contain the same active ingredients, yet many consumers are willing to pay the extra amount for the brand name. Some argue that consumers pay a premium for branded products because past advertising successfully convinced consumers that Centrum, for example, is a superior product. Instead of creating a new market demand, the advertising attempts to draw consumers away from competitors.

According to the anticompetitive view, product differentiation manipulates the demand for a product. Successful advertising can manipulate consumers' preferences, thus influencing the position of the demand curve for the product. The demand curve may shift up because consumers may be willing to pay more for the product, and the demand curve may become more inelastic with respect to price, giving the firm some ability to reduce output and raise price. This phenomenon was seen in in-store experiments for retail advertising by Bemmaor and Mouchoux (1991).

As an example, many public health professionals claim that the purpose behind cigarette advertising is to manipulate the demand for cigarettes. Of major concern is the advertising aimed at teenagers' demand for cigarettes. A report by the Centers for Disease Control and Prevention found that, among smokers aged 12 to 18, preferences were greater for Marlboro, Newport, and Camel, three brands that are heavily advertised (Ruffenach, 1992). The effect of cigarette advertising on increased use of smoking by teens was seen by Hanewinkel, Isensee, Sargent, and Morgenstern (2011) and by Pechmann and Shih (1999). Internationally, the restriction of tobacco ads resulted in lower tobacco consumption (Laugesen & Meads, 1991).

Existing firms may also use advertising or other types of product differentiation to create barriers to entry. If existing firms control the market through advertising, new firms may find it difficult to enter the market because they are unable to sell a sufficient amount of output to break even financially. It implies that product differentiation aimed at creating artificial wants, habit buying, or barriers to entry results in the misallocation of resources (Holmer, 2002; Wolfe, 2002). For example, in an extensive study, Gilbody, Wilson, and Watt (2005) found that direct-to consumer advertising for pharmaceuticals was associated with increased prescription of advertised products and a substantial increase in patients' requests for particular drugs over less familiar drugs. Resources are misused if they are employed to create perceived rather than real value.

When evaluating the social desirability of product differentiation, most consumers prefer diversity and enjoy choosing among a wide variety of goods and services selling at different prices. In this scenario, the higher-than-competitive price that is paid for product differentiation may simply reflect the premium consumers pay for variety.

OLIGOPOLY

Oligopoly involves a market model with a few large firms and relatively high barriers to entry. There may be a large number of firms in the industry, but the other firms may be small price takers with limited market share. The dominant firms must be sufficiently sized and limited in number that the pricing or output decisions of one firm affect the decisions for the other dominant firms in the market. This mutual interdependence among the firms distinguishes the oligopoly structure from other market models. This mutual interdependence varies and results in no one model of oligopoly behavior. An example of an oligopoly in the healthcare market is the proliferation of integrated delivery systems in regional markets (Malone, 1998) or more simply the presence of hospital systems in a community. These systems are organizations that provide a continuum of healthcare services, with the characteristics of oligopolies.

According to the Collusive Oligopoly Model, all firms cooperate rather than compete on price and output and jointly maximize profits by collectively acting like a monopoly. It follows that a deadweight loss and misallocation of society's scarce resources result from a collusive oligopoly as in the case of a monopoly structure.

Collusion among the firms may be overt or tacit. Overt collusion refers to a situation where firm representatives formally meet to coordinate prices and market shares. Tacit collusion occurs when firms informally coordinate their prices. Price leadership is an example of tacit collusion, where firms in the market agree that one firm will be the price maker. The other firms in the market match or parallel the price behavior of the leader. This market behavior can mimic the monopoly outcome as overt collusion.

There are several factors that make collusion difficult. First are the legal and practical considerations. The Sherman Antitrust Act prohibits overt collusion. Firms found in violation of overt pricing behavior can be subjected to severe financial penalties and their chief financial officers may be imprisoned. However, antitrust officials do not pursue cases of tacit collusion because there is a burden of proof. Firms in a market may parallel their actions simply because they experience the same market shocks as other firms. However, a tacit collusive agreement has its own difficulties. Other firms may have trouble interpreting price changes set by the leader. Also, cost differences make it harder for firms to cooperate and agree on a common price. High-cost firms will desire a higher price than lower-cost firms. However, the success of the collusion depends on the agreement on a common price. Collusion is also less successful when entry barriers are low. Lastly, collusion is more likely when only a few firms exist in the market. Low negotiation costs exist with fewer firms. Further, the potential for cheating behavior is greater when more firms exist in the industry because of high monitoring costs. For these reasons, it is very difficult to form and maintain a collusive oligopoly structure.

Competitive Oligopoly

Competitive oligopolies occur when firms act competitively, do not cooperate, and seek to maximize their own profits. If the market consists of goods or services that are relatively homogeneous, firms will seek to set price equal to MC because there are many close substitutes for the product. With this pricing scheme, each firm will have some of the market share and will not be undersold. If firms behave in this way, market price equals MC, and resources are efficiently allocated—even though there are a few dominant firms in the market.

SUMMARY

The model of a pure monopoly is the exact opposite of the perfectly competitive market. This market model is characterized by one seller with one product and perfect barriers to entry. Due to the downward-sloping demand and the fact that the monopolist has market power, this results in the monopolist restricting output and a misallocation of society's resources.

Monopolistic competition is noted as an intermediate market model, with its main distinguishing feature being its differentiated product. Differentiated products allow the firm to raise the price slightly without losing all market shares. Because barriers to entry are nonexistent in the long run, the monopolistically competitive firm makes normal economic profits in the long run. Given that variety is valued by consumers, the only real criticism of this model is in the use of differentiation. If differentiation through branding, advertising, or trademark can provide cheap information and therefore a more competitive solution, it can also be argued that these same features impede competition through brand loyalty and habitual buying behavior.

Oligopoly is also considered an intermediate market model. A few dominant firms and mutual interdependence between the firms distinguish oligopoly from the other market models. The efficiency of an oligopolistic market depends on the level of competition or cooperation among the firms in the market. Cooperation or collusion leads to monopolistic outcomes and a misallocation of resources. Competition leads to efficient allocation of resources.

KEY WORDS

- **Average total cost**
- **Long-run average total cost**
- **Marginal revenue**
- **Pareto efficiency**

Questions

1. Show graphically and explain verbally how a monopoly results in deadweight loss. Also discuss the redistribution in society as a result of a monopoly.

2. Explain why economic profits are zero in the long run in a monopolistically competitive market.

3. Discuss the two ways that product differentiation affects demand for the product.

4. Explain the difference between collusive and competitive oligopolistic market models.

PROFILE: MICHAEL GROSSMAN

Michael Grossman was born in 1942 in New York City and graduated with a bachelor's degree from Trinity College in 1962. He received his graduate training from Columbia University, which resulted in a PhD in economics in 1970.

In 1966, Grossman was appointed as a research assistant by Victor Fuchs at the National Bureau of Economic Research and, in 1972, he was hired by the City University of New York (CUNY) Graduate Center as a visiting assistant professor of economics. He became professor of economics at CUNY in 1978 and, in 1988, he earned the rank of distinguished professor of economics.

Grossman's work focuses on the economic models of the determinants of health, substance abuse, and interest rates on tax-exempt hospital bonds. His research projects include moral hazard in less invasive surgical technology for coronary artery disease, the effects of food prices and food advertising on the body composition of children, and the causal relationship between schooling and health. His body of work is highly influential in health economics and resulted in Grossman receiving the Victor Fuchs Award for Lifetime Contributions to the Field of Health Economics by the American Society of Health Economists in 2008.

Data from Mullner, R. M. (2009). "Grossman, Michael". *Encyclopedia of Health Services Research*. Los Angeles: Sage. pp. 450–451; https://wfs.gc.cuny.edu/MGrossman/www/mike%20grossman%20profile.pdf, accessed March 20, 2014.

REFERENCES

Bemmaor, A. C., & Mouchoux, D. (1991). Measuring the short-term effect of in-store promotion and retail advertising on brand sales: A factorial experiment. *Journal of Marketing Research, 28*(2), 202–214.

Cady, J. F. (1976). An estimate of the price effects of restrictions on drug price advertising. *Economic Inquiry, 14*(4), 493–510.

Gilbody, S., Wilson, P., & Watt, I. (2005). Benefits and harms of direct to consumer advertising: A systematic review. *Quality and Safety in Health Care, 14*(4), 246–250.

Hanewinkel, R., Isensee, B., Sargent, J. D., & Morgenstern, M. (2011). Cigarette advertising and teen smoking initiation. *Pediatrics, 127*(2), e271–e278.

Holmer, A. F. (2002). Direct-to-consumer advertising—Strengthening our health care system. *New England Journal of Medicine, 346*(7), 526–528.

Klein, B., & Leffler, K. B. (1981). The role of market forces in assuring contractual performance. *Journal of Political Economy, 89*(4), 615–641.

Kwoka, J. E., Jr. (1984). Advertising and the price and quality of optometric services. *American Economic Review, 74*(1), 211–216.

Laffont, J. J. (2008). Externalities. In S. N. Durlauf & L. E. Blume (Eds.), *The New Palgrave Dictionary of Economics* (2nd ed.). Retrieved from www.dictionaryofeconomics.com/ article?id=pde2008_E000200

Laugesen, M., & Meads, C. (1991). Tobacco advertising restrictions, price, income and tobacco consumption in OECD countries, 1960–1986. *British Journal of Addiction, 86*(10), 1343–1354.

Malone, T. A. (1998). Integrated delivery systems: Evolving oligopolies. *Physician Executive, 24*(2), 30–32.

McCarthy, M. S., & Norris, D. G. (1999). Improving competitive position using branded ingredients. *Journal of Product and Brand Management, 8*(4), 267–285.

Morris, S., Devlin, N., & Parkin, D. (2007). *Economic analysis in health care.* West Sussex, England: John Wiley & Sons.

Pechmann, C., & Shih, C-F. (1999). Smoking scenes in movies and anti-smoking advertisements before movies: Effects on youth. *Journal of Marketing, 63*(3), 1–13.

Ruffenach, G. (1992). Study says teenagers' smoking habits seem to be linked to heavy advertising. *The Wall Street Journal*, p. B8.

Wolfe, S. M. (2002). Direct-to-consumer advertising—Education or emotion promotion? *New England Journal of Medicine, 346*(7), 524–526.

The Role of Government

INTRODUCTION

While the perfectly competitive market is the gold standard in determining optimal market behavior, earlier chapters have shown that, particularly in health care, failures of the competitive framework are plentiful in the health economy. In this chapter, the role of government as a corrective agent in the market for health care is described and analyzed.

THEORIES OF GOVERNMENT INTERVENTION

The public interest and special interest group theories describe the motivation behind government intervention in the healthcare market. The public interest theory, first presented by Pigou (1920), states that the government intervenes in the best interests of society to promote efficiency and equity in the market. It assumes that the markets are fragile and will not reach an optimal solution on their own without the government as a neutral arbiter. An efficient allocation of resources occurs when, for a given distribution of income, **marginal social benefit** is equal to **marginal social cost** (MSB = MSC). In the presence of market failures, such as imperfect information or monopolistic behaviors, markets fail to allocate resources efficiently as seen in the competitive market.

The public interest is served when the government attempts to restore efficiency or to distribute income equitably by encouraging competition, providing information, reducing harmful externalities, or redistributing income in society. Therefore, the public interest theory of government behavior predicts that the laws, regulations, and other government interventions enhance efficiency and equity that cannot be achieved naturally in the private market behaviors.

The special interest theory (Becker, 1983) states that the political venue can be treated like any private market for goods and services so that amounts and types of legislation are determined by supply and demand for such legislation. Vote-maximizing legislators are the suppliers of legislation while wealth-maximizing special interest groups are demanders of such legislation. In this structure, incumbent politicians increase the likelihood of getting reelected by moving wealth or resources away from the general public and toward the powerful and influential special interest groups. In return, politicians expect votes, support, and political contributions. Professional lobbyists representing special interest groups negotiate with the legislators and arrive at market clearing types of legislation. This form of legislation changes over time with relative power shifts among different interest groups. Power or political pressure is determined by the amount of resources the group controls, the size of the group, and the efficiency with which the group transforms resources into pressure to achieve specific goals or resource allocations.

The successful politician stays in office by combining legislative programs of various special interest groups into an overall fiscal package to be advanced in the political arena. The beneficiaries are the special interest groups, but the costs fall on the general public. Special interest forums and politicians are made better off by the legislation—otherwise it would not occur. The politicians retain or acquire elected positions and the special interest groups receive wealth-enhancing legislation.

The general public is made worse off by the legislation. Individuals are rationally ignorant about the wealth implications of government activities because the cost of acquiring such information is high and the private benefit is low. The wealth transfer from the public to the special interest group is low in per capita terms. To challenge the special interest group legislation, a group or an individual must organize a legitimate counterpolitical movement, inform others, circulate a petition, and engage in lobbying. All of these activities entail sizable personal and monetary costs, and the public is generally unorganized, thus making these activities unfeasible.

The special interest model of government behavior implies that the typical consumer is taken by wealth-transferring legislation. The political negotiations leading to the wealth transfer involve scarce resources such as politicians' time and professional lobbyists. As more resources are diverted to political negotiations, fewer resources are left for productive purposes. Therefore, inefficiencies are associated with this model.

To protect the public, government intervention includes regulations and laws because some special interest groups benefit at the expense of the general public. Individuals in a special interest group are collectively powerful because they share a common concentrated interest. Consumers as a group, however, are generally diverse and powerless. Organization and time costs prohibit the general public from taking action even when wealth transfers to the special interest groups are known.

The public interest and special interest group theories are contrasting models regarding the reasons why the government intervenes in a market-based system. In the real world, the government intervenes for both reasons. In some cases, market failures occur and the government intervenes to promote efficiency and equity. In other cases, government policies enhance the well-being of specific groups at an overall cost to society and therefore a misallocation of resources and inequitable distribution of income occurs. It is important to remember that both the government and the market can have imperfections or failures. In the real world, the role of informed consumers or analysts is to determine which institution can accomplish which objectives in a more equitable and efficient manner.

FORMS OF GOVERNMENT INTERVENTION

The government can promote efficiency and equity by providing public goods, levying taxes, correcting for externalities, imposing regulations, enforcing antitrust laws, operating public enterprises, and sponsoring redistribution programs. As an example of a public good, a public health sanitation officer inspects the conditions at restaurants to protect the public's health. To correct for externalities, the government taxes the emissions of firms to reduce the level of air or water pollution in an area, or provides subsidies for people to obtain routine vaccinations. The Sherman Antitrust Act of 1890 prohibits independent physicians from discussing their pricing policies to prevent monopolistic practices, such as price fixing. A hospital operated by Veterans Affairs is an example of government enterprise. The social insurance programs of Medicaid and Medicare are examples of public medical care distribution programs. Each example influences the allocation of resources and the distribution of output in the healthcare economy.

Antitrust Issues

Economists, as well as courts dealing with **antitrust** cases, often use the concept of cross-price elasticity of demand to measure whether a firm has monopoly power in supplying a good or service in the given market. The cross-price elasticity of demand measures the degree to which the quantity demanded of good X is related to the price of another good Y. It is defined as the

$$\frac{(\% \text{ change in quantity of X demanded})}{(\% \text{ change in price of Y})}$$

If the coefficient is negative, this provides evidence that the goods in question are complements, otherwise the goods are substitutes. A **complementary good** is good that is used in companion to the good in question; a **substitute good** is a good that is used instead of the good in question. If the coefficient of cross-price elasticity of demand for a good is positive and large enough in magnitude to be of some consequence, the firm likely has effective monopoly power.

As seen in Chapter 4, the contemporary market for physician services provides some examples of behavior associated with collusive oligopoly or cartels, which are organizations that set output quotas and sometimes directly set prices. Examples of vertically and horizontally integrated physician networks have attained a virtual monopoly over local or even regional provision of physician services (Greenberg, 1998). Antitrust law allows clinically integrated groups to jointly contract. In ruling such cases, the Federal Trade Commission has argued that, even if physician networks are not financially integrated, they can receive special treatment under the Rule of Reason. Under this rule, the circumstances in which the restraining action was committed must be considered.

However, a series of Supreme Court decisions beginning in the 1970s have interpreted antitrust law as applying to hospitals (Alpert & McCarty, 1984). The belief that consolidation was associated with lower costs was maintained by the courts throughout the 1970s and early 1980s (*United States v. Carilion Health System and Roanoke Valley Hospital*). Since the late 1980s, the Justice Department has become critical of hospital mergers (Noether, 1998; Rust, 2012; Whitesell & Whitesell, 1995). Further, government regulators have responded to the apparent change in the effects of concentration on hospital markets and now tend to see competition as beneficial. Difficulty in defining the relevant geographic markets in which hospitals operate has led to very limited success on the part of the government in blocking large hospital mergers to date, but government policy remains suspicious of increasing concentration in the hospital sector. Since 1997, the Justice Department has largely been unsuccessful in the courts in blocking the majority of hospital mergers that it has attempted to forestall (Gaynor, 2006; Greaney 2002, 2006; McDermott & Emery, 1999). However, the future is changing for hospitals engaging in anticompetitive conduct (Dranove & Sfekas, 2009), with less amenable receptions of antitrust cases in the courtroom.

Social Insurance Programs

The principles of **social insurance** are quite different from those that pertain to the private market. Social insurance programs are generally funded by mandatory contributions through some form of taxation. They usually have goals in addition to pooling of risk, which include transfers of benefits between groups, from the more affluent to the poor, from younger adults to senior citizens, from adults to children, or from the able-bodied to the disabled. Therefore, the goal is to

© iStockphoto/Thinkstock

equate marginal social benefits with marginal social costs in the provision of optimal insurance packages.

Social insurance in the United States is limited to certain categories of citizens and residents, such as senior citizens, a segment of the poor, and people with qualified disabilities, who are covered by Medicare and Medicaid. A few other special groups are covered by public insurance programs, including Native Americans on reservations, veterans of armed forces, members of Congress, and low-income families with children. Some states have also expanded social insurance programs for families who would not otherwise be covered by federal programs.

Provision of Information

When market failure in health care arises due to imperfect information, the government may help to correct the problem via provision of information. An example is the provision of information for the general public on the benefits of certain types of health care, such as the safety of the mumps, measles, and rubella vaccine. Other forms of information can include public announcements or advertisements concerning the outcomes of certain activities, such as smoking and its health consequences.

Regulations

Regulations in the healthcare sector can take many forms and generally aim to protect and improve the public good. These regulations can be health and safety mandates such as seat belt utilization. They can also take the form of price controls or oversight of fee structures in insurance firms to assure that the public is not charged unusually high fees for services.

One growing concern for the protection of public goods is the regulation of health information technology. In this instance, the development and diffusion of technology surpasses the speed with which regulations concerning the use of medical information can be developed and implemented. For example, consider the case of mHealth, or mobile information technology. Here, applications are developed for consumers to provide biomarkers to providers on a regular basis. This technology is so new that it is important for application developers and providers to understand the influence that government regulations have on this industry (Silberman & Clark, 2012).

There is a notable gap between healthcare information systems and government regulations. This is seen in the violation of the **Health Insurance Portability and Accountability Act (HIPAA)**, where breaches in electronic health records cannot only violate confidentiality but also create economic losses due to resulting job loss in regard to discovery of a particular health issue of the employed person (Wu, Ahn, & Hu, 2012).

Another major issue in data security that requires government oversight is the use of cloud computing in the storage of medical records. This data storage can be superior to traditional electronic records, but the development of this new technology is constrained by federal and state regulators (Schweitzer, 2012). In both cases, while the goal of government regulation is to protect the privacy and misuse of sensitive health information, the regulations often lag behind the technological developments.

SUMMARY

Government intervention is based on the special interest or public interest theories. The public interest theory focuses on efficiency in the market, and the special interest theory levels the playing field in the legislative marketplace. All government interventions focus on either improvements in efficiency or equity in the market through the provision or financing of goods or services, promoting competition or providing information.

KEY WORDS

- **Antitrust**
- **Complementary good**
- **Health Insurance Portability and Accountability Act (HIPAA)**
- **Marginal social benefit**
- **Marginal social cost**
- **Social insurance**
- **Substitute good**

Questions

1. Compare and contrast the special interest and public interest theories of government intervention.

2. What are the controversies in enforcing antitrust legislation?

3. What are the main differences between social and private insurance?

PROFILE: GARY BECKER

Gary Becker was born in Pottsville, Pennsylvania, and later moved to New York City, where he attended elementary school and high school. Due to lively household discussion about politics and justice, he developed competing interests with mathematics and social issues.

In his freshman year at Princeton University, he began to appreciate economics and was intrigued by the mathematical rigor of the subject that dealt with social organization. His heavy investment in mathematics helped his studies in economics, which he completed in 3 years.

In 1951, he attended the University of Chicago for graduate work in economics. His work with Milton Friedman helped him to develop an appreciation for economics as a powerful tool to analyze real-world phenomena. It was here that he really learned what economics was all about, and he published a book related to his dissertation in 1957—a systematic use of economic theory to analyze the effects of prejudice on the labor market participation of minorities. This was his first published work on the economics of social issues.

In Becker's third year of graduate study, he was appointed an assistant professor at the University of Chicago but left after 3 years for a position at Columbia University and the National Bureau of Economic Research in Manhattan. This move gave him more intellectual self-confidence. During his time in Manhattan, he wrote articles on allocation of time, crime and punishment, and irrational behavior.

In 1970, Becker returned to the University of Chicago, where he renewed his interest in developing the theoretical model for the role of special interest groups in the political process. However, during this time, he mainly worked on family issues, such as marriage, divorce, altruism toward other members, investments by parents in children, and long-term changes in family dynamics. This latter work culminated in *A Treatise on the Family* published in 1981 and expanded in 1991.

Currently, Becker is university professor in the Department of Economics and Sociology, and professor in the Graduate School of Business, at the University of Chicago. He is also senior fellow at the Hoover Institute at Stanford University and research associate at the National Opinion Research Center.

For many years, Becker's work was ignored or disliked by leading economists, and he was often considered not to be a real economist. However, younger generations of economists are more sympathetic: They may disagree with the analytical style but accept the problems addressed as legitimate. Evidence of this shift in opinion of Becker's work is seen in the awards bestowed to him, including the Seidman Award, the first social science Award of Merit from the National Institutes of Health, and the 1992 Sveriges Riksbank Prize in Economic Sciences in Memory of Alfred Nobel.

Data from Nobelprize.org. (2015). *Gary S. Becker: Biographical.* Retrieved February 15, 2014, from http://www.nobelprize.org/nobel_prizes/economic-sciences/laureates/1992/becker-bio.html.

REFERENCES

Alpert, G., & McCarty, T. R. (1984). Beyond Goldfarb: Applying traditional antitrust analysis to changing health markets. *Antitrust Bulletin, 29,* 165–204.

Becker, G. S. (1983). A theory of competition among pressure groups for political influence. *Quarterly Journal of Economics, 98*(3), 371–400.

Dranove, D., & Sfekas, A. (2009). The revolution in health care antitrust: New methods and provocative implications. *Milbank Quarterly, 87*(3), 607–632.

Gaynor, M. (2006). Why don't courts treat hospitals like tanks for liquefied gases? Some reflections on health care antitrust enforcement. *Journal of Health Politics, Policy and Law, 31*(3), 497–510.

Greaney, T. L. (2002). Wither antitrust? The uncertain future of competition law in health care. *Health Affairs, 21*(2), 185–196.

Greaney, T. L. (2006). Antitrust and hospital mergers: Does the nonprofit form affect competitive substance? *Journal of Health Politics, Policy and Law, 31*(3), 511–529.

Greenberg, W. (1998). Marshfield Clinic, physician networks, and the exercise of monopoly power. *Health Services Research, 33*(5 Pt 2), 1461–1476.

McDermott, W., & Emery, L. (1999). *Health Law Update, 16,* 3.

Noether, M. (1998). Economic issues in the antitrust assessment of hospital competition: Overview. *International Journal of the Economics of Business, 5*(2), 133–141.

Pigou, A. C. (1920). *The economics of welfare.* London, England: Macmillan.

Rust, M. E. (2012). From HCQIA to ACA: The 180° arc of provider antitrust concerns in healthcare over 25 years. *Journal of Legal Medicine, 33*(1), 21–42.

Schweitzer, E. J. (2012). Reconciliation of the cloud computing model with US federal electronic health record regulations. *Journal of the American Medical Informatics Association, 19*(2), 161–165.

Silberman, M. J., & Clark, L. (2012). M-health: The union of technology and healthcare regulations. *Journal of Medical Practice Management, 28*(2), 118–120.

Whitesell, S. E., & Whitesell, W. E. (1995). Hospital mergers and antitrust: Some economic and legal issues. *American Journal of Economics and Sociology, 54*(3), 305–321.

Wu, R., Ahn, G-J., & Hu, H. (2012). *Towards HIPAA-compliant healthcare systems.* Retrieved from www.public.asu.edu/~ruoyuwu/IHI2012.pdf

© zhu difeng/Shutterstock

PART **III**

Demand

The Demand for Health

LEARNING OBJECTIVES

By the end of this chapter, the student will be able to:

1. Distinguish between the determinants of individual and population health status.
2. Develop the models for investment and consumption aspects of health.
3. Use Grossman's model in determining individual health status.
4. Compare health status measures between the United States and other developed countries.

INTRODUCTION

Most everyone desires good health both for the sake of quality of life and because it contributes to productivity and earning income. Yet a great deal of study has gone into determining which factors affect health, and a formal model of investment in health is used by economists. Health is viewed as a stock of capital that yields a stream of healthy days just as wealth is a stock of financial capital that yields a stream of income.

Improving health is not the only characteristic of health care that health economics takes into account. Many types of health care may affect other aspects of a person's well-being. For example, health care can be seen as providing reassurance or reducing anxiety about an individual's state of health. But for most types of health care, their most important and interesting characteristic is that they are intended to alter health, not that they are services provided by the healthcare industry (Morris, Devlin, & Parkin, 2007).

This chapter presents a model of the demand for health, with health care as an input for the production of health. It also takes into account that there may be negative conse-

quences in the production of health. Formulating the basis for the demand for health provides the foundation for the demand for health care, which is derived from the demand for health.

HEALTH AS A FORM OF HUMAN CAPITAL

The most important and powerful insight is that in addition to health care being an economic good, health itself can be thought of as a good. It can be regarded as a fundamental commodity from an economic and policy perspective: one of the true objects of people's wants and for which other tangible goods and services—such as health care—are simply a means to create it. This theory originates from the work of Becker (1965) and Grossman (1972) but can be traced to 18th-century economists such as Jeremy Bentham (1780/1970), who wrote that "the relief of pain" is a "basic pleasure."

If it is accepted that health is a fundamental commodity, we can analyze the demand for improvements in health in very similar ways to the analysis of demand for other goods and services. A key difference is that, because health is not tradeable or purchased directly, it is not possible for it to be analyzed in the market framework. Instead, the production of health is the key means in which people express their demand for it, which may involve the purchase of goods and services, thereby indirectly purchasing health improvements. Health care is therefore derived from the demand for health. Such analysis can be used for almost any goods or services, but it is of particular importance in health because the consumption of health care is usually not pleasurable in and of itself but is undertaken simply to improve or maintain health (Morris et al., 2007).

A model of the demand for health, developed in the 1970s by Michael Grossman, treats investment in health as a form of investment in **human capital** (Culyer & Newhouse, 2000). The general model of human capital was originally developed by Gary Becker (1975) in the context of investment in education, and it was logical to extend it to health.

Consider what is involved in the investment in any capital good. The analogy between health care and machine repair has often been made. A person might buy a machine in order to earn income as a consultant. In this case, the machine is a computer, which is a capital good. Or one might buy a computer to work and do pleasurable things, such as using the Internet or playing games. In this case, the computer is also a capital good that provides a stream of services over time that has monetary value and value of utility or consumption aspects. The consumption aspects would be the joy of playing a favorite game on the weekend.

To improve or maintain the investment in a computer, some preventive maintenance is necessary, such as keyboard cleaning, virus protections, and so on. Sometimes, costly repairs are needed, such as a drive failure. In this case, the repair and maintenance of the computer is not unlike that of maintaining health. The amount of repairs needed by the computer depend on how it was treated. Routine maintenance of and repairs to the computer are performed to offset depreciation. This is part of the gross investment to the computer over the life of the machine. Gross investment includes the cost of purchasing the computer and its upkeep.

Grossman's Investment Model of Health

The principle contribution of Grossman's model (1972) is the distinction between health as an output (e.g., a fundamental commodity), which is a source of utility to people, and medical care as an input to the production of health. In Grossman's model, health is both demanded and produced by individuals. Health is demanded because it affects the total time available for the production of income and because it is a source of utility in itself. Ill health reduces both our happiness, or perceptions of ourselves, and our ability to earn a living and purchase other goods and services to maximize utility.

Health is modeled as being produced by individuals using a variety of means such as environment, lifestyle choices, and medical care. How efficient people are in the production of health depends on their knowledge and education. Medical care is but one input to the production of health. Each individual is modeled as starting life with a "stock" of health driven by biology and other exogenous factors, such as demographics including race and gender, which has characteristics similar to capital: Health depreciates through time with age but can also be increased through investments in environmental changes, time, effort, knowledge, or by seeking health care.

Grossman's model captures two important insights. First, health care is but one input in generating improvements in health: It is now widely accepted that medical care is not the major determinant of health. Second, individuals do not demand health care for its own sake: The utility received from consuming health care is not generated from health care but from the improvements in health that result. Therefore, the demand for health care is a derived demand from the demand for health itself.

The investment model of health views the demand for health as being conditional on both the cost of health capital and the rate of depreciation of the health stock. As in the investment in any capital good that has a limited life, the difference between the gross (total) and net investment depends on the rate at which the capital good wears out or depreciates.

The **marginal efficiency of capital** (MEC) is a measure of how much extra output can be produced with an extra unit of capital input. **Figure 6-1** depicts the MEC schedule of health capital. It shows how much extra expenditure is required to produce an additional unit of health stock. One measures the stock of health capital on the horizontal axis and the costs along the vertical axis. The MEC curve slopes downward because additional units of investment are assumed to yield smaller marginal improvements in the production of

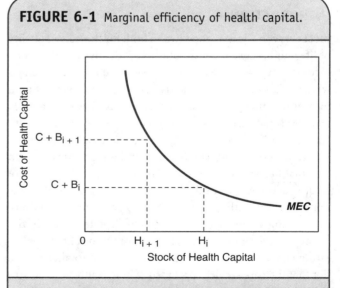

FIGURE 6-1 Marginal efficiency of health capital.

health. In other words, assume that the production of health is subject to **diminishing marginal returns**. H_i and H_{i+1} are two levels of health stock chosen by an individual at different levels of health costs. The total cost of producing any health stock includes the cost of offsetting depreciation and the cost of incremental units of health stock, C.

One can think of the MEC schedule as the demand curve for health. It can also be seen as a production function for health because it relates inputs and the output of the stock of health. Once we know the MEC schedule, it is possible to determine the level the individual will choose to produce. A rational person will invest extra resources in the production of health to the point where the value of additional degrees of healthiness is equal to the marginal cost of producing it. This can also be seen as the total investment in health stock.

The MEC schedule is specific to an individual. The location of the MEC schedule depends on a person's initial stock of health at the beginning of the time period. An individual with a lower endowment of health will require more inputs to achieve the same health stock than will an individual with a higher initial endowment. In that case, the MEC curve will be located to the left of the one that describes someone who begins life in a healthier state. The model does not assume that a given increase in inputs into the health production function will generate the same marginal improvement in different people due to the differences in individual health production functions.

The Wage Effect

The change in the wage rate is treated as a shift in the MEC schedule because it changes the return from the stock of health. It does so because the wage rate measures an individual's market efficiency, the rate at which healthy days are converted into monetary earnings, and also the opportunity cost of nonmarket time as measured by the earnings foregone per hour or day. A stock of health is a better investment for high-wage earners because the individual's healthy working hours yield more income, and the opportunity cost of his or her nonmarket time is also greater.

The Consumption Model

For some purposes, it makes sense to shift a model that focuses on budget allocation (income) between investment in health and expenditure on consumer goods at any given time. In **Figure 6-2**, the straight line is the budget line. It shows the different combinations of health and consumption goods that one can purchase with a particular budget or income level. The quantity of goods that may be purchased from a budget depends on the prices of the goods and income. The slope

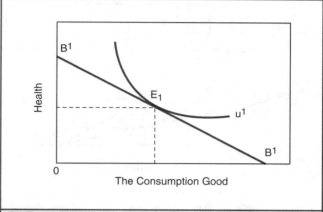

FIGURE 6-2 Trade-off among the investment good, health, and consumption good.

Folland, Sherman; Goodman, Allen C.; Stano, Miron, *Economics of Health and Health Care*, 5th Edition, © 2007. Reprinted/Adapted and Electronically reproduced by permission of Pearson Education, Inc., New York, New York.

of the budget line is determined by the relative prices of the goods, which are the consumer composite good and health.

U is an individual's **indifference curve**. Each indifference curve shows the various combinations of health and consumption goods that provide an individual with an equal amount of satisfaction or utility. A higher indifference curve represents a higher level of total utility. The standard assumption is that both the consumption good and health are subject to **diminishing marginal utility**. In other words, as a person increases consumption of a good or service while keeping consumption of other goods at a constant level, there is a decline in the marginal utility that person derives from consuming each additional unit of the good or service in question. Therefore, one can draw the indifference curves in the usual way, which is convex to the origin. Because one's productivity in the workplace is likely to be affected by one's health, investment in health could increase earnings to the extent that one might spend money on health care without reducing his or her consumption of other goods. Then there would be no trade-off between the two.

ADDITIONAL FACTORS THAT AFFECT THE INVESTMENT IN HEALTH

Age

As one ages, it takes more resources to obtain or maintain a given stock of health. In contrast, older people are generally not charged higher prices for most consumer goods. In fact,

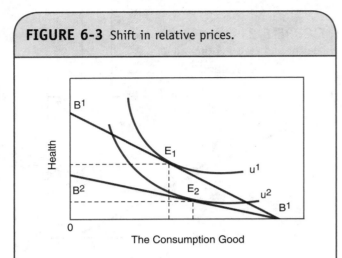

FIGURE 6-3 Shift in relative prices.

Folland, Sherman; Goodman, Allen C.; Stano, Miron, *Economics of Health and Health Care*, 5th Edition, © 2007. Reprinted/Adapted and Electronically reproduced by permission of Pearson Education, Inc., New York, New York.

some goods may be subject to senior citizen discounts, such as air travel and some restaurant meals. Therefore, the relative pricing of producing health versus purchasing consumer goods tends to increase with age. The substitution effect (relative price effect) would encourage the substitution of other consumer goods for investment in health as one ages. In **Figure 6-3**, an increase in the relative price of health investment is shown by a decrease in the slope of the budget line from B_1B_1 to B_0B_1. This results in a new optimal combination of health and other goods as in E_1. However, a person with a very serious illness may decide that it is not worth investing in the minimal health stock necessary to stay alive.

Education

Both the investment and consumption models can be used to analyze the effects of education on the demand for health. Considerable evidence exists that more highly educated people are more efficient in the production of health (Ederington & Minier, 2008). In the investment model, education shifts the MEC curve to the right by raising the productivity of the inputs into the production of health.

This effect seems to be true not only in the United States and similarly developed countries but also in countries that have much lower per capita income and education and less advanced technologies. One hypothesis is that education is correlated with a lower rate of depreciation in the stock of health (Muurinen, 1982). This can be shown as a downward movement along the MEC curve associated with a reduction in the cost of producing

health stock. It is expected that the increase in the demand for health is associated with an increase in education.

Education may not only make investment in health less costly, it may also be associated with different time preferences. **Time preference** is a term that refers to the extent to which people discount the future. The person who is preoccupied with the present ignores the future— that is, discounts it very heavily. Such a person is not likely to save or invest much in either education or health (Fuchs, 1980).

Lifestyle Effects of Wealth

The MEC curve may shift to the left as people become wealthier, eating rich foods and decreasing exercise. These are negative inputs into the production of health. Research has shown that there is a negative relationship between upturns in the economy and the level of healthiness in society (Grossman, 1972). In low-income countries, however, periods of prosperity would be expected to reduce malnutrition and lead to better health outcomes.

Chemical Dependency

In the case of addictive drugs, additional insight may be gained by utilizing both the investment and consumption models of health. Addiction might be viewed as shifting the marginal efficiency of health capital curve to the left, and it can also be viewed as causing a change in taste that would result in the substitution of the additive good for an expenditure on health. For example, one may reduce preventive care in order to afford more illegal drugs. A common view of drug addiction associates it with a very short time horizon in decision making, which is consistent with a diversion of resources away from investing in health to purchasing "utility-producing" addictive goods due to time preferences that are opposite of those who are health producing.

Following this reasoning, anything that increases the stock of health value will tend to reduce chemical dependency. In the case of addiction, better opportunities in the labor market, which increase the value of healthy days, would tend to discourage chemical dependency because the market value of health is higher.

Environment

The MEC curve may shift to the right as people become wealthier and achieve greater socioeconomic status and better physical environments. These are positive inputs into the production of health. Research has shown a positive relationship between upturns in household wealth and income and level of healthiness in society. Conversely, the health consequences of poverty include the exposure to and effect of environmental health risks such as hazardous wastes, pollutants, noise, and neighborhood conditions (Evans & Kantrowitz, 2002).

Biology

The MEC curve may lie closer to the left for people with poorer genetic profiles or family histories of disease. These are negative inputs into the production of health. Generally, a poorer initial endowment of health stock will lead to a lower level of healthiness for the individual holding all other inputs constant in the health production function.

UNDERSTANDING THE INVESTMENT ASPECTS OF THE GROSSMAN MODEL

Grossman's theory (1972) is based on the idea of household and production. The true objectives are the fundamental commodities that are created within households by using time and market goods and services. The total time available can be used either for direct production of these commodities or for work to obtain income for market goods. For example, in creating the fundamental commodity related to eating, a household can have home-cooked, restaurant, take-out, or prepared meals. Each involves different combinations of the household's time and market goods. Analogously, health can be produced by diverse activities and goods such as exercise, diet, medical care, and lifestyle changes. Drawing from Grossman's model, the theory of health demand starts by assuming that, for simplicity, people derive utility from two goods: health (H) and a composite of all other fundamental commodities (O), such that

$$U = U(H,O)$$

Both H and O are sums over time, weighted by the person's time preference: Different people have different preferences for when to obtain benefits, some being more impatient than others. H is therefore a weighted sum of the number of healthy days that the person enjoys over a lifetime. These healthy days derive from a person's stock of health (HS) so that the greater health stock will lead to a greater number of healthy days. The health stock as a particular time (HS_t) is determined by the health stock in the previous period (HS_{t-1}) less any depreciation in health stock that has taken place over that period (d_t) plus any investment in health (I_t) that the person has undertaken, such that

$$HS_t = HS_{t-1} - d_t + I_t$$

Health, in this way of thinking, is analogous to other types of capital, such as a machine. For example, one's health can depreciate over time owing to excessive alcohol use or the effects of aging. But this can be offset by other investments that will improve health, such as lifestyle changes or medical care consumption. Both O and I are produced within the household, and we can define a production function for each of them. Production of O and I uses market goods, medical care (M), and all other market goods (X), respectively, and time spent on either in the production of health (T_H) or in the production of other goods (T_O). A third input to both is human capital, usually characterized as the level of education (E). The production functions are therefore

$$I_t = I(M_t, T_H, E_t)$$
$$O_t = O(X_t, T_O, E_t)$$

It is assumed that a person will attempt to maximize his or her utility, but there are two constraints upon this: a time budget and an expenditure budget. The time budget (T) is fixed at 365.25 per year, where time is further constrained to time spent working (T_W) and time spent being sick (T_S), such that

$$T_t = T_{Ht} + T_{Ot} + T_{Wt} + T_{St}$$

The constraint on the expenditure budget is income, which depends on how much time is spent working and the wage rate (W). How much is spent depends on the cost of the market goods, M and X and their prices, and it is assumed that all income is spent, such that

$$P_M (M) + P_X (X) = T_W(W)$$

Both sides of the equation are in terms of present discounted values because they refer to a person's lifetime income and expenditures and are discounted at interest rate, r.

Maximization of the utility function, subject to these constraints and taking into account the production function, leads to an equilibrium condition that can be interpreted as a person equalizing the marginal benefits of health capital and its marginal cost (Grossman, 1972).

EMPIRICAL EVIDENCE CONCERNING THE GROSSMAN MODEL

Several studies have been performed to determine the effects of age, schooling, and wealth on the demand for health (Murrinen, 1982). Researchers have constructed dynamic models to study the investment in health changes over the life cycle (Wagstaff, 1993) and have introduced uncertainty into the investment model. For example, if illness is defined as a state in which the stock of health falls beneath a critical level, the value of investing more in health stock is to reduce the likelihood of entering an illness state (Cropper, 1977). Therefore, health status results from a process in which the individual can only influence the probability of transitions from one health state to another (Zweifel & Breyer, 1997).

Critics of the Grossman Model

Critics of the Grossman model have argued that decisions about health care as part of a rational strategy for investing in health is belied by the facts. One argument states that expenditures on medical care are, in fact, correlated with ill health. Higher expenditure on health is simply a result of responses to negative shocks to the state of health. Others have posited that the great amount of uncertainty associated with the onset of illness makes it impossible to develop a rational plan for investing in health, or a case of rational ignorance. Although it is undeniable that external shocks alter the stock of health during an individual's lifetime, dynamic models should be able to take this into account.

Other critics noted that, while economic studies found an association between poor health and low socioeconomic status in older age groups, epidemiological studies did not. This finding is consistent with the Grossman model but can really be caused by the fact that these health indicators yield different results based on the derived models used due to the latent health at older ages (Salas, 2002). This can be explained as a misspecification of the model.

INTERNATIONAL HEALTH STATUS COMPARISONS

The United States, while spending 13.5% per capita on health care relative to 7.5% in Organisation for Economic Co-operation and Development (OECD) countries, has a ranking on health indicators that is in the bottom half of the OECD countries and has been falling since 1960 (Anderson & Poullier, 1999; Mathers, Sadana, Salomon, Murray, & Lopez, 2001). As seen in Chapter 1, the United States is one of the major spenders on health care in the world but has very poor results related to such expenditures. Much of this is due to socioeconomic disparities and maldistribution of care in the population.

These inequality issues are common in other developed countries, such as the European Union. Research among European countries found that lower socioeconomic status played a role in higher rates of death and poorer health assessments. Among these countries, inequalities in socioeconomics status and health outcomes are associated with inequalities in death due to smoking or alcohol use or appropriate medical interventions (Lazzarino, Yiengprugsawan, Seubsman, Steptoe, & Sleigh, 2014; Mackenbach et al., 2008). Lazzarino and colleagues have also concluded that mental or psychological stress may be the true indicator of socioeconomic differences in health status. These findings are similar to what is understood to be the case in the United States.

Focusing on developing countries, research shows that low income adversely affects health, regardless of age (Cameron & Williams, 2009). This finding is consistent with that in developed countries and may be due to the fact that acute illness plays a dominant role in the health–income relationship, while chronic illness is a major determinant in developed countries such as the United States.

In these international comparisons, it is clear that Grossman's model of health status holds in many of the associations, with new information that stress and coping can play a dominant role in health status determination across countries (Lazzarino et al., 2014).

SUMMARY

Economists see the demand for health as an investment decision. Using this model, health care is not a consumer good but an input into the production of the capital good, the stock of health. This chapter presented the widely used model of the demand for health developed by Michael Grossman, with empirical evidence of the model and numerous international comparisons of health status.

KEY WORDS

- **Diminishing marginal returns**
- **Diminishing marginal utility**
- **Human capital**
- **Indifference curve**
- **Marginal efficiency of capital**
- **Time preference**

Questions

1. Which factors make people more efficient in the production of stock of health?

2. Graphically show the change in demand for health when the wage rate increases.

3. What are the differences between the investment and consumption aspects of the investment in health?

4. How does aging affect the cost of acquiring health capital?

PROFILE: AMARTYA SEN

Amartya Sen spent his life on college and university campuses with parents who were academics. He was born in Santiniketan and spent his early childhood years in Mandalay, Burma, where his father had a visiting faculty position. Long intrigued with social and political issues and debates, Sen held numerous positions throughout his career. These appointments included serving as professor of economics at Jadavpur University Calcutta, the Delhi School of Economics, and the London School of Economics, as well as Drummond Professor of Political Economy at Oxford University. Currently he is Thomas W. Lamont University Professor, and professor of economics and philosophy, at Harvard University, as well as Senior Fellow at the Harvard Society of Fellows. He served as the Master of Trinity College, Cambridge, until 2004.

Sen's research includes social choice theory, economic theory, ethics and political philosophy, welfare economics, theory of measurement, decision theory, development economics, public health, and gender studies. For his vast breadth and depth of work, he received numerous awards including but not limited to Commandeur de la Legion d'Honneur (France), the National Humanities Medal (United States), Honorary Companion of Honour (United Kingdom), Edinburgh Medal (United Kingdom), the George Marshall Award (United States), and the Nobel Prize in Economics in 1998.

Data from Harvard University. (2015). Biographical note: Amartya Sen. Retrieved April 28, 2014, from http://scholar.harvard.edu/sen/biocv; Nobelprize.org. (2015). Amartya Sen: Biographical. Retrieved April 28, 2014, from http://www.nobelprize.org/nobel_prizes/economic-sciences/laureates/1998/sen-bio.html.

REFERENCES

Anderson, G. F., & Poullier, J. P. (1999). Health spending, access, and outcomes: Trends in industrialized countries. *Health Affairs, 18*(3), 178–192.

Becker, G. S. (1965). A theory of the allocation of time. *The Economic Journal, 75*(299), 493–517.

Becker, G. S. (1975). *Human capital: A theoretical and empirical analysis, with special reference to education* (2nd ed.). Chicago, IL: University of Chicago Press.

Bentham, J. (1970). *The collected works of Jeremy Bentham: An introduction to the principles of morals and legislation* (J. H. Burns & H. L. A. Hart, Eds.). New York, NY: Oxford University Press. (Original work published 1780)

Cameron, L., & Williams, J. (2009). Is the relationship between socioeconomic status and health stronger for older children in developing countries? *Demography, 46*(2), 303–324.

Cropper, M. L. (1977). Health, investment in health, and occupational choice. *Journal of Political Economy, 85*(6), 1273–1294.

Culyer, A. J., & Newhouse, J. P. (2000). *Handbook of health economics* (Vol. 1A). New York, NY: Elsevier.

Ederington, J., & Minier, J. (2008). Reconsidering the empirical evidence on the Grossman-Helpman model of endogenous protection. *Canadian Journal of Economics, 41*(2), 501–516.

Evans, G. W., & Kantrowitz, E. (2002). Socioeconomic status and health: The potential role of environmental risk exposure. *Annual Review of Public Health, 23*, 303–331.

Fuchs, V. (1980). *Time preference and health: An exploratory study* (NBER Working Paper No. 539). Cambridge, MA: National Bureau of Economic Research.

Grossman, M. (1972). On the concept of health capital and the demand for health. *Journal of Political Economy, 80*(2), 223–255.

Lazzarino, A. I., Yiengprugsawan, V., Seubsman, S. A., Steptoe, A., & Sleigh, A. C. (2014). The associations between unhealthy behaviours, mental stress, and low socio-economic status in an international comparison of representative samples from Thailand and England. *Globalization and Health, 10*(1): 10.

Mackenbach, J. P., Stirbu, I., Roskam, A. J. R., Schaap, M. M., Menvielle, G., Leinsalu, M., Kunst, A. E. (2008). Socioeconomic inequalities in health in 22 European countries. *New England Journal of Medicine, 358*, 2468–2481.

Mathers, C. D., Sadana, R., Salomon, J. A., Murray, C. J. L., & Lopez, A. D. (2001). Health life expectancy in 191 countries, 1999. *The Lancet, 357*(9269), 1685–1691.

Morris, S., Devlin, N., & Parkin, D. (2007). *Economic analysis in health care.* West Sussex, England: John Wiley & Sons.

Muurinen, J. M. (1982). Demand for health: A generalised Grossman model. *Journal of Health Economics, 1*(1), 5–28.

Salas, C. (2002). On the empirical association between poor health and low socioeconomic status at old age. *Health Economics, 11*(3), 207–220.

Wagstaff, A. (1993). The demand for health: An empirical reformation of the Grossman model. *Health Economics, 2*(2), 189–198.

Zweifel, P., & Breyer, F. (1997). *Health economics.* New York, NY: Oxford University Press.

CHAPTER 7

The Demand for Health Care

By the end of this chapter, the student will be able to:

1. Understand the role of health care as an input to the production of health.
2. Identify the relation of income to demand for health care.
3. Calculate the responsiveness of demand for health care with respect to time, price, and income.
4. Distinguish between individual demand for health care and aggregate demand for health care.

INTRODUCTION

Having established that we can construct a production function for health, we can consider the demand for health care, one of the inputs into the production function. Health care is different from the other inputs in the production of health in several ways. It has no utility apart from promoting health, unlike clothes, cars, and other consumption goods. While some health care is predictable, such as routine preventive services, a least part of the demand for health care is unpredictable in that it is conditional on declines in health status. The level of healthcare expenditure is correlated to the type of health condition and can be very high relative to household income.

This chapter will explore the individual determinants of healthcare demand and the responsiveness of demand to key determinants such as the price of healthcare goods and services, as well as income. Individual and aggregate demand for health care are presented, as well as the implications of a major market failure due to the information problem that consumers face in demanding health care, are explored through the theoretical and empirical research nationally and internationally in supplier-induced demand.

THE DEMAND FOR HEALTH CARE

Anything that increases the demand for health should increase the demand for health care, other things being equal. For instance, higher wages, which make healthy days more valuable, should increase the demand for health and health care because productive days are more valuable. The demand for health care also depends on the particular production function for health. Production functions are always constructed assuming a particular technology. Technological inputs in health care have increased the use of medical inputs in the production of health. They have also increased expectations about improvements in attainable health and therefore have increased the demand for health itself. Individuals

© Odua Images/Shutterstock

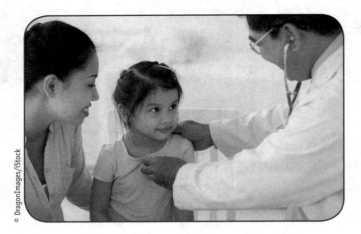

© DragonImages/iStock

do not want to age gracefully in general but to live longer, fuller lives with the most vigor possible (Ebrahim, 2002). This, then, increases the demand for health care in order to decrease the rate of health stock depreciation.

The effect of education on the demand for health care is not as straightforward. If education makes a person more efficient in producing health, an increased awareness of the value of good nutrition and disease prevention will reduce the quantity of health care required to produce a given stock of health. Education can also increase the demand for health itself. The more educated will demand more health but less health care due to efficiencies in obtaining health care if the effect of education on the productivity of inputs into health outweighs the shift in the demand for health. Empirical research provides evidence of the ambiguity of education on the demand for health care (Pohlmeier & Ulrich, 1995; Suziedelyte, 2012; Wagstaff, 1986).

The effect of age on the demand for health care has been found to vary by type of health care required. The demand for ambulatory care—for example, seeing a physician during a given year—decreases significantly with age, but the demand for inpatient services increases (Newhouse & Phelps, 1976) due to the growing complexity of health conditions as people age. Although it has been commonly believed that pharmaceutical expenses increase among the elderly, research has shown that spending growth for these products expands fastest among younger age groups for whom insurance coverage is more extensive (Meara, White, & Cutler, 2004). However, when health status is factored into the estimation, including age on the demand for health care, age is no longer significant. It appears that the deterioration in health status that accompanies age, rather than age itself, increases the demand for health care (Reinhardt, 2003; Zweifel, 1985).

The effect of insurance on the demand for health care is very important. It primarily influences the price of health care, which is a movement along a given demand curve for health care. More insurance coverage decreases the out-of-pocket costs of obtaining care, thus increasing the quantity demanded of care at every market price.

In analyzing the demand for health care, it is important to take into account the concept of need. This is not only true when considering an individual's consumption for health care, but it is also the case that a characteristic of health policy is usually the concept of need, rather than demand, that dominates views about the aims of health services.

If you ask most people what determines their demand for health care, their answer will most likely be that people go to the doctor when they need it. By contrast, the straightforward economics answer would be because they want to do so, which sounds peculiar because no one wants health care for its own sake (Evans, 1984). On face value, Grossman's theory provides a reconciliation of these two views because people want health improvements and demand care that will produce these improvements, holding other related factors constant. However, need is more complicated than that. Need implies that there is an imperative to having health care because it will deal with health problems. In contrast, demand simply implies the willingness and ability to pay for health care. In addition, people have limited knowledge about such needs—about the existence of health problems and the health care that will deal with them. By contrast, the usual assumption of economics is that, in making demands, people are the best judge of their own wants.

Needs and demands can therefore be regarded as two very different ways of viewing healthcare consumption. Two extreme positions may arise. Sometimes there might be a demand with no need. People might be pessimistically mistaken about their health state or optimistically mistaken about the possibilities for improving it. This is the case of the worried well. More important, in practice, there might be need where there is no demand, and if health services only respond to demand, then there is unmet need. Some of the unmet need will be due to deficiencies in information. Unmet needs may also be due to barriers to health care, such as supply factors, which are the availability of services to meet needs, and demand factors, such as prices, incomes, and insurance coverage, which affect the consumer's ability to financially access services (Morris, Devlin, & Parkin, 2007).

ASYMMETRY OF INFORMATION AND IMPERFECT AGENCY

A characteristic of the healthcare market is uncertainty about diagnoses, available treatments, and effectiveness (Arrow, 1963). Some of the uncertainty is irreducible (Pauly, 1978),

© michaeljung/Shutterstock

where neither the doctor nor the patient can know with certainty what the consequences of treatment will be. This leads to the problem of unmet need. However, much of the uncertainty is one sided: The consumer lacks the medical training and knowledge to make informed choices and relies on the healthcare provider to guide him or her through healthcare choices and consumption levels to improve health status.

Information is itself an economic good: Obtaining information—for example, by engaging in consumer research to compare prices and qualities of alternative healthcare providers, or checking the relative costs and efficacies of alternative treatments—is worthwhile if the benefits exceed the costs. When the costs of obtaining information are too high, if information is highly specialized or difficult to obtain, or the likely benefits too low, consumers may choose to be rationally ignorant and to delegate decision making to the service provider. Typically, it is during the patient's contact with the provider that the provider tells the patient what he or she should do (McGuire, 2001), where the provider is acting as an agent for the patient in the healthcare market. As an agent, the provider is attempting to maximize the patient's utility in consumption of healthcare goods and services. In other words, the provider is acting in the best interests of the patient.

This relationship between provider and patient is often presented as a principal–agent problem. The provider is the agent acting on behalf of a principal, who is the patient, in making decisions about which health care to purchase. If providers made these decisions in a manner fully consistent with patients' preferences, unaffected by the consequences for themselves, they would be acting as perfect agents—essentially making the healthcare decisions that the patients would if they had access to the same information. Much of the economics literature has focused on the possibility that providers either cannot or do not act as perfect agents. Specifically, the hypothesis of supplier-induced demand (Evans, 1984) is

that providers engage in some persuasive activity to shift the patient's demand curve in or out depending on the provider's self-interest (McGuire, 2001).

Extensive theoretical and empirical literature exists on this subject. Early studies focused on testing the effects of increased availability of providers on the utilization of health care. A problem with this literature is that many of the findings may be consistent with a noninducement model of how utilization is determined (Morris et al., 2007; Rice, 1998). In research from centrally planned healthcare systems such as Norway (Carlsen & Grytten, 1998; Sorensen & Grytten, 1999), it was found that, once changes in the physician-to-population ratio were accounted for, there was no evidence of inducement for selected outpatient services. In general, and based on most studies, it seems that there is no way in which observed movements in prices and quantities can prove inducement. Of course, this also means that there are no data to disprove it.

However, some findings are clear: A comprehensive review of the literature (McGuire, 2001) and later research (Mulley, 2009; Richardson & Peacock, 2006; Van de Voorde, Van Doorslaer, & Schokkaert, 2001) demonstrate that physicians do respond to financial incentives, and they do appear to influence demand and to do so partly in response to self-interest. Even with this research, the definitive understanding of supplier-induced demand remains elusive. To understand whether patients are being induced to demand more services than they really want, it is necessary to know how much they would have demanded if they were as well informed as the physician. No such study has yet been conducted (Mooney, 1994; Rice, 1998).

Estimates of the Price Elasticity of Demand for Health Care

Responsiveness of consumer demand for health care is measured to changes in the price of a good or service by the **price elasticity of demand**. When measuring the degree of elasticity, a coefficient of -3 is a higher degree of elasticity than that of -0.1 because the coefficient of -3 represents a 300% decrease in quantity demanded for a 100% increase in price, whereas a coefficient of -0.1 reflects only a 10% decrease in quantity demanded associated with a 100% increase in price. The formula for elasticity of demand with respect to price is as follows:

$$\frac{(\% \text{ change in the quantity of health care demanded})}{(\% \text{ change in price of health care})}$$

In general, goods and services that are close substitutes have higher price elasticities because one good or service can be used instead of the other. Complementary goods and services have lower price elasticities because these goods or services are used jointly. The demand elasticity for a good that constitutes a higher proportion of income is also generally higher because the increase in the price of the good or service requires curtailing more consumption expenditures on other goods. An example of this is the price elasticity of demand for high-cost medical procedures. In these cases, the patient may forego the technology if there is no insurance cost share.

The highest price elasticity estimates have been seen for those demanding hospital inpatient and outpatient services and for nursing home services (−1.00, −0.73, and −2.40, respectively). Nursing home services have substitutes in home care and family care services, and these costs represent a high proportion of the budget, which is another reason why elasticities are higher for these services (Zweifel & Breyer, 1997).

Researchers have also estimated price elasticity on sensitivity to variations in prices and among physicians and hospital services. These are culled from specific demand elasticity. A lower number of substitutes for hospitals causes the elasticity for hospital services to be lower than for physician services. Once a physician is chosen, this also limits the number of hospitals that the patient can utilize. Further, health status changes requiring inpatient services may be less discretionary than outpatient services such as office visits.

In international work, researchers (Farag et al., 2012) have found that healthcare demand is least responsive to changes in income in low-income countries and most responsive in middle-income counties. However, for the developing country of Burkina Faso, Sauerborn, Nougtara, and Latimer (1994) found that, among those with the lowest incomes and among infants and children, price elasticities were highest (−1.4, −3.6, and −1.7, respectively). These elasticities were substantially greater than the overall elasticity of −0.79 for this country. Further, in a centrally planned health economy such as Norway, there is no relationship between income and demand for outpatient services such as dental care (Grytten, Holst, & Skau, 2012).

Time Costs and Time Price Elasticities

The time cost is the value of time used in a given activity. Estimates of the price elasticity of demand for any good or service that requires time will tend to be biased if one does not also take into account the time and money costs. The time cost of consuming a healthcare service would be the time involved in waiting for the appointment as well as the travel time. The total cost of services that require time will be higher for patients with higher wage rates because they have a higher opportunity cost of time. Any factor that increases the value of time will increase the opportunity cost of time. For example, when insurance pays for a portion of the market price of health care, the time component of the cost becomes relatively large as a component of total cost. Insurance coverage has been shown to make time a more important consideration in the decision about how much medical care to seek and which providers to use (Acton, 1973). Studies have found that time costs are more important than money costs in healthcare decisions (Coffey, 1983; Murray & Berwick, 2003). Specifically, advanced access to care cannot be sustained if waiting times for appointments for primary care, for example, are always greater than the ability of the providers to accommodate the demand for services (Murray & Berwick, 2003).

AGGREGATE DEMAND FOR HEALTH CARE

Researchers have found that, using healthcare spending per person as a proxy measure for aggregate demand, most of the variation in healthcare demand between countries can be explained using just one variable: the country's income, generally measured as the gross domestic product (GDP) per person. It is clear that there is a positive relation between income and the demand for health care: The richer the country, the more health care will be demanded because health care is a normal or superior good as defined next.

An influential paper on this issue by Newhouse (1977), using simple linear regression analysis in 13 countries, found that GDP per person of a country explains 92% of the variance in the level of spending between countries. These original findings and conclusions were the catalyst for a vast literature that reexamined the determinants of healthcare spending. More recent contributions have focused on econometric issues arising from time series and panel data properties of the data sets used, testing for unit roots and co-integration. The results have either been confirmed (Blomqvist & Carter, 1997; Roberts, 2000) or contradicted (McCoskey & Selden, 1998). A review of the literature by Gerdtham and Jönsson (2001) suggests that the most likely reason for the variation in results is differences in methods. Lago-Peñas, Cantanero-Prieto, and Blázquez-Fernández (2013) found that the relationship between GDP and healthcare expenditures is positive but related to GDP cycles rather than trends. These results imply that further research is required to provide a definitive answer to the income and expenditure relationship.

HEALTH CARE: A NORMAL OR SUPERIOR GOOD?

A **normal good** is a good for which income elasticity is positive but less than 1. This means that, if income increases by a given percentage, the quantity of the good consumed increases but at a lower percentage than associated with the income increase. If the percentage increase in the quantity consumed is greater than the associated percentage increase in income, the good is called a **superior good**.

The answer differs depending on whether studies based on individual responses or those utilizing aggregate data are examined. Several studies in the 1960s through the 1990s provide estimates of income elasticities for health care based on survey data derived from individual responses. A review of these studies shows consensus that most healthcare services have coefficients of income elasticity that are positive and in the r range of 0–1 and can be classified as normal goods. By contrast, studies using macroeconomic data yield considerably higher income elasticity coefficients for health care. A wide range of studies have generally found health care to be a superior good. This is true for both industrialized and developing countries (Scheiber, 1990).

SUMMARY

The demand for health care depends on age, education, income, insurance, the price of other goods and services, and health state. The demand for health care is generally sensitive to price and income, but price elasticities have values ranging between 0 to −1. Health care for which substitutes exist have higher price elasticities than those with fewer substitutes, such as an acute care hospitalization. The association between income and the amount of health care utilized shows that health care can be a normal good when studies are based on individual responses. However, the macroeconomic data that compare country-wide aggregates in income and healthcare spending show that health care is a superior good. This is true for industrialized nations and comparisons between industrialized nations and developing countries.

KEY WORDS

- **Normal good**
- **Price elasticity of demand**
- **Superior good**

Questions

1. How would you expect the price elasticity of demand for health care to vary with health status?

2. Would the demand for health care increase or decrease with an improvement in educational attainment in the community? Explain.

3. Compare the time price elasticity of demand if people reduce their physician visits by 20% when the travel time to get the nearest physician is from 15 to 45 minutes.

4. What are some reasons for variations in the estimates of healthcare expenditures?

PROFILE: DANIEL L. McFADDEN

Daniel L. McFadden was born in 1937 in North Carolina. His early years were spent in a rural part of the state, where he lived on a farm and was an avid reader. He attended rural North Carolina public schools and went on to receive a BS in physics with the highest honors at the age of 19 from the University of Minnesota. His interests shifted to human behavior and he pursued graduate studies at Minnesota under the prestigious Ford Foundation Behavioral Science Training Program that was designated to produce social science scholars. He then earned his PhD in economics in 1962 from this same institution.

His first academic appointment was at the University of Pittsburgh in 1962 as a Mellon postdoctoral fellow; the following year he went on to the University of California, Berkeley. In 1977, he joined the economics department at MIT and was given the James Killian Chair of that department. In 1986, he served as director of the Statistics Research Center at MIT but later felt a better fit back at Berkeley.

Throughout his career, McFadden was influenced by many economics scholars and this shaped his research interests in the economic theory of choice behavior. Most of his papers have origins in applied problems and the development of statistical tools for applied economists. His work has influenced areas such as the adequacy of housing arrangements, financial planning, and the delivery and costs of health services.

McFadden is currently a professor in the graduate school at the University of California, Berkeley's College of Letters and Science. He is widely honored in his field and was the recipient of the Sveriges Riksbank Prize in Economic Sciences in Memory of Alfred Nobel in 2000.

Data from University of California, Berkeley, College of Letters and Science. (2015). Daniel L. McFadden. Retrieved April 28, 2014, from http://eml.berkeley.edu/~mcfadden/; Novelprize.org. (2015). Daniel L. McFadden: Biographical. Retrieved April 28, 2014, from http://www.nobelprize.org/nobel_prizes/economic-sciences/laureates/2000/mcfadden-bio.html.

REFERENCES

Acton, J. P. (1973). *Demand for health care when time prices vary more than money prices*. Santa Monica, CA: RAND Corporation.

Arrow, K. J. (1963). Uncertainty and the welfare economics of medical care. *American Economic Review, 53*(5), 941–973.

Blomqvist, A. G., & Carter, R. A. L. (1997). Is health care really a luxury? *Journal of Health Economics, 16*(2), 207–229.

Carlsen, F., & Grytten, J. (1998). More physicians: Improved availability or induced demand? *Health Economics, 7*(6), 495–508.

Coffey, R. M. (1983). The effect of time price on the demand for medical-care services. *Journal of Human Resources, 18*(3), 407–424.

Ebrahim, S. (2002). The medicalization of old age. *British Medical Journal, 324*(7342), 861–863.

Evans, R. G. (1984). *Strained mercy: The economics of Canadian health care*. Toronto, Canada: Butterworths.

Farag, M., NandaKumar, A. K., Wallack, S., Hodgkin, D., Gaumer, G., & Erbil, C. (2012). The income elasticity of health care spending in developing and developed countries. *International Journal of Health Care Finance and Economics, 12*(2), 145–162.

Gerdtham, U-G., & Jönsson, B. (2001). International comparisons of health expenditure. In A. J. Culyer & J. P. Newhouse, *Handbook of health economics* (Vol. 1A, pp. 11–54). New York, NY: Elsevier.

Grytten, J., Holst, D., & Skau, I. (2012). Demand for and utilization of dental services according to household income in the adult population in Norway. *Community Dentistry and Oral Epidemiology, 40*(4), 297–305.

Lago-Peñas, S., Cantanero-Prieto, D., & Blázquez-Fernández, C. (2013). On the relationship between GDP and health care expenditure: A new look. *Economic Modeling, 32*, 124–129.

McCoskey S. K., & Selden, T. M. (1998). Health care expenditures and GDP: Panel data unit root test results. *Journal of Health Economics, 17*(3), 369–376.

McGuire, T. G. (2001). Physician agency. In A. J. Culyer & J. P. Newhouse, *Handbook of health economics* (Vol. 1A, pp. 461–536). New York, NY: Elsevier.

Meara, E., White, C., & Cutler, D. M. (2004). Trends in medical spending by age, 1963–2000. *Health Affairs, 23*(4), 176–183.

Mooney, G. (1994). *Key issues in health economics*. New York, NY: Pearson.

Morris, S., Devlin, N., & Parkin, D. (2007). *Economic analysis in health care*. West Sussex, England: John Wiley & Sons.

Mulley, A. G. (2009). Inconvenient truths about supplier induced demand and unwarranted variation in medical practice. *British Medical Journal, 339*, b4073.

Murray, M., & Berwick, D. M. (2003). Advanced access: Reducing waiting and delays in primary care. *Journal of the American Medical Association, 289*(8), 1035–1040.

Newhouse, J. P. (1977). Medical-care expenditure: A cross-national survey. *Journal of Human Resources, 12*(1), 115–125.

Newhouse, J. P., & Phelps, C. E. (1976). New estimates of price and income elasticities of medical care services. In R. N. Rosett (Ed.), *The role of health insurance in the health services sector* (pp. 261–320). Cambridge, MA: National Bureau of Economic Research.

Pauly, M. (1978). Is medical care different? In W. Greenberg (Ed.), *Competition in the health care sector: Past, present, and future* (pp. 11–35). Germantown, MD: Aspen Systems.

Pohlmeier, W., & Ulrich, V. (1995). An econometric model of the two-part decisionmaking process in the demand for health care. *Journal of Human Resources, 30*(2), 339–361.

Reinhardt, U. E. (2003). Does the aging of the population really drive the demand for health care? *Health Affairs, 22*(6), 27–39.

Rice, T. (1998). *The economics of health reconsidered.* Chicago, IL: Health Administration Press.

Richardson, J. R., & Peacock, S. J. (2006). Supplier-induced demand: Reconsidering the theories and new Australian evidence. *Applied Health Economics and Health Policy, 5*(2), 87–98.

Roberts, J. (2000). Spurious regression problems in the determinants of health care expenditure: A comment on Hitiris. *Applied Economics Letters, 7*(5), 279–283.

Sauerborn, R., Nougtara, A., & Latimer, E. (1994). The elasticity of demand for health care in Burkina Faso: Differences across age and income groups. *Health Policy and Planning, 9*(2), 185–192.

Scheiber, G. J. (1990). Health expenditures in major industrialized countries, 1960–87. *Health Care Financing Review, 11*(4), 159–167.

Sorensen, R. J., & Grytten, J. (1999). Competition and supplier-induced demand in a health care system with fixed fees. *Health Economics, 8*(6), 497–508.

Suziedelyte A. (2012). How does searching for health information on the Internet effect individuals' demand for health care services? *Social Science and Medicine, 75*(10), 1828–1835.

Van de Voorde, C., Van Doorslaer, E., & Schokkaert, E. (2001). Effects of cost sharing on physician utilization under favourable conditions for supplier-induced demand. *Health Economics, 10*(5), 457–471.

Wagstaff, A. (1986). The demand for health: Some new empirical evidence. *Journal of Health Economics, 5*(3), 195–233.

Zweifel, P. (1985). The effect of aging on the demand and utilization of medical care. In C. Tilquin (Ed.), *Systems sciences in health-social services for the elderly and disabled.* Toronto, Canada: Pergamon Press.

Zweifel, P., & Breyer, F. (1997). *Health economics.* New York, NY: Oxford University Press.

CHAPTER **8**

The Market for Health Insurance

LEARNING OBJECTIVES

By the end of this chapter, the student will be able to:

1. Identify the characteristics of the insurance market.
2. Determine the amount of moral hazard in the insurance market.
3. Analyze the role of and implications of employer-based insurance.
4. Relate the trends in insurance markets.

INTRODUCTION

People buy insurance because they are risk averse. Buying insurance allows a person to pay a certain known amount in order to transfer the risk of a much larger expenditure (in the case of an adverse event such as an illness) to an insurer, known as a third-party payer. Firms sell insurance because they are paid to assume a risk that can be managed by spreading it over a large pool of the insured, with the range such that some have no utilization of care nor adverse events while others have a moderate to large number of adverse health events and subsequent need for utilization of care. Insurance markets exist where consumers are willing to pay enough to transfer risk to induce insurance companies to assume the risk. This chapter examines the characteristics of insurance markets.

THE INSURANCE MARKET

There are several types of risk associated with health. There is the risk to one's health and life associated with illness or disease, such as a sudden bone fracture. There is the additional risk that, if one undertakes treatment, it may or may not cure or alleviate the symptoms of disease, such as the use of an experimental drug. There are also the costs associated with the treatments of illness and disease, such as treatments with iatrogenic effects. A person can take action to reduce the risk of illness, such as getting vaccines, avoiding unhealthy environments, and leading a healthy lifestyle. However, one cannot insure against bad health outcomes. In addition, people do not generally self-insure themselves by saving money when well to use in times of illness. Much of this is due to the fact that people cannot save enough for catastrophic illnesses. Even those with extensive wealth buy insurance due to the fact that most people are **risk averse**.

Economists define risk aversion as a characteristic of people's utility functions. Consumers' attitudes toward risk depend on the marginal utility of an extra dollar that may be different in different ranges of wealth. If the marginal utility of wealth decreases as wealth increases, that is a situation of risk aversion. After a certain wealth level, the additional utility or satisfaction of holding more wealth declines as wealth holdings expand due to such things as increased costs of managing the new wealth accumulations. Given this, it is assumed that people are more likely to buy insurance to cover low-probability events involving large losses or events that follow a hypergeometric distribution.

Setting Insurance Premiums

Insurance is a mechanism for assigning risk to a third party. It is also a mechanism for pooling risk over a large group of insured persons. The price that an insurance company charges for an insurance policy, or premium, is based on the expected payout (amount paid out on average for a large group of insured) plus administrative costs, reserve funds, and profits or surpluses of the insured company. As a result, premiums charged generally exceed the fair value of the risk that the insurance company has assumed, where the fair value is the expected payout or actuarially fair premium.

The part of the insurance premium that exceeds the fair value of the insurance is called the *loading fee*. It is theoretically correct to think of the load, not the premium, as the price of insurance. The price of insurance is the cost of transferring risk. Particularly when comparing different insurance policies, it is convenient to express the loading fee as a percentage based on the ratio of premium to expected payout:

$$L = 100 \times [(\text{premium}/E) - 1], \text{ where}$$
$$E = \text{probability of illness} \times \text{treatment costs}$$

Due to risk aversion, insurance suppliers will be more willing to enter market situations where they can make a reasonable estimate of their payouts, or where they can assess the degree of risk they are assuming. They will also be more willing to insure risky events about which the probability of occurrence is better known.

Experience Versus Community Rating

One common method of pricing insurance is **experience rating**. This occurs when insurance companies base premiums on past levels of payouts, which is often done in the case of car or homeowners insurance. Drivers who have been in an auto accident will find their rates increased, as will homeowners who have had a claim. In the case of health insurance, age and preexisting conditions may be good predictors of future utilization of healthcare services and may be used to determine premiums. Here, the price of insurance is more efficient because insurer profit is based on actual utilization patterns.

Community rating applies when each member of an insurance pool pays the same premium per person or per family for the same coverage, which results in an equitable premium structure. Community rating is inefficient in the sense that the price of insurance to an individual subscriber does not reflect the marginal costs of that individual to the insurer. However, the trade-off between equity and efficiency is usually also considered. Not only do more societies support some intertemporal risk sharing but also some sharing of risk between healthy (or low-risk) and ill (high-risk) individuals.

Moral Hazard

Moral hazard refers to the phenomenon of a person's behavior being affected by his or her insurance coverage. Moral hazard is known to exist in all types of insurance markets. For example, people may be more careless with property that is insured. The main way that moral hazard comes into play in the health insurance market is through an increase in demand for healthcare services utilized in terms of the intensity or quantity of the services regardless of health status and due to the fact that the out-of-pocket costs to consumers of services are lower than the market price for those services.

Moral Hazard and the Structure of Health Insurance Contracts

The reason that in health insurance moral hazard operates differently than in other insurance markets is that health insurance contracts differ from most other forms of insurance. Instead of paying a sum of money to the insured in the case of an adverse event, the price of the health care associated with the adverse event or illness is reduced.

Moral hazard, in the context of the health insurance market, is illustrated in **Figure 8-1**. An individual's demand for health care when he or she has no insurance is denoted

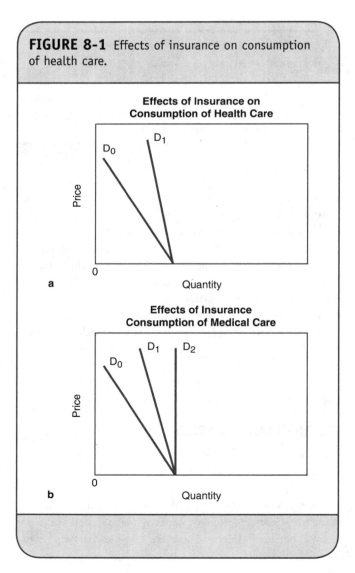

FIGURE 8-1 Effects of insurance on consumption of health care.

by D_0D. If insurance pays 100% of the healthcare bill, the demand curve will shift to D_2D because the individual treats the service as free. D_1D depicts a situation where insurance covers only part of the price charges for the service. The price on the axis is the full market price of care as shared by the insurer and the insured. Therefore, the insured has not had a shift in demand for healthcare services per se but is responding to the decline in out-of-pocket price that results from the insurance company paying all or part of the medical bill.

Some degree of moral hazard exists when the price elasticity of demand for covered healthcare services is greater than zero. In theory, the problem of moral hazard should be greater in the case of policies covering a broader range of services, including more discretionary or elective ones because the price elasticity of demand for these services is believed to be higher than for urgent care, for example. Under these conditions, the consumer is more price sensitive and can be more discretionary in the consumption of the healthcare service in question.

Major healthcare service contracts also differ from most types of insurance in that they generally cover more than unlikely catastrophic events, also fulfilling a function analogous to that of a service contract on an automobile. For example, they include reimbursement insurance for annual physical exams, vaccinations, treatment for chronic conditions, and various types of routine tests. The demand for these services is neither unpredictable nor does it usually entail catastrophic levels of expenditures.

Cost Sharing to Offset the Effects of Moral Hazard

Deductibles. A deductible is a level expenditure that must be incurred before any benefits are paid out. Homeowners and auto insurance policies generally have a deductible per event. The difficulty in deciding what is a separate event in the case of health problems makes this kind of deductible impractical in health care. Health insurance policies generally have yearly deductibles, which is less effective in removing moral hazard. As is typical of all kinds of insurance, the load factor tends to be higher on a health insurance policy with low deductibles because administrative costs constitute a higher proportion of the total cost of the policy to the insurer due to the greater number of claims that will be processed for the period.

Coinsurance. Coinsurance is the proportion of the total expenditure that is paid by the insured. Coinsurance helps to reduce the moral hazard factor for the insured who has spent more than his or her deductible because health care is not free to the consumer.

Use of Usual, Customary Fees to Limit Payments. It has become common practice for insurance policies that reimburse on the basis of fee-for-service to limit reimbursement or insurance payment for covered services to a customary or usual fee within given geographic markets. If a provider charges higher that customary fees, the insured is responsible for the balance of the fee as well as the copayment on the covered portion. It discourages consumer insensitivity to price.

Managed Care. Managed care is a catch-all phrase that describes a variety of different kinds of insurance instruments. Care is actually managed or rationed using such mechanisms as gatekeepers who are primary care physicians who make all referrals to specialists, limiting coverage to service providers with whom the insurance company has a contractual agreement, and requiring precertification or approval from the insurance company before services are rendered. Controls are on the supply side as well as the use of risk-sharing arrangements with healthcare providers.

Stop-Loss Provisions. Many policies also have annual limits on out-of-pocket expenditures (per person or per family) that must be borne by the insured. This is called a *stop-loss provision*. After the insured has paid out an amount equal to the stop-loss threshold, the insurance company pays 100% of additional coverage to healthcare expenses during the year. This increases moral hazard for those with an annual level of expenditures that exceed the stop-loss limit.

Adverse Selection. **Adverse selection** exists when people with different health-related characteristics than the average person increase the amount of health insurance purchased. People know more about their own health status than insurers, and this inequality of information is the basis for risk to insurers due to adverse selection.

In the health insurance market, high-risk people are those with more severe health problems than the average person. These people, who are rationally choosing more comprehensive plans, would be overrepresented in the insurance markets, particularly those with more inclusive policies. This would drive up the premium because the high-risk persons would use more health care, which is greater than their premiums, and drive off those with better health from buying the insurance policies, thus leaving only cost-increasing higher-risk insured in the pool. The existence of adverse selection argues for a single-payer plan because those with higher risk would not be able to pick their insurance plan, and everyone would have the same insurance pool.

Insurer Responses to Selection Problems

Insurers engage in positive selection, where the companies structure coverage to both avoid adverse selection and also to attract lower-than-average risk subscribers. Marketing efforts may be concentrated in communities known to have younger and healthier subscribers. In some cases, insurance companies do not enter or limit participation in markets with large amounts of adverse selection. Because insuring groups of people has the effect of offsetting adverse selection, insurers often avoid the individual or direct pay insurance market.

The disappearance of insurance options due to the spiraling costs associated with adverse selection has been a serious problem in the market for individual, direct pay policies in regions that require community rating. However, New York State's move in 1993 to require community rating for all insurance companies selling policies to individuals or small groups does not appear to have had much effect. A study found no difference in the percentage change in individuals or small groups covered by health insurance in New York State before and after this reform when compared to Connecticut and Pennsylvania that did not impose community rating in the small group and individual market (Buchmueller & DiNardo, 1999).

Offsetting Adverse Selection

The condition necessary for insurance markets to function, even with the problems of adverse selection, was summarized 25 years ago. It is still relevant today: Neither insurance firms nor their consumers have to be perfectly informed about the differences in risk properties that exist among individuals. What is required is that individuals with different risk properties differ on some characteristic that can be linked to the purchase of insurance and that there is some way that an insurance company can discover the link (Rothschild & Stiglitz, 1976).

EMPLOYER-BASED INSURANCE

Advantages of Employer-Based Insurance

The majority of nonretired Americans who have private health insurance are covered by group policies that are part of employer contracts. Employer-based insurance has dominated the market since the 1950s, when price controls on wages made fringe benefits an important part of increasing worker compensation. Group insurance is important for offsetting adverse selection. Community rating applies within the employment group, which results in some degree of risk sharing. Economies of scale in administrative rates are lower than those for individual or direct pay policies. This leads to lower load and lower premium than smaller pool policy groups.

Insurance companies may still use experience rating to charge higher prices to higher-risk groups. The success of this strategy depends on both the stability within the group of the insured and the duration of the group's insurance coverage with the same carrier. Federal law now prohibits employer-based insurance from excluding coverage for preexisting health conditions, even when workers change jobs. It does not, however, regulate which premiums can be charged to groups, although state regulatory agencies may impose restrictions. Over time, as selections and choices among insurance plans have come to be offered within firms to employee groups, adverse selection has emerged as a problem not limited to the individual and small group market.

Disadvantages of Employer-Based Insurance

When health insurance is tied to employment, job loss involves the risk of losing access to affordable health insurance. The Consolidated Omnibus Budget Reconciliation Act of 1985 requires employers to offer former employees an option of purchasing their former group health insurance coverage for up to 18 months after termination of employment. This provides only a temporary solution and may be unaffordable because the employee must pay the entire premium plus a 2% fee.

The tying of health insurance to employment reduces labor mobility and results in what is considered to be job lock. Research leads to the conclusion that employer-provided insurance has reduced labor mobility by about 25% to 30% (Gruber, 2000). The Health Insurance Portability and Accountability Act (HIPAA) of 1996 addresses part of the problem by making it illegal for insurers to exclude any employee from a group plan on the basis of health-related factors or past claims history. However, it may not be possible to find a new job with health benefits and, for an individual who has left employment due to ill health, it may not be possible to get employment at all. In addition, employers may be unwilling to hire a worker whose preexisting conditions may drive up the group health insurance premiums. Under the Affordable Care Act of 2010 (ACA), Americans could cut back on work hours or end unsatisfying jobs (thus ending job lock) because health insurance is now portable (Tanner, 2014). However, the problem with this consequence of the ACA is that people quitting their positions would be subsidized by other taxpayers who may also be in less optimal employment situations. With both acts, unintended consequences exist in that people can be financially penalized due to the fact that they may be unable to get affordable insurance either through lack of access to plans or due to uninsurability (under HIPAA) or higher marginal tax rates with better jobs (under ACA).

Tax Treatment of Employer-Based Insurance

Under federal and state income tax law, health insurance premiums paid by employers as part of the workers' compensation package have been tax-free income to employees and tax-deductible labor costs for firms. It has led to worker preferences for higher proportions of their compensation packages in the form of health insurance because firms can offer workers compensation that represents more after-tax benefits that a cash wage package costing the firm an equal amount. There are further savings to firms and workers in the form of payroll tax (FICA) exclusions on the portion of compensation paid in health insurance premiums rather than wages.

The income-tax free status of employer-based insurance has income distribution effects. Because the federal income tax is progressive, workers with higher wages and salaries who pay higher marginal tax rates receive a larger subsidy.

OPTIMAL INSURANCE CONTRACTS

A problem with constructing an optimal insurance policy is associated with adverse selection. Where there is a menu of health insurance plans available, the less healthy people will be attracted to the more generous plans. A common form of partial risk sharing requires the more generous plans to charge only for the extra cost associated with the extra benefits. In this strategy, it is assumed that the health-related characteristics of members of different plans are on average the same. This method is often used for pricing employer-based insurance.

Optimal insurance also must consider the degree of risk sharing between healthcare providers and insurers. Optimality requires a balance such that the providers neither provide more than medically appropriate nor withhold care.

One problem in modeling the optimal insurance contract is that the degree of moral hazard may vary by type of illness or type of healthcare service. This may lead to very complicated insurance contracts with different degrees of copayments for different services.

There are a wide variety of results associated with empirical research involving optimal insurance contracts. Estimates of optimal coinsurance rates vary from 58% to 25%. Estimates of optimal stop-loss limits vary from $1,000 to greater than $25,000. Using the RAND Health Insurance Experiment Data, Blomqvist (1997) constructed an optimal policy that features coinsurance rates that vary by level of spending. In this plan, up to an expenditure of $1,000 out of pocket, one would pay a 27% coinsurance rate. Beyond that level, coinsurance rates would be reduced. When the out-of-pocket expenses rise above $30,000, the coinsurance rate is reduced to 5% (Aron-Dine, Einav, & Finkelstein, 2012; Cutler & Zeckhauser, 2000). Moral hazard was also seen to be reduced with a simulation that charges copayments for higher-cost treatments and subsidies for low-cost treatments in the example of prostate cancer treatment (Chernew,

Encinosa, & Hirth, 2000). As well, the use of a system of deductibles allows the reduction of moral hazard in health states associated with the largest healthcare expenditures (Drèze & Schokkaert, 2013).

REIMBURSEMENT

The method of reimbursement relates to the way in which healthcare providers are paid for the services they offer. It is useful to distinguish between reimbursement methods because they can affect the quantity and quality of health care. Here, the focus is on methods for reimbursing hospitals.

Retrospective Reimbursement

Retrospective reimbursement at full cost means that hospitals receive payment in full for all healthcare expenditures incurred in some prespecified period of time. Reimbursement is retrospective in the sense that not only are hospitals paid after they have provided treatment but also in that the size of the payment is determined after treatment is provided. Total reimbursement, p, is given either by

$$P = W \times AC$$

Or by

$$P = W \times (S \times I)$$

where W = workload (e.g., number of cases treated), AC = average cost of service provided per case, S = number of services provided per case, and I = fee per item of service. Which model is used depends on whether the hospital is reimbursed on actual costs incurred or on a fee-for-service basis.

The main features of retrospective reimbursement are that, in the actual costs model, hospital income depends on workload and actual costs incurred. In the fee-for-service model, reimbursement depends on workload and the services provided and may be set by competition or by the third-party payer. Because hospital income depends on actual costs incurred or on the volume of services provided, there are few incentives to minimize costs. For example, hospitals might encourage excessively long lengths of stay or may over-order diagnostic tests to boost revenue received.

Prospective Payment

Prospective payment implies that payments are agreed in advance and are not directly related to the actual costs incurred. This does not mean that the hospital received the payment in advance, only that the size of the payment is determined in advance. Because payment is not directly related to the actual costs incurred, incentives to reduce costs are greater, but payers may need to monitor the quality of care provided and access to services. If the hospital receives the same income regardless of quality, there is a financial incentive to provide low-quality care for minimum effort and minimum cost.

Prospective reimbursement can take two forms. With global budgeting, the size of the budget paid to the hospital is set prospectively across the whole range of treatments provided. It is unrelated to the actual costs incurred and to workload. This provides a financial incentive to constrain total expenditure (= W × AC). Global budgeting gives overall expenditure control to the third-party payer, but because the way in which the global budget is distributed throughout the hospital is not specified, the allocation of the global budget within the hospital may not be efficient. The size of the global budget might be set historically with an additional adjustment made each year to account for inflation and changes in case mix, or it might be set according to a resource allocation formula based on the size of the need-weighted population served by the provider. In the latter case, the incentives of the global budget will depend on the precise components of the formula.

With prospectively set cost per case, the amount paid per case (S × I) is determined before treatment is provided. By setting the costs per case prospectively, reimbursement is divorced from the costs incurred (AC) or the services provided per case (S), which generates incentives for the cost containment. Total reimbursement can still be increased by raising workload. Unlike global budgeting, this method does not provide overall expenditure control to the third-party payer.

An example of prospectively set costs per case is the diagnosis-related groups (DRGs) pricing scheme introduced by Medicare in 1984 and later used in other countries. Under this methodology, DRG payments are based on average costs per case in each diagnostic group derived from a sample of hospitals. Total reimbursement achieved by a hospital is given by

$$P = W \times (DRG)$$

where DRG is the DRG-based prospective payment.

The precise effect of this type of reimbursement will depend on the actual costs incurred by the hospital. If DRG < AC, hospitals will reduce AC until DRG = AC; hospitals have an incentive to minimize costs. If DRG > AC, hospitals will increase costs until DRG = AC. They will spend more on amenities in order to improve their competitive position in the healthcare market, which will cause AC to rise.

Predicted effects of the DRG pricing method are cost shifting, patient shifting, and DRG creep. Cost shifting and patient shifting are ways of circumventing the cost-minimizing effects of DRG pricing by shifting patients or some of the services provided to patients out of the DRG pricing method and into other parts of the system not covered by DRG pricing (i.e., shifting inpatient care to outpatient care or nursing homes, which is reimbursed retrospectively). This shift to nursing home services was seen more quickly as DRG payments fell among Medicare recipients (Qian, Russell, Valiyeva, & Miller, 2011). However, for obstetric services, there was no significant association between DRG and the number of outpatient visits post discharge (Shon, Chung, Yi, & Kwon, 2011). DRG creep arises when hospitals deliberately or inadvertently classify cases into DRGs that carry a higher payment, indicating that they are more complicated than they really are.

INTEGRATION BETWEEN THIRD-PARTY PAYERS AND HEALTHCARE PROVIDERS

There are three different kinds of integration between third-party payers and healthcare providers. First, the third-party payer and provider are separate entities with separate aims and objectives. Second, there is selective contracting, with the third-party payer agreeing to steer individuals insured on their plans to selected providers, and, in turn, the selected providers charge lower prices to the insurers. Third, there is vertical integration in which the insurance provider and the healthcare provider merge to become different parts of the same organization. Vertical integration means that a single organization provides health care in return for payment of an insurance premium. Because the two entities are parts of the same organization, they have common goals with respect to cost and quality of care. This is a key feature of managed care.

Managed care organizations (MCOs) have arisen predominantly in the private health insurance sector in the U.S. healthcare system as a means to control spiraling healthcare costs arising from the traditional private health insurance model (sometimes called the *indemnity plan*). Typically, health care is provided by an MCO to a defined population at a fixed rate per month. The payments made by individuals are lower than the direct out-of-pocket payment or indemnity plans. In return for lower premiums, enrollees are required to receive health care from a limited number of providers with whom the MCO has negotiated lower reimbursement rates. There are several broad types of MCOs, reflecting the extent of integration between third-party payers and healthcare providers.

Preferred Provider Organizations

In return for payment of the insurance premium, preferred provider organizations (PPOs) offer insured individuals two options when they require treatment. First, they can use the PPO's providers—those with which it contracts selectively in return for lower reimbursement rates. By using a preferred provider, individuals face lower user charges, and so the reduced costs of care with the preferred provider are passed on to the consumer. Second, individuals may choose to use a different provider outside of the network of preferred providers but with higher user charges. Patients can choose freely because there are no gatekeepers restricting the choices, but there is a clear financial incentive to stay within the network of preferred providers.

Health Maintenance Organizations

In its simplest form, the main feature of a health maintenance organization (HMO) is that the insurance company and the healthcare provider vertically integrate to become different parts of the same organization. The HMO provides health care to the individual in return for a fixed fee, therefore combining the role of the third-party payer and the healthcare provider. HMO members are assigned a primary care provider who serves as a gatekeeper and authorizes any healthcare provided, and the individual must pay the additional charge for any treatment not authorized.

There are four broad types of HMOs, reflecting different relationships between the third-party payer and the healthcare provider. In the staff model, the HMO employs physicians directly. In the group model, the HMO contracts with a group practice of physicians for the provision of care. In the network model, the HMO contracts with a network of group practices. In the case of independent practice associations, physicians in small independent practices contract to service HMO members.

Point-of-Service Plans

Point-of-service (POS) plans are a mixture of PPOs and HMOs. As with PPOs, in return for payment of an insurance premium, patients have two options when they require treatment: use the preferred provider network and have lower charges, or use the non-networked providers on less favorable terms. Unlike PPOs, however, POS plans employ primary care physician gatekeepers who authorize any health care offered by the preferred provider network. In this way, POS plans are like HMOs (Morris, Devlin, & Parkin, 2007).

Patient-Centered Medical Homes

The Patient-Centered Medical Home (PCMH) is a model for the organization of primary care, not just primary care delivery. The care is comprehensive in that it includes preventive, acute, mental health, and chronic care through a team approach in order to reap efficiencies and enhance quality and coordination of care. While the goals are not finance driven, the efficiency, quality, and safety objectives of the PCMH lead to lower costs in healthcare delivery. In the model, payers reward providers with a per member per month bonus for improving primary care services for PCMH patients (Council of Accountable Physician Practices, 2013). In the Patient-Centered Primary Care Collaborative study (2014), researchers found that the PCMHs across the United States made impressive gains in cost and utilization control, health outcomes, and access to care. While there is a gap in clinical satisfaction with the model, the PCMH plays a major role in strengthening accountable care organizations and is very influential in payment reform developments.

Accountable Care Organizations

Accountable care organizations (ACOs) are one of the solutions proposed in the ACA to address the gaps in quality and unrestrained costs of the U.S. healthcare delivery system as seen through the Medicare fee-for-service system (Berwick, 2011). An ACO is a set of healthcare providers that works together and accepts group responsibility for the cost and quality of the care delivered to its patient base. An ACO can be developed with a new team of providers or can evolve from existing organizational structures such as independent practice associations. Insurers are also creating incentives for ACO development for more organized provider groups in their market share or by purchasing physician providers to improve care delivery (Burke, 2011). The Council of Accountable Physician Practices (2013) believes that these organizations should be primary-care centric, with strong specialty and physician-led alliances. They further believe that payments made by insurers or the government should create incentives to control costs and improve quality, not just for the Medicare population but for all patients equally.

Like the PCMH, the ACO is primary-care based but consists of many PCMHs that work together. The major financial difference between the PCMH and ACO models is that the ACOs must be accountable for the cost and quality of care within and beyond the primary care transactions—in other words, the entire care continuum for an episode of care. The benefit of this broader view is that it allows for overall cost management and the ability to determine trends for quality (Council of Accountable Physician Practices, 2013). The real cost savings of ACOs have yet to be determined (Devers & Berenson, 2009; Fisher & Shortell, 2010; Fisher, Staiger, Bynum, & Gottlieb, 2007).

OPTIONS FOR HEALTHCARE FINANCING

The exposition in this section draws from Mossialos, Dixon, Figueras, and Kutzin (2002).

Private Health Insurance

This type of insurance has all of the main features of the basic health insurance model developed in the first part of this chapter. Individuals enter into contracts with insurance providers voluntarily and pay premiums out of pocket, or are paid by their employers as part of their salary package, or both. Private health insurance is usually supplied by providers for profit, although it can also be offered by nonprofit organizations that may have other goals, including prestige or community service such as maximization of covered lives. Most private insurance in the United States is offered through employer-based plans, which are most affordable because they have large and relatively healthy pools of insured. However, this avenue for obtaining private insurance has eroded over time, leading to such reforms such as the ACA. Employer-based coverage is noted for problems in job lock, high administrative costs, and basic inability to cover large groups in the population by the fact that only employees and their dependents can be covered under the policies offered. While this is not an optimal situation, and even with reforms such as the ACA, researchers have concluded that the presence of Medicare and Medicaid and their ability to cover many of the uninsurable weaken political pressure for true universal coverage for all (Enthoven & Fuchs, 2006).

The size of the insurance premium under private insurance is usually based on the risk status of the insured individual or the "community" (i.e., the demographic or geographic utilization group of the insured pool, usually classified by gender and age). Patients may be required to pay user charges, in the form of copayments or deductibles, to cover all or part of the costs of their health care. This helps to reduce the level of moral hazard.

Private insurance can be substitutive, when it provides the only form of insurance coverage for the individual relative to paying for services out of pocket completely; complementary, where it provides coverage for health care that is excluded or not fully covered by compulsory insurance systems; or supplementary, when its role is to increase subscriber choice of provider and improve access to services financially or through an increased approved network of providers.

Social Insurance

Here, workers, employers, and government all contribute to the financing of health care by paying into a social insurance fund. Payments by employees can be fixed, or related to the size of their income, but not to their individual risk. Many countries finance their social insurance funds by means of a payroll tax, with each firm paying an amount depending on the number of people it employs. Social insurance funds are usually independent of direct government control.

Membership of social insurance funds may be assigned according to occupation or region of residence, or individuals may be free to choose a fund. Children are covered through their parents' funds, and husbands and wives who do not work are covered by their spouses' funds. Contributions can be made into social insurance funds for retired and unemployed individuals either by the state or via pension funds and unemployment funds. Often, the premiums are subsidized by the government and are more affordable than premiums under private insurance plans.

HEALTH INSURANCE AND THE CONSUMPTION OF HEALTH CARE

Health insurance operates to increase the quantity demanded of health care by lowering the effective price to consumers. The magnitude of the effect will depend on how much the policy reduces the out-of-pocket payment below the market price and the price elasticity of demand for health care. There is a potential problem that the amount of insurance coverage people choose may not be independent of their demand for health care. The RAND Health Insurance Experiment provided estimates that are free from this bias, and the study design allows estimation of the effects of marginal rates of insurance coverage on the quantity of health care consumed. The RAND study found a range of coinsurance elasticity estimates for health care centering on -0.2 (Newhouse, 1988). This means that when coinsurance rates change by 10%, the quantity of health care utilized changes by 2%. This estimate is widely used in economic studies (Zweifel & Manning, 2000) but has been challenged based on differing modeling strategies and assumptions of insurance contracts (Aron-Dine et al., 2012).

Insurance Coverage and Time Costs

When insurance coverage lowers the monetary costs of healthcare services to people, the time cost becomes a more important component of total cost. This will tend to increase the time price elasticity of demand for health care, with the result that consumers may shift to using healthcare services that have higher monetary costs but fewer time costs (i.e., waiting time or travel time). Growth in wages or salaries increases the opportunity cost of time, which will lead to a tendency to substitute away from time-intensive health care. To the extent that insurance coverage is positively correlated with earnings, the substitution from time-intensive healthcare services to more expensive services will be enhanced.

Insurance Coverage and the Market Price of Health Care

More extensive insurance coverage on the part of a community will tend to increase the quantity of health care that will be consumed at a given market price. This implies that there will be a shift in demand. **Figure 8-2** shows that a hypothetical increase in a community's demand for health care will depend on the change in its market price as well as the change in insurance coverage. This also depends on the nature of the supply of services in the market. The supply curve is upward sloping as the change in the price of health care causes a rise

in the quantity supplied of health care. Over time, the out-of-pocket prices of health care for the community will rise as the market price of health care rises. Insurance companies will also experience higher payouts, and they will respond by raising premiums charged for the same coverage or by holding premiums constant and reducing coverage.

Health policy analysts are interested in what happens to the community's total expenditures on health care as insurance coverage increases. In Figure 8-2, the community's expenditure on health care, not including insurance costs, is represented by $P_1 \times Q_1$—before expansion of insurance coverage—and $P_2 \times Q_2$ after demand shifts outward. Total expenditures on health care rise with an increase in insurance coverage, even though there may be little change in total out-of-pocket expenditures. A full consideration of healthcare expenditures should also include an analysis of the expenditure on insurance. For instance, research based on the RAND Health Insurance Experiment data estimate that only 10% of the increase in U.S. healthcare expenditures between the end of World War II and the mid-1980s was associated with an increase in insurance coverage (Aron-Dine et al., 2012; Newhouse, 1988).

The majority of economists have agreed that the favorable tax treatment given to health insurance created a welfare loss to society by encouraging workers to purchase more extensive insurance coverage than was socially optimal (Arrow, 1963). The argument was that tax-free status of employee health insurance led people to be insured to the point where the marginal value of insurance benefits is less than the marginal cost of the insurance in taxable dollars (Feldstein & Friedman, 1977).

The cost to society of subsidizing health insurance was considered to be a function of the price elasticity of demand for health care and the elasticity of supply for healthcare services. The lower the elasticity of supply, the greater the social cost because the effect of increased demand for health care will then cause a corresponding increase in price (see Figure 8-2).

A counterargument is that the favorable tax treatment of health insurance, which has also stimulated the growth of employer-based insurance, has increased access to group insurance for those who may not have purchased individual or direct pay insurance. Therefore, the correct measure of welfare loss due to moral hazard would calculate how much extra health care a consumer would demand if he or she purchased an actuarially fair contract when ill (Nyman, 2001). A study by Nyman that addressed the issue of providing health insurance coverage to those previously uninsured found that favorable tax treatment of employer-based insurance would

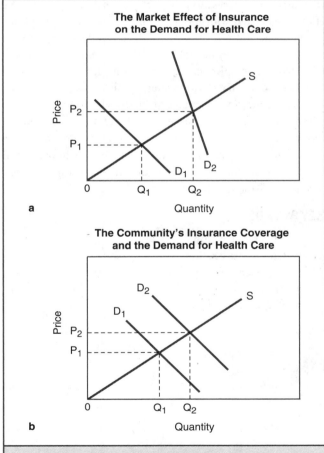

FIGURE 8-2 The market effect of insurance on the demand for health care and the community's insurance coverage and the demand for health care.

The Market Effect of Insurance on the Demand for Health Care

The Community's Insurance Coverage and the Demand for Health Care

Data from Johnson-Lans, S. (2004). *A Health Economics Primer*. Boston: Pearson, Addison Wesley.

reduce healthcare spending by considerably less than had been predicted in most of the literature and that more than half of the reduction in spending would result from a decline in the number of people having any coverage rather than from a reduction in coverage.

INSURANCE TRENDS

Over the past 20 years there has been a noticeable decrease in the amount that employers are willing to pay for insurance premiums. Firms increasingly offer only base-level insurance plans and give employees the option of paying the difference if they choose more extensive coverage. Several reasons have been given for this phenomenon in addition to the rise in health insurance premiums: the recession in the late 1980s and early 1990s, then extension of Medicaid coverage to more low-income worker families, and the growth of dual-earner families, which reduced the pressure of employers to cover dependents. The decline in unionizations has been found to explain approximately one-quarter of the reduction in the generosity of plans (Buchmueller, Dinardo, & Valletta, 2002).

Health insurance coverage has declined in large part because workers have not exercised options to purchase it. The rise in insurance premiums and the cutback in the proportion of the premiums that employers are willing to pay have left many workers with unaffordable premium costs. Cutler (2002) found a significant drop in take-up rates on the part of employees offered insurance during the period 1998 to 2001. There are important policy implications associated with the fact that a growing proportion of the 44 million uninsured Americans in 2004 were workers and families of employed persons. This growth in the uninsured has risen to 50 million (Dvorak, 2013) and has led to numerous attempts at reforming the health insurance system in the United States at the state and national levels. The key reform at the national level to close the coverage gap is the ACA of 2010. However, critics of this act conclude that it is more incremental than sweeping as a goal for universal coverage and has many opportunities for unsustainable spending.

SUMMARY

The demand for health insurance exists because of the uncertainty associated with a person's state of health and the risk of very large expenditures in the case of illness. Health insurance provides risk sharing between the insured and the insurer, pooling risks among the insured, and sometimes risk sharing between the insurer and healthcare providers. Insurance is a mechanism for transferring funds from the state in which a person is well to the costly state of illness, as well as between people who are well to those requiring health care. Because most private insurance is purchased through the workplace in employer-based plans, there is a degree of community rating involved in the pricing of insurance policies. Group insurance is a mechanism for dealing with adverse selection.

Insurance increases the demand for health care as well as its price. After decades of discussion, questions still remain about the welfare effects of subsidizing employer-based insurance through favorable tax treatment. Recent literature suggests that there are positive welfare effects associated with increasing access to group insurance as well as negative effects associated with moral hazard. Increases in premiums and cutbacks in the proportion of the premiums that employers are willing to pay have shifted the focus of policy concerns from whether employees have typical insurance coverage to whether too few have any coverage at all.

Trends in coverage have shifted away from employer-based plans and created more incentives for job lock and the risk of uninsurability if people become unemployed. This has led to more activity for health insurance reforms and the passage of attempts to create universal coverage through mechanisms such as the ACA.

KEY WORDS

- **Adverse selection**
- **Community rating**
- **Experience rating**
- **Moral hazard**
- **Risk averse**

Questions

1. How would you define a risk-neutral person in the context of making decisions about health insurance?

2. What is meant by a loading fee when considering the price of an insurance policy? Why is the loading fee a higher proportion of the premium when people choose low deductibles?

3. Define moral hazard and provide an example.

4. What are the advantages and disadvantages of community rating of health insurance? Consider both equity and efficiency.

PROFILE: ERIC S. MASKIN

Eric S. Maskin was born in New York City in 1950 and spent his early years in Alpine, New Jersey. While in high school, he stumbled upon economics in a topics course and was drawn to the applied mathematics of the field, earning both an AB and PhD (1976) in economics from Harvard University.

Maskin's first academic appointment was at MIT, which he held from 1977 to 1984; he returned to Harvard from 1985 to 2000. After 15 years at Harvard, he was offered and accepted a position at the Institute for Advanced Study, which he held from 2000 to 2011 as the Albert O. Hirschman Professor of Social Science. He is currently the Adams University Professor at Harvard.

Maskin has a diverse portfolio of research that includes game theory, the economics of incentives, and contract theory. His most renowned work is in dynamic games, which has applications to health economics. He has been highly influenced by well-known economists and he himself had numerous honors, including receiving the Sveriges Riksbank Prize in Economic Sciences in Memory of Alfred Nobel in 2007.

Data from Nobelprize.org. (2015). *Eric S. Maskin: Biographical.* Retrieved May 10, 2014, from http://www.nobelprize.org/nobel_prizes/economic-sciences/laureates/2007/maskin-bio.html; Harvard University. (2015). Eric S. Maskin. Retrieved from May 10, 2014, http://scholar.harvard.edu/maskin/home.

REFERENCES

Aron-Dine, A., Einav, L., & Finkelstein. A. (2012). *The RAND health insurance experiment, three decades later* (NBER Working Paper No. 18642). Cambridge, MA: National Bureau of Economic Research.

Arrow, K. J. (1963). Uncertainty and the welfare economics of medical care. *American Economic Review, 53*(5), 941–973.

Berwick, D. M. (2011). Launching accountable care organizations—The proposed rule for the Medicare Shared Savings Program. *New England Journal of Medicine, 364*(32), 1–3.

Blomqvist, A. (1997). Optimal non-linear health insurance. *Journal of Health Economics, 16*(3), 303–321.

Buchmueller, T., & DiNardo, J. (1999). *Did community rating induce an adverse selection death spiral? Evidence from New York, Pennsylvania and Connecticut* (NBER Working Paper No. 6872). Cambridge MA: National Bureau of Economic Research.

Buchmueller, T. C., Dinardo, J., & Valletta, R. G. (2002). Union effects on health insurance provision and coverage in the United States. *Industrial and Labor Relations Review, 55*(4), 610–627.

Burke, T. (2011). Accountable care organizations. *Public Health Reports, 126*(6), 875–878.

Chernew, M. E., Encinosa, W. E., & Hirth, R. A. (2000). Optimal health insurance: The case of observable, severe illness. *Journal of Health Economics, 19*(5), 585–609.

Council of Accountable Physician Practices. (2013). *Accountable care organizations: Frequently asked questions and research summary.* Retrieved from http://c0024345.cdn1.cloudfiles.rackspacecloud.com/LegislativeDownload.pdf

Cutler, D. M. (2002). *Employer costs and the decline in health insurance coverage* (NBER Working Paper No. 9036). Cambridge, MA: National Bureau of Economic Research.

Cutler, D. M., & Zeckhauser, R. J. (2000). The anatomy of health insurance. In A. J. Culyer & J. P. Newhouse, *Handbook of health economics* (Vol. 1A, pp. 563–644). New York, NY: Elsevier.

Devers, K. J., & Berenson, R. A. (2009). *Can accountable care organizations improve the value of health care by solving the cost and quality quandaries?* Washington, DC: Urban Institute.

Drèze, J. H., & Schokkaert, E. (2013). Arrow's theorem of the deductible: Moral hazard and stop-loss in health insurance. *Journal of Risk and Uncertainty, 47*(2), 147–163.

Dvorak, D. (2013, April 15). Beyond Obamacare: How a single payer system can save health care in the United States. *Minnesota Medicine.* Retrieved from www.pnhp.org/news/ 2013/april/beyond-obamacare

Enthoven, A. C., & Fuchs, V. R. (2006). Employment-based health insurance: Past, present, and future. *Health Affairs, 25*(6), 1538–1547.

Feldstein, M., & Friedman, B. (1977). Tax subsidies: The rational demand for insurance and the health care crisis. *Journal of Public Economics, 7*(2), 155–178.

Fisher, E. S., & Shortell, S. M. (2010). Accountable care organizations: Accountable for what, to whom, and how. *Journal of the American Medical Association, 304*(15), 1715–1716.

Fisher, E. S., Staiger, D. O., Bynum, J. P. W., & Gottlieb, D. J. (2007). Creating accountable care organizations: The extended hospital medical staff model. *Health Affairs, 26*(1), w44–w57.

Gruber, J. (2000). Health insurance and the labor market. In A. J. Culyer & J. P. Newhouse, *Handbook of health economics* (Vol. 1A, pp. 645–706). New York, NY: Elsevier.

Morris, S., Devlin, N., & Parkin, D. (2007). *Economic analysis in health care.* West Sussex, England: John Wiley & Sons.

Mossialos, E., Dixon, A., Figueras, J., & Kutzin, J. (Eds.). (2002). *Funding health care: Options for Europe.* Buckingham, England: Open University Press.

Newhouse, J. P. (1988). Has the erosion of the medical market place ended? *Journal of Health Politics, Policy and Law, 13*(2), 263–278.

Nyman, J. A. (2001). The income transfer effect, the access value of insurance and the RAND health insurance experiment. *Journal of Health Economics, 20*(2), 295–298.

Patient-Centered Primary Care Collaborative. (2014). *The medical home's impact on cost and quality: An annual update of the evidence, 2012–2013*. New York, NY: Milbank Memorial Fund.

Qian, X., Russell, L. B., Valiyeva, E., & Miller, J. E. (2011). "Quicker and sicker" under Medicare's prospective payment system for hospitals: New evidence on an old issue from a national longitudinal survey. *Bulletin of Economic Research, 63*(1), 1–27.

Rothschild M., & Stiglitz, J. (1976). Equilibrium in competitive insurance markets: An essay on the economics of imperfect information. *Quarterly Journal of Economics, 90*(4), 629–649.

Shon, C., Chung, S., Yi, S., & Kwon, S. (2011). Impact of DRG payment on the length of stay and the number of outpatient visits after discharge for cesarean section during 2004–2007. *Journal of Preventive Medicine and Public Health, 44*(1), 48–55.

Tanner, M. (2014, March 1). In fighting the "job lock," Democrats opened a poverty trap. *New York Post*. Retrieved from http://nypost.com/2014/03/01/in-fighting-the-job-lock-democrats-opened-a-poverty-trap/

Zweifel, P., & Manning, W. G. (2000). Moral hazard and consumer incentives in health care. In A. J. Culyer & J. P. Newhouse, *Handbook of health economics* (Vol. 1A, pp. 409–460). New York, NY: Elsevier.

CHAPTER **9**

Health Disparities

INTRODUCTION

The United States spends more on health care than any other country in the world, whether measured in total dollars spent, per capita expenditures, or as a share of the gross domestic product. For all of this spending, it is unclear whether the United States is healthier than its foreign counterparts. Critics of the system say that life expectancy is lower than in other countries, and the higher infant mortality combined with the extreme healthcare spending bolster their argument that the system is in need of a major overhaul. In this chapter, the student will learn about the measures for health disparities and the associated affect on health outcomes, as well as a growing concern in America regarding the obesity epidemic.

HEALTH DISPARITIES

Health disparities is a multidimensional concept that includes such aspects of the population as race, ethnicity, gender, geographic location, and **socioeconomic status (SES)**, to name a few. In general, if a health outcome has variation within a population, then there is a health disparity.

In 2008, the U.S. population of 304 million had a profile as follows (U.S. Department of Health and Human Services, 2014):

- Thirty-three percent identified themselves as part of a racial or ethnic minority group.
- Fifty-one percent were women.
- Twelve percent of the noninstitutionalized population identified themselves as having a disability.
- Twenty-three percent of the population lived in rural areas.

Given these characteristics and the fact that differences in health status along racial or socioeconomic lines are considered unjust in society (Adler & Stewart, 2010), the movement is toward **health equity**, or the attainment of the best health status of all people regardless of gender, racial, ethnic, socioeconomic, or geographic diversity. Historically, the attainment of health equity focused on the treatment of disease and access to health services.

The incentive to move toward health equity is due to the fact that people who are poorer and who have less education are more likely to suffer from diseases and to experience loss of functioning and higher morbidity and mortality rates (Crimmins, Hayward, & Seeman, 2004; Marmot, Ryff, Bumpass, Shipley, & Marks, 1997). People in higher SES are much less likely to have health conditions, and these health disparities are also found in other countries (Crimmins, et al., 2004; Crimmins & Saito, 2001). This is because people in different SES strata have very different experiences, opportunities, and environmental and social exposures

(Williams & Collins, 1995). SES is more than income or wealth or educational attainment, it is access to opportunities over the life course (Oakes & Rossi, 2003). At times, these complex interrelationships lead to great differences in access to care and associated health outcomes.

Pathways of the Effect of SES on Health Status

Several environmental, social, and behavioral pathways exist in the way that SES affects health status and results in health disparities. First, healthcare access gets most of the public's and policymaker's attention because those with less income and inadequate health insurance will be unable to access affordable quality care, resulting in poorer health outcomes. However, financial access to care through improved or universal insurance coverage does not alleviate all health disparities because time costs are also involved, such as travel time, flexibility in making appointments, and self-control, all of which are difficulties faced by those disenfranchised in the system. A second pathway is environmental, with those in lower SES often exposed to hazardous occupational and residential environments. People faced with **environmental injustice**, or inequities in environmental factors, have fewer resources to cope with these effects on health. Third, nearly all health behaviors and habits, such as diet, exercise, and smoking, are associated with SES and contribute to increased **morbidity** or illness among those in lower educational and income classes (Adler & Stewart, 2010). Due to these multiple variables, researchers must spend more effort in understanding how health disparities arise and the true pathways that need correction to eliminate health status inequalities.

SES and the Life Course

SES and health status can be both causes and consequences of one another. For example, health problems that arise in adulthood can affect work life, earnings, and wealth accumulation (Shea, Mikes, & Hayward, 1996). In older years, wealth can be depleted due to chronic health conditions requiring large amounts of healthcare resources (Smith, 1999). Further, SES is a complex driver of racial differences in health status (Williams, Mohammed, Leavell, & Collins, 2010). Therefore, the relationship and causality of SES and health can vary significantly over the age of the individual.

The perspective of the effect of SES over the life course on health status explains a large amount of the variation in health across many social strata. Warner and Hayward (2002) found that childhood social circumstances and SES explain much of the gap in mortality rates between blacks and whites. There appears to be a strong protective effect of intact families on the health status of individuals in later life. As well, individuals who are raised in higher SES families and environments have better access to information, nutrition, and lower hazardous exposures that usually lead to improved career and housing opportunities. Further, these higher-status individuals are usually treated better when obtaining healthcare services and have better lifestyle choices (Winkleby, Kraemer, Ahn, & Varady, 1998). Haas, Krueger, and Rohlfsen (2012) have also found that a large amount of racial and ethnic health disparities in adults are affected by SES disadvantages in childhood and young adulthood. Therefore, when examining health disparities, the link between both SES and health status, as well as SES and the mechanisms in the life course it influences, must be examined. This further suggests that disparities can be alleviated in many points in life and through a variety of pathways. However, identifying the mechanisms in which SES affects the health status of individuals is particularly challenging because many of the data elements for the life course are not available in surveys or other administrative sources.

One group that appears to have a consistent result concerning SES and health than what was previously presented is the U.S. Hispanic population. Even though Hispanics have higher poverty rates, poorer educational attainment, and poorer healthcare access, the health outcomes for this subgroup are at least as good as for non-Hispanic whites. This is known as the **epidemiological paradox**, or the Hispanic health paradox. Morales, Lara, Kington, Valdez, and Escarce (2002) found substantial support for this paradox and note that more research is needed to better understand the protective factors of this subgroup in maintaining health status.

THE OBESITY EPIDEMIC

Obesity is at epidemic proportions in the United States and is strongly associated with SES at least among whites (Centers for Disease Control and Prevention [CDC], 2011). Specifically, the CDC presented the following findings:

- For most sex–age groups in the United States, whites have a lower prevalence of obesity than blacks or Mexican Americans.
- Along gender lines, black women have the highest prevalence of obesity, while Mexican-American males aged 20 or younger have the highest prevalence.
- There is a strong negative association between family income and the prevalence of obesity among whites, but there is a weaker association in the other groups or a positive association among black or Mexican-American men (Ogden, Lamb, Carroll, & Flegal, 2010).
- These racial and ethnic differences in obesity prevalence occur after controlling for family income.

Further, results of an evaluation of *Healthy People 2010* objectives found that little progress was made in nutrition and weight goals for the U.S. population (Moyer, 2011). For example, the percentage of obese adults increased from 23% during 1988–1994 to 34% during 2005–2008. More troubling is that the obesity rate among children increased in these periods from 11% to 17%. Because health disparities in obesity exist (Chang & Lauderdale, 2005), the public and policymakers must develop and implement practical interventions such as information on good nutrition (Kumanyika & Krebs-Smith, 2000) and lifestyle choices in order to reduce morbidity due to obesity-related conditions such as diabetes and cardiovascular disease. Research also needs to use a disparities lens to examine the multiple pathways to being the advantaged or disadvantaged, the deprived, or the socially excluded (Braveman, 2009). However, the challenge in implementing such recommendations can be seen in inequalities in environments that may preclude those disadvantaged from being able to access built environments to exercise safely or appropriate venues to obtain nutritious foods. This has been shown by Gordon-Larsen, Nelson, Page, and Popkin (2006) where low SES and high-minority areas were associated with reduced access to exercise facilities and safe walking, which resulted in increased weight.

Minority Youth: A Growing Target for Obesity

Childhood obesity has been associated with an increased prevalence of precursors for cardiovascular disease, type 2 diabetes, metabolic syndrome, and certain cancers (Weiss et al., 2004). More concerning is that, over the past 20 years, minority youth have had growing proportions of obese members. Given these statistics, it is imperative that interventions are put into place for minority youth in particular in order to eliminate health disparities across many chronic diseases.

Minority children experience disparities in access to quality care, insurance access, and referrals to specialists, as well as racial differences regardless of SES (Wilson, 2009). Moreover, minority youth have disparities over the life course, with adult minorities having significantly worse mortality rates than whites from cardiovascular disease, most

cancers, diabetes, and cerebrovascular disease, for example (Sorlie, Rogot, Anderson, Johnson, & Backlund, 1992), which are all obesity related as well.

Obesity Prevention Paradigms

In the United States, treatment is often at the individual level. This is politically neutral and does not challenge the more collective orientation of broad-based policies on food choices such as sugary drinks. These approaches also focus on the individual's responsibility for his or her actions and ultimate health status.

According to Kumanyika (2005), however, these personal actions are performed within a cultural and environmental context where those in lower SES are faced with a range of eating or physical activity choices that can be quite different from those in higher SES classes. Therefore, population-oriented interventions are more appropriate because they are geared more for aggregate control rather than punishing the victim if his or her choice sets are limited, leading to poorer health outcomes.

SUMMARY

SES is related to nearly all health outcomes, but as people age the direction of the causal relationship is unclear. For example, for older people the relationship between SES and health is a combination rather than a strict causation. There are also complex pathways that exist between SES and health status, particularly so for the growing obesity epidemic. Finally, population-oriented policy and intervention to reduce obesity prevalence in society is preferred, especially for those who are disadvantaged by race, ethnicity, or SES.

KEY WORDS

- **Environmental injustice**
- **Epidemiological paradox**
- **Health disparities**
- **Health equity**
- **Morbidity**
- **Socioeconomic status (SES)**

Questions

1. What are the main determinants of health disparities and how can these be modified to improve health status in society?

2. Why is health equity important in society and why would it be financially feasible in the health economy?

3. What are the pros and cons of interventions that are individually based versus population based?

PROFILE: JOHN R. HICKS

John R. Hicks was born in 1904 in Warwick, England, and attended Clifton College and Baillol College in Oxford to study mathematics under a scholarship. He eventually earned a degree in philosophy, politics, and economics at Oxford, which was not held in very high esteem there as it was a new and rather unsuccessful program. His first appointment was at the London School of Economics, where he initially focused on labor economics but later moved into analytical economics.

Hicks held numerous appointments at Cambridge University and Oxford University and was as a research fellow at All Souls College. During this time, he researched welfare economics and in later years he contributed to the field of theoretical economics as well as several areas in applied economics.

Hicks's work is broad and highly acclaimed. Notable honors include being named a Fellow of the British Academy in 1942,

being knighted in 1964, and being named honorary doctor in several British universities. He also received the Sveriges Riksbank Prize in Economics in Memory of Alfred Nobel in 1972 for his far-reaching work in elasticity of substitution, macroeconomics, one of the first works on general equilibrium theory, and compensation tests in welfare economics. Specifically, he received the Nobel Prize for general equilibrium theory and welfare theory.

Data from Nobelprize.org. (2015). *John R. Hicks: Biographical.* Retrieved July 10, 2014, from http://www.nobelprize.org/nobel_prizes/economic-sciences/laureates/1972/hicks-bio.html; Library of Economics and Liberty. (2008). *John R. Hicks: The concise encyclopedia of economics.* Retrieved July 10, 2014, from http://www.econlib.org/library/Enc/bios/Hicks.html.

REFERENCES

Adler, N. E., & Stewart, J. (2010). Health disparities across the lifespan: Meaning, methods, and mechanisms. *Annals of the New York Academy of Sciences, 1186,* 5–23.

Braveman, P. (2009). A health disparities perspective on obesity research. *Preventing Chronic Disease: Public Health Research, Practice, and Policy, 6*(3), A91–A97.

Centers for Disease Control and Prevention. (2011). CDC health disparities and inequalities report—United States, 2011. *Morbidity and Mortality Weekly Report, 60.* Retrieved from www.cdc.gov/mmwr/pdf/other/su6001.pdf

Chang, V. W., & Lauderdale, D. S. (2005). Income disparities in body mass index and obesity in the United States, 1971–2002. *Archives of Internal Medicine, 165*(18), 2122–2128.

Crimmins, E. M., Hayward, M. D., & Seeman, T. E. (2004). Race/ethnicity, socioeconomic status, and heath. In N. B. Anderson, R. A. Bulatao, & B. Cohen (Eds.), *Critical perspectives on racial and ethnic differences in health in late life* (pp. 310–352). Washington, DC: National Academies Press.

Crimmins, E. M., & Saito, Y. (2001). Trends in health life expectancy in the United States, 1970–1990: Gender, racial, and educational differences. *Journal of Social Science and Medicine, 52*(1), 1629–1641.

Gordon-Larsen, P., Nelson, M. C., Page, P., & Popkin, B. M. (2006). Inequality in the built environment underlies key health disparities in physical activity and obesity. *Pediatrics, 117*(2), 417–424.

Haas, S. A., Krueger, P. M., & Rohlfsen, L. (2012). Race/ethnic and nativity disparities in later life physical performance: The role of health and socioeconomic status over the life course. *The Journals of Gerontology Series B: Psychological Sciences and Social Sciences, 67B*(2), 238–248.

Kumanyika, S. (2005). Obesity, health disparities, and prevention paradigms: Hard questions and hard choices. *Preventing Chronic Disease: Public Health Research, Practice, and Policy, 2*(4), 1–9.

Kumanyika, S. K., & Krebs-Smith, S. M. (2000). Preventive nutrition issues in ethnic and socioeconomic groups in the United States. In A. Bendich & R. J. Deckelbaum (Eds.), *Nutrition, Volume II: Primary and secondary prevention* (pp. 325–356). Totowa, NJ: Humana Press.

Marmot, M., Ryff, C. D., Bumpass, L. L., Shipley, M., & Marks, N. F. (1997). Social inequalities in health: Next questions and converging evidence. *Social Science and Medicine, 44*(6), 901–910.

Morales, L. S., Lara, M., Kington, R. S., Valdez, R. O., & Escarce, J. J. (2002). Socioeconomic, cultural, and behavioral factors affecting Hispanic health outcomes. *Journal of Health Care for the Poor and Undersesrved, 13*(4), 477–503.

Moyer, C. S. (2011, October 24). Healthy People 2010 misses targets on obesity and health disparities. *Amednews.com.* Retrieved from www.amednews.com/article/20111024/ health/310249947/4/

Oakes, J. M., & Rossi, P. H. (2003). The measurement of SES in health research: Current practice and steps toward a new approach. *Social Science and Medicine, 56*(4), 769–784.

Ogden, C. L., Lamb, M. M., Carroll, M. D., & Flegal, K. M. (2010). *Obesity and socioeconomic status in adults: United States, 2005–2006* (NCHS Data Brief No. 50). Washington, DC: U.S. Department of Health and Human Services.

Shea, D. G., Mikes, T., & Hayward, M. (1996). The health–wealth connection: Racial differences. *The Gerontologist, 36*(3), 342–349.

Smith, J. P. (1999). Healthy bodies and thick wallets: The dual relation between health and economic status. *Journal of Economic Perspectives, 13*(2), 145–166.

Sorlie, P., Rogot, E., Anderson, R., Johnson, N. J., & Backlund, E. (1992). Black-white mortality differences by family income. *The Lancet, 340*(8815), 346–350.

U.S. Department of Health and Human Services. (2014). *Disparities: Healthy People 2020.* Retrieved from www.healthypeople.gov/2020/about/foundation-health-measures/ Disparities

Warner, D. F., & Hayward M. D. (2002, May). *Race disparities in men's mortality: The role of childhood social conditions in a process of cumulative disadvantage.* Paper presented at the annual meeting of the Population Association of America, Atlanta, GA.

Weiss, R., Dziura, J., Burgert, T. S., Tamborlane, W. V., Taksali, S. E., Yeckel, C. W. Allen, K., . . . Caprio, S. (2004). Obesity and the metabolic syndrome in children and adolescents. *New England Journal of Medicine, 350,* 2362–2374.

Williams, D. R., & Collins, C. (1995). U.S. socioeconomic and racial differences in health: Patterns and explanations. *Annual Review of Sociology, 21,* 349–386.

Williams, D. R., Mohammed, S. A., Leavell, J., & Collins, C. (2010). Race, socioeconomic status and health: Complexities, ongoing challenges and research opportunities. *Annals of the New York Academy of Sciences, 1186,* 69–101.

Wilson, D. K. (2009). New perspectives on health disparities and obesity interventions in youth. *Journal of Pediatric Psychology, 34*(3), 231–244.

Winkleby, M. A., Kraemer, H. C., Ahn, D. K., & Varady, A. N. (1998). Ethnic and socioeconomic differences in cardiovascular disease risk factors: Findings for women from the Third National Health and Nutrition Examination Survey, 1988–1994. *Journal of the American Medical Association, 280*(4), 356–362.

zhu difeng/Shutterstock

PART **IV**

Supply

CHAPTER **10**

Healthcare Supply

INTRODUCTION

The supply of health care can be approached in a similar way as the demand for health care. Suppliers include hospitals and physicians, who provide health care directly, for example, and medical supply and pharmaceutical companies, who provide inputs to the healthcare production process. The supply side of the market is heavily dependent on theories of how firms behave, and the topic is often called the *theory of the firm* (Morris, Devlin, & Parkin, 2007). This chapter will explore the determinants of the supply of healthcare services and the responsiveness of the supply curve with respect to price changes.

THE NATURE OF SUPPLY

Analysis of **supply** in economics is often dominated in neoclassical frameworks by theories of the firm that are based on an assumption that the firm's main goal is to maximize profits. Such theories can be reasonable descriptions of the aims of some firms and can therefore be used to generate predictions about the ways that firms and markets operate. In the case of health care, firms may have more altruistic motives such as providing charity care or maximizing the number of covered lives in order to improve access to health care. However, an important aspect of healthcare provision is that, typically, firms do not aim to maximize profits nor do they aim to earn any profits at all. This is very different from the neoclassical view of firm behavior. However, the goal of most pharmaceutical companies and many insurance companies is to generate profits, and profit maximization may be a reasonable goal for them. By contrast, most hospitals and nursing homes and some insurance companies do not aim to maximize profit but aim instead to maximize other more altruistic goals such as the number of covered lives. Theories based on profit maximization have another use in that they provide a helpful set of performance benchmarks against which firms' actual performance can be compared. Therefore, given the reduced incentive for profit maximization in health care for many firms, other theories will be more appropriate.

Figure 10-1 shows an upward-sloping supply curve for office visits. It illustrates, for example, that physicians would be willing to offer 10 office visits if the price were $90 per visit. At a higher price, say $100, more would be offered.

Factors That Affect Supply

The price schedule and **quantity supplied** are directly related. In other words, as price increases, the amount of the good or service offered for sale also increases. This is denoted as a movement along a given supply curve.

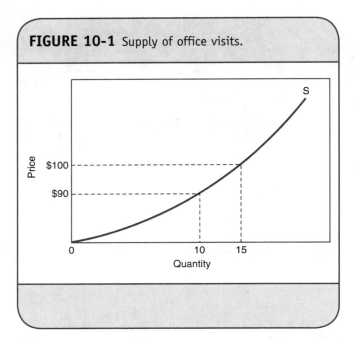

FIGURE 10-1 Supply of office visits.

In addition to the market price schedule of the healthcare good or service, a list of supply shifters may be generated from a set of exogenous determinants. According to Schafermeyer (2000), the following are factors underlying the supply curve:

- *Technological change.* As technology improves for producing a healthcare product, the good becomes cheaper to produce. As the product becomes cheaper to produce, suppliers are willing to offer more for sale at a given market price. This increases quantity supplied at every market price, thus shifting the supply curve to the right.
- *Input prices.* If physicians' wages were to rise, this increase in labor cost would result in suppliers' decreased willingness to offer as much for sale at the original price. The quantity supplied would decrease at every market price, shifting the curve to the left.
- *Prices of production-related goods.* The price of a good related in production, such as a rise in the price of radiology services related to physician services, also would be relevant. Because physicians can use radiology for diagnosis as well as treatment, this will cause the quantity supplied to decrease at every market price, thus shifting the supply curve to the left. This is due to the complementary nature of the goods or services in question.

- *Size of the industry.* As more firms enter the market, the **aggregate supply** of the product will be greater at every price. Aggregate supply is the total quantity supplied by all firms in the market at a given price schedule. Therefore, entry of firms will cause supply to shift to the right.
- *Weather.* For several products, natural occurrences such as weather will tend to affect production. The direction of the effect is obvious: Good weather increases quantity supplied at every price, causing a rightward shift in the supply curve.

ELASTICITY OF SUPPLY

The price **elasticity of supply** is calculated in the same manner as the elasticity of demand. Here, the quantities are the quantity supplied rather than the quantity demanded. The formula for calculating the elasticity of supply is

$$\frac{(\% \text{ change in quantity supplied})}{(\% \text{ change in price})}$$

Factors that influence the elasticity or responsiveness of supply to percent changes in the price of the good or service in question is driven by short- and long-run ability to change production or decision making. For example, the responsiveness depends on the ability to switch production processes or even the good or service produced, barriers to entry or exit in the market (as seen in Chapter 3), and the time frame in which to make production decisions in response to the price changes. As the time period lengthens, the flexibility of the firm to change production increases because inputs can change in intensity or quantity. Such production changes can include a change in technology, labor force, or capital (e.g., plant or equipment). This implies that the elasticity of supply is greater as the time period increases in the production decision-making time frame.

In the healthcare economy, as in many other markets, if the firm has a high capital-to-labor ratio, it is less responsive to changes in price due to the inability to easily switch production capacity because of the fixed nature of capital or the substitutability of labor for capital. For example, a home health firm would be much more responsive to fee changes relative to a hospital serving the same gerontological population.

EMPIRICAL ESTIMATES OF SUPPLY

There has been considerable growth and progress in the field of study of the market for healthcare services. Competition in the market is now modeled in static and dynamic frameworks, and estimates are made for the responsiveness of price changes in the markets as they are influenced by the quality and breadth of the provider network (Gaynor & Town, 2011). Other research (Jacobson, Earle, & Newhouse, 2011) has shown that physicians' services alter due to price changes as a result of other professional and personal debts (e.g., loans and mortgages). In both cases, there are significant levels of price elasticity of supply in play.

PAY FOR PERFORMANCE AND SUPPLY AND QUALITY

Pay for performance consists of developing and implementing financial incentives to supply improved quality services in the market for physician or hospital services. However, it seems inconclusive that the incentives actually improve quality care (Lindenauer et al., 2007; Peterson, Woodward, Urech, Daw, & Sookanan, 2006; Rosenthal, Fernandopulle, Song, & Landon, 2004; Rosenthal & Frank, 2006; Ryan, Blustein, & Casalino, 2012). Further, it is unclear if this mechanism for improving quality of the supplied of services in the long term can be accomplished without significant lags.

SUMMARY

In this chapter, the characteristics and concepts pertaining to the supply of healthcare services were presented. In any market, including the market for healthcare services, there is a direct relationship between price and quantity supplied. That is, as price increases, the quantity offered for sale in the market will increase. Several other underlying factors affect the position of the supply curve, shifting it to the left or right as noted earlier. Elasticity of supply was also explored, with a comparison of firms that are labor versus capital intensive.

KEY WORDS

- **Aggregate supply**
- **Elasticity of supply**
- **Quantity supplied**
- **Supply**

Questions

1. Suppose that licensure requirements become more stringent so that fewer physicians will be able to practice medicine. What would happen to the supply curve for physician services? Explain.

2. Suppose that there is a high demand for a new diet drug on the market. What would happen to the supply of the drug?

3. Suppose that you are a manager of a large healthcare system and the reimbursement fees for services rendered has changed significantly during the period. What is your short-run elasticity with respect to price and would this change over a longer planning horizon? How?

PROFILE: ELINOR OSTROM

Elinor Ostrom was born in 1933 in Los Angeles into a family of modest means during the Great Depression. The family lived near Beverly Hills and she attended Beverly Hills High School. It was during this time that she realized the challenges of being poor among those with much greater financial means.

Ostrom attended UCLA through self-funding and studied the social sciences. However, this training did not lead to advanced employment positions but rather clerical jobs. It was this job search experience that led her to learn to move past initial rejections in achieving goals.

Ostrom was accepted into the PhD program in economics at UCLA but only after some heated discussions within the department about the role of women in the program and field. After hard work in the department, she received her PhD in 1965 and accepted an academic position at Indiana University Bloomington in the Department of Political Science. Here, she studied police industries in the United States for 15 years, after which she returned to her work on economics.

In the early 1970s, Ostrom and her husband formed the Workshop in Political Theory and Policy Analysis, which spanned social economics and politics and how they affect behavior. This venue explored police agencies, irrigation systems, and forest resources.

Ostrom was not actually an economist in her work at Indiana, and her research focused mainly on government regulation of public resources. Her significant contributions in political science had major influence on economics and public goods, which led her to be the only woman to receive the Nobel Prize in Economics in 2009. Ostrom died of cancer in 2012 at the age of 78.

Data from Nobelprize.org. (2015). Elinor Ostrom: Biographical. Retrieved May 1, 2004, from http://www.nobelprize.org/nobel_prizes/economic-sciences/Laureates/2009/ostrom-bio.html; Rampell, C. (2012, June 12). Elinor Ostrom, winner of Nobel in Economics, dies at 78. The New York Times. Retrieved May 1, 2014, from http://www.nytimes.com/2012/06/13/business/elinor-ostrom-winner-of-nobel-in-economics-dies-at-78.html?_r-0.

REFERENCES

Gaynor, M., & Town, R. J. (2011) *Competition in health care markets* (NBER Working Paper No, 17208). Cambridge, MA: National Bureau of Economic Research.

Jacobson, M., Earle, C. C., & Newhouse, J. P. (2011). Geographic variation in physicians' responses to a reimbursement change. *New England Journal of Medicine, 365*, 2049–2052.

Lindenauer, P. K., Remus, D., Roman, S., Rothberg, M. B., Benjamin, E. M., Ma, A., & Bratzler, D. O. (2007). Public reporting and pay for performance in hospital quality improvement. *New England Journal of Medicine, 356*, 486–496.

Morris, S., Devlin, N., & Parkin, D. (2007). *Economic analysis in health care.* West Sussex, England: John Wiley & Sons.

Peterson, L. A., Woodward, L. D., Urech, T., Daw, C., & Sookanan, S. (2006). Does pay-for-performance improve the quality of health care? *Annals of Internal Medicine, 145*(4), 265–272.

Rosenthal, M. B., Fernandopulle, R., Song, H. R., & Landon, B. (2004). Paying for quality: Providers' incentives for quality improvement. *Health Affairs, 23*(2), 127–141.

Rosenthal, M. B., & Frank, R. G. (2006). What is the empirical basis for paying for quality in health care? *Medical Care Research and Review, 63*(2), 135–157.

Ryan, A. M., Blustein, J., & Casalino, L. P. (2012). Medicare's flagship test of pay-for-performance did not spur more rapid quality improvement among low-performing hospitals. *Health Affairs, 31*(4), 797–805.

Schafermeyer, K. W. (2000). Health economics II: Some unique aspects of health economics. *Journal of Managed Care Pharmacy, 6*(2), 173–180.

CHAPTER 11

Healthcare Production and Costs

LEARNING OBJECTIVES

By the end of this chapter, the student will be able to:

1. Describe the various production characteristics, including marginal and average productivity.
2. Calculate the elasticity of substitution among inputs.
3. Derive the short-run and long-run costs of production.
4. Determine economies and diseconomies of scale and scope.

INTRODUCTION

Production and sale of healthcare goods takes place in a world of scarce resources, and theories are needed to understand the operation and planning process of medical firms. In this chapter, various economic principles will be used to guide the production and cost behavior of medical firms.

THE NATURE OF PRODUCTION

According to Santerre and Neun (2006), five assumptions are made to simplify the discussion of short-run production:

1. The firm produces a single output of medical services.
2. Initially, two inputs exist: labor hours and a composite capital good.
3. Capital is fixed during the period because short run is defined as a period where at least one input is fixed.
4. The firm initially has the incentive to produce as efficiently as possible.
5. Initially, the firm possesses perfect information regarding the demands for its product.

A **production function** identifies how various inputs can be combined and transformed into a final output. The

short-run production function for healthcare services can be mathematically generalized as $q = f(n, k)$, where q is output, n is labor input, and k is capital (which is fixed in the short run). The production function allows for the possibility that each level of output may be produced by several different combinations of the personnel and capital inputs. Each combination is assumed to be technically efficient because it results in the maximum amount of output that is feasible given the state of technology.

The Healthcare Production Function

The analysis begins by examining the level of healthcare services, q, as it relates to a greater quantity of variable labor input, n, given that the capital amount, k, is assumed to be fixed. One important microeconomic principle from production

FIGURE 11-1 The total productive curve.

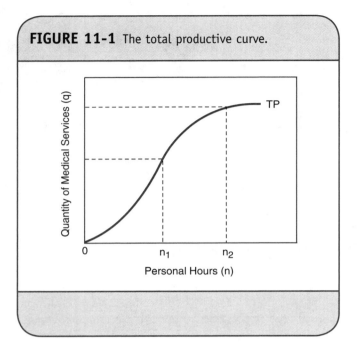

theory is the law of **diminishing marginal returns**. This phenomenon is where total output at first increases at an expanding rate but after some point increases at a decreasing rate with respect to a greater quantity of a variable input, holding all other inputs constant.

Figure 11-1 presents the **law of diminishing productivity**. It shows a graphical relation between the quantity of healthcare services on the vertical axis and the number of labor input on the horizontal axis. The curve is the total product curve, TP, because it depicts the total output produced by different levels of variable input, holding all other inputs constant. The output first increases at an expanding rate over the range of labor input of 0 to n_1. Beyond point n_1, further increases in labor cause healthcare services to increase at a decreasing rate. That is the point in which diminishing productivity sets in. Beyond n_2, there is a possibility that too many labor inputs can lead to a reduction in the quantity of healthcare services due to inefficiencies in production. Therefore, the slope of the total product curve is negative beyond n_2.

Economists point to the fixed short-run inputs as a basis for diminishing productivity. For example, when labor input is increased at first, there is initially a considerable amount of capital, the fixed input, with which to produce healthcare services. The abundance of capital enables increasingly greater amounts of healthcare services to be generated from the employment of additional labor. At some point, however, the fixed capital becomes limited relative to the variable input, and additional labor inputs lead to successively fewer incremental units of healthcare output due to increased inefficiencies. In the extreme, as more labor is crowded into a medical facility, the quantity of services produced may begin to decline as congestion sets in and creates unwanted production problems.

Elasticity of Input Substitution

Realistically, however, the medical firm operates with more than one variable input in the short run. Therefore, there may be some form of substitutability between variable inputs. For example, licensed practical nurses often substitute for registered nurses in the production of inpatient services. The actual degree of substitutability between any two inputs depends on technical and legal considerations. For example, physician assistants are prohibited by law from prescribing medications in most states.

In general terms, the elasticity of substitution between any two variable inputs that are substitutable equals the percent change in input ratio divided by the percent change in the ratio of the inputs' marginal productivities, holding the level of output constant. In other words, the formula for this elasticity is

$$\sigma = \frac{\Delta(I_i/I_2)}{I_i/I_2} \div \frac{\Delta(MP_2/MP_i)}{MP_2/MP_i}$$

where i is the quantity employed of each input. The ratio of marginal productivities is referred to as the **marginal rate of technical substitution**, which illustrates the rate at which one input substitutes for the other in the production process at the margin. The marginal product is the additional quantity of output associated with an additional unit of a variable input. For example, suppose that two licensed practical nurse hours are needed to substitute completely for one registered nurse hour.

Theoretically, σ takes on the value between 0 and $+\infty$ and identifies the percent change in the input ratio that results from a 1% change in the marginal rate of technical substitution. At the extremes, there is either no substitutability (e.g., 0), or infinite, or perfect substitutability.

SHORT-RUN COSTS FOR A MEDICAL FIRM

According to Santerre and Neun (2006), economists and accountants refer to costs differently. The accountant considers only the **explicit costs** of doing business when determining the accounting profits of a medical firm. Explicit costs are easily identified because a recent market transaction is available to provide an accurate measure of costs or money spent for the goods or services acquired. Wage payments to labor, utility bills, and medical supply expenses are all examples of explicit costs of healthcare firms.

Economists consider both the explicit and **implicit costs** of production. Implicit costs reflect the opportunity costs of using any resources the medical firm owns. For example, a general practitioner (GP) may own the physical assets used in producing physician services. In this case, a recent market transaction is unavailable to determine the cost of using these assets. However, an opportunity cost is incurred when using them because the physical assets could have been rented out for the next best alternative use. For example, the clinic could be remodeled and rented as a psychological counseling center, and the medical equipment could be rented by another physician. Therefore, the foregone rental payments reflect the opportunity cost of using the physical assets owned by the GP.

When determining the economic profit of a firm, economists consider the total costs of doing business, including both the explicit and implicit costs. Economists believe that

© AbleStock

it is important to determine whether sufficient revenues are available to cover the costs of using all rented and owned inputs. For example, if the rental return on the physical assets is greater than the return on actual use by the GP, the GP might do better by renting out the assets rather than retaining them for personal use.

Short-Run Cost Curve

Cost theory relates the quantity of output to the cost of production. As such, it identifies how total costs respond to changes in output. If we continue to assume the two inputs of labor, n, and capital, k (still fixed), the short-run total costs, STC, of producing a given level of medical output, q, can be written as

$$\text{STC}(q) = wn + r\bar{k}$$

where w and r represent the wage for labor and the rental costs of capital, respectively. Input prices are assumed to be fixed, which means that the single competitive medical firm is small enough that it can purchase these inputs without affecting their market prices.

This equation implies that the short-run total costs of production are dependent on the quantities and prices of inputs employed. The wage rate multiplied by the number of labor inputs equals the total wage bill and represents the total variable costs of production. Variable costs respond to changes in total output. The product of the rental price and the quantity of capital represent the total fixed costs of production. This cost component does not vary with the level of production because the quantity of capital is fixed.

The total product curve not only identifies the quantity of healthcare output produced by a particular number of labor inputs but also shows, reciprocally, the number of labor inputs necessary to produce a given level of healthcare output. With this information, the short-run total cost can be determined for various levels of healthcare output. First, through the production function, is the necessary number of labor inputs, n, for each level of medical output. Second, the quantity of labor inputs are multiplied by the wage to get the **short-run total variable costs**, STVC, of production, or w_n. Third, the **short-run total fixed costs** are added, STFC or rk to the STVC to derive the short-run total costs, STC, of production. This three-step procedure for each level of output can be used to derive the short-run total cost curve such as the one in **Figure 11-2**.

There is a reciprocal relationship between the short-run total **cost function** in Figure 11-2 and the short-run total product curve in Figure 11-1. For example, when total product is increasing at an expanding rate up to point n_1 in Figure 11-1, short-run total costs are increasing at a decreasing rate up to output q_1 in Figure 11-2.

FIGURE 11-2 Short-run total cost curve.

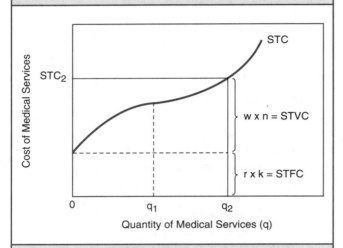

Factors Affecting the Position of the Short-Run Cost Curve

A variety of short-run circumstances affect the position of the total cost curve. Among them are the prices of variable inputs, the quality of care, the patient case mix, and the amounts of the fixed inputs. When any one of these variables changes, the position of the cost curve changes through either an upward or a downward shift depending on whether costs increase or decrease. A properly specified short-run total cost function for medical services should include the following variables: STC = f (output level, input prices, quality of care, patient case mix, quantity of the fixed inputs).

LONG-RUN COSTS

Long-run **economies of scale** refer to the notion that average costs fall as a medical firm gets physically larger due to specialization of labor and capital. Larger medical firms such as hospitals are able to utilize greater and more specialized labor involved in the production process. For example, people generally become very proficient at a specific task when they perform it repeatedly. Therefore, specialization allows larger firms to produce increased amounts of output at lower costs. The downward-sloping portion of the **long-run average total cost curve** (LRATC) in **Figure 11-3** reflects economies of scale.

Another way to conceptualize long-run economies of scale is through direct relation between inputs and output,

or returns to scale, rather than output and costs. Consistent with long-run economies of scale is **increasing returns** to scale. Increasing returns to scale result when an increase in all inputs results in a more-than-proportionate increase in output. For example, a doubling of all inputs that result in three times as much output is a sign of increasing returns to scale. Similarly, if a doubling of output can be achieved without doubling of all inputs, the production process exhibits long-run increasing returns, or economies of scale.

Most economists believe that economies of scale are exhausted at some point and **diseconomies of scale** set in. Diseconomies of scale result when the medical firm becomes too large and experiences managerial inefficiencies. Bureaucratic red tape becomes common, and top-to-bottom communication flows break down. As a result, poor decisions are sometimes made when the firm gets too large, and long-run average costs

FIGURE 11-3 Long-run average cost curve.

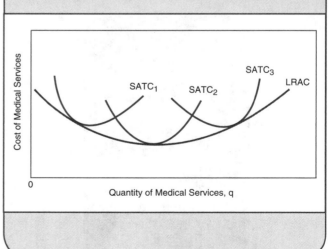

increase. Diseconomies of scale are reflected in the upward-sloping segment of the LRATC curve in Figure 11-3.

Diseconomies of scale can also be interpreted as meaning that an increase in all inputs results in a less-than-proportionate increase in output, or **decreasing returns** to scale.

Another possibility shown in Figure 11-3 is that the production process exhibits constant returns to scale. **Constant returns to scale** occur when, for example, a doubling of inputs results in a doubling of output. In terms of long-run costs, constant returns imply a horizontal LRATC curve.

Shifts in the Long-Run Average Cost Curve

The position of the long-run average cost curve is determined by a set of long-run circumstances that include the price of all inputs, quality, and patient case mix. When these circumstances change on a long-run basis, the long-run average cost curve shifts up or down depending on whether the change involved higher or lower long-run costs of production. For example, a cost-saving technology tends to shift the long-run average cost curve down.

PATIENT SAFETY AND PRODUCTION

Patient safety and quality improvement can have profound effects on the production of healthcare services. Many studies have shown that there is an incentive to improve patient safety and health outcomes. However, not all initiatives work. In California, Assembly Bill 394 mandated a lower nurse-to-patient ratio in hospital settings, but the implemented

© iStockphoto/Thinkstock

improved staffing ratios did not appear to be associated with patient safety enhancements in the participating hospitals (Cook, Gaynor, Stephens, & Taylor, 2012). Moreover, in a meta-analysis conducted by Morello and colleagues (2012), even for a variety of culture-change interventions to improve patient safety, there was limited evidence to support that there was a significant improvement in patient safety. However, one study of five economic analyses of acute care safety interventions investigated by Etchells and colleagues (2012) found that pharmacist-led medication reconciliation, certain intensive care unit interventions, and standard surgical sponge counts, for example, were economically feasible in improving patient safety and outcomes. These results combined are inconclusive in determining whether patient safety is improved with a variety of interventions.

SUMMARY

In this chapter, the characteristics and concepts pertaining to the costs of producing healthcare services were presented. First, the underlying production behavior of a single medical firm was described. The short-run production function that resulted from this examination relates productivity to input usage. Second, the inverse relation between productivity and costs was presented. Finally, some concepts such as economies of scale and returns to scale were defined.

KEY WORDS

- **Constant returns to scale**
- **Cost function**
- **Decreasing returns**
- **Diminishing marginal returns**
- **Diseconomies of scale**
- **Economies of scale**
- **Explicit costs**
- **Implicit costs**
- **Increasing returns**
- **Law of diminishing productivity**
- **Long-run average total cost curve**
- **Marginal rate of technical substitution**
- **Production function**
- **Short-run total fixed costs**
- **Short-run total variable costs**

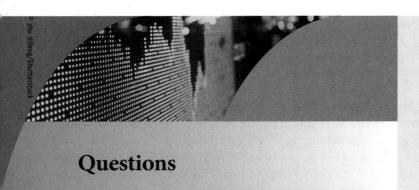

Questions

1. Suppose that you are to specify a short-run production function for counseling services. Which inputs might you include in the production function? Which would be variable inputs and which would be fixed inputs?

2. What does the elasticity of substitution illustrate?

3. Explain the difference between explicit and implicit costs of production.

4. Explain the reasoning behind the u-shaped long-run average cost curve.

5. From the LRATC, how would you identify areas of economies and diseconomies of scale?

PROFILE: STUART ALTMAN

Stuart Altman was born in 1937 and is an economist who has made major contributions in federal and state health policy, Medicare, and health system reform. He earned a BBA from the City College of New York and pursued graduate work at UCLA, where he received a PhD in economics.

One of Altman's significant professional achievements is his service for 12 years as chair of the Prospective Payment Assessment Commission formed to advise Congress and the Executive Branch on the performance of the diagnosis-related group system of Medicare and other system reforms. Further, from 1997 to 1999 he served on the National Bipartisan Commission on the Future of Medicare that advised President Bill Clinton.

Altman is a prolific author of books and articles and has received numerous accolades and honors. His two edited books, *Politics for an Aging Society* and *Power, Politics, and Universal Health Care*, focus on the history of health care in the United States and provide context for the Affordable Care Act of 2010.

Altman is currently the Sol C. Chaiken Professor of National Health Policy at Brandeis University.

Data from Brandeis University. (2015). The Heller School faculty and researchers: Stuart Altman. Retrieved May 1, 2014, from http://heller.brandeis.edu/facultyguide/person.html?emplid=cf63e5b4 29988290b1667469d90e-9f9ae4eefe8a.

REFERENCES

Cook, A., Gaynor, M., Stephens, M., Jr., & Taylor, L. (2012). The effect of a hospital nurse staffing mandate on patient health outcomes: Evidence form California's minimum staffing regulation. *Journal of Health Economics, 31*(2), 340–348.

Etchells, E., Koo, M., Daneman, N., McDonald, A., Baker, M., Matlow, A., . . . Mittman, N. (2012). Comparative economic analyses of patient safety improvement strategies in acute care: A systematic review. *British Medical Journal of Quality and Safety, 21*, 448–456.

Morello, R. T., Lowthian, J. A., Barker, A. L., McGinnes, R., Dunt, D., & Brand, C. (2012). Strategies for improving patient safety culture in hospitals: A systematic review. *British Medical Journal of Quality and Safety, 22*(1), 11–18.

Santerre, R. E., & Neun, S. P. (2006). *Health economics: Theories, insights and industry studies* (4th ed.). Independence, KY: Thomson South-Western.

CHAPTER **12**

The Healthcare Workforce Market

By the end of this chapter, the student will be able to:

1. Understand the role of the market in analyzing workforce shortages.
2. Calculate the projections of the physician market.
3. Derive the monopsony model for the market for nurses.
4. Determine the role of incentives in market surpluses and shortages.

INTRODUCTION

Two differing points of view have characterized American attitudes toward medical professionals in the United States. One focuses on the high monetary and psychic costs of the lengthy training period and the long hours and great responsibility that being a practicing physician entails and concluded that the economic returns to practicing medicine are not excessive. The other asserts that physicians and other healthcare providers have been able to extract economic rents by charging fees that are higher than those that prevail in a reasonably competitive market (Tyson, 2001).

This chapter will focus on the supply of physicians and nurses and, in particular, their decisions to undertake training and enter the field of medicine. Health planners define the adequacy of supply of doctors and nurses in relation to the community's health needs. Economists use supply and demand to analyze the market for doctors and nurses. This analysis is applied to understanding why shortages and surpluses may exist.

THE PHYSICIAN'S MARKET

The supply of physicians depends on a combination of individual career decisions and public policy. Since the mid-19th century, medical associations have interacted with state and federal governments to regulate the practice of medicine. Medical schools and hospitals with residency programs also make decisions that affect training opportunities. As a result, individuals' ability to enter the profession and the financial returns from doing so are not left to the invisible hand of supply and demand in the private market.

According to Kessel (1958) and others, the professionalization of medical training and the practice of medicine date from the mid-19th century, when, under the urging of the **American Medical Association (AMA)**, state licensing boards were established to set examinations for doctors of medicine. Licensing limited the scope of activity of other medical practitioners such as homeopaths, osteopaths, chiropractors, and midwives. In the 20th century, the AMA also began to oversee the quality of medical education. In 1910, a commissioned study that came to be known as the Flexner Report offered a highly critical review of medical education that led to the closure of many U.S. medical schools and the addition of a second requirement for becoming a licensed physician graduating from an accredited medical school (Cooke, Irby, Sullivan, & Ludmerer, 2006; Duffy, 2011).

A medical degree requires 4 years of medical school plus a year of practical training in hospitals. Physicians must pass examinations in a particular state in order to be licensed to practice medicine in that state. Most U.S. physicians also undertake additional postgraduate training in the form of hospital residency in some specialty. This is now often combined with the practical training in hospitals. In addition, many become board-certified specialists. A board-certified specialist must complete one or more residencies and pass an examination in one of two specialist fields. A physician can practice in a specialist field such as cardiology without being board certified, but the certification carries with it prestige and the likelihood of higher earnings. Some specialties, such as neurosurgery, require very long residencies. In 2012, approximately 75% of the more than 815,000 actively practicing physicians in the United States were board-certified specialists (AMA, 2013).

Health Planners' Evaluation of Physician Supply

Health planners evaluate the supply of physicians by examining the theoretical number of physicians required to perform the health procedures needed by a community, estimating need by reference to statistics on incidence of disease in a population of a given size. According to Rimlinger and Steele (1963), it was determined that there was a physician shortage, particularly in certain regions, given the uneven geographical distribution of practicing physicians.

Economic Analysis of Physician Supply

Economists define a shortage as a situation in which quantity supplied is less than quantity demanded at a given market price. Shortages are not easy to measure in a profession where a high proportion of the members are self-employed. Except for young physicians in training employed by hospitals, there are few data on vacancy rates. Researchers studying markets for professionals therefore study relative returns to training.

A study conducted by MedScape (2012) of 24,216 U.S. physicians across 25 specialty areas found that 49% of doctors believe that they are not fairly compensated. Of primary care physicians, this percentage increased to 54%. This is mainly due to the large debt incurred in training relative to the controlled earnings of physicians relative to other professions. Further, higher earnings in one professional field do not necessarily indicate barriers to entry into that field. The return to training is a preferred instrument to use. It is also a useful measure for individual decisions to enter healthcare training and choices about which medical field to pursue (Becker, 1965). Incorporating the human capital model into the analysis of the supply of physicians led to an approach that focused on returns over the lifetime in training rather than current earnings.

A medical degree can be thought of as a stock of human capital that yields a stream of returns over time. A way to evaluate the return on any form of investment is to find its discounted present value (DPV), where

$$DPV = \sum [R_{t=} + R_{t+} /(1 + r) + \ldots + R_{t+n} /(1 + r)^{t+n-1})]$$

with R as the return on investment, r as the interest rate on a risk-free asset, and n as the number of periods in the time frame. The concept of internal rate of return is defined as the discount rate that will equate the (discounted) present value of the return streams with the (discounted) present value of the training costs. Higher rates of return may be an indication of what are considered to be dynamic shortages. In a physician's career, where training can take more than 10 years, the lags can be lengthy and there can be miscalculations about the economic return on the part of those entering the field.

In the 1950s and 1960s, it was generally found that physicians were found to receive higher internal rates of return on their training compared with other professions. However, with greater cost controls in the healthcare market, this is no longer the case in terms of physicians' earnings (MedScape, 2012). The issue in the current physician market is the lack of primary care gatekeepers, with a disproportionate number of specialists entering the market due to higher DPV than primary care providers. Therefore, economists and health planners concurred that there was a shortage of physicians. In reality, there is an overall surplus of physicians but gross maldistributions geographically and between primary care physicians and specialists.

Barriers to Entry

One reason for the higher returns to medical training is a result of the **barriers to entry** to practicing medicine. Some economists linked the high returns to profit-maximizing behavior on the part of the AMA (Friedman & Kuznets, 1945). The AMA was viewed as a guild that imposed strict apprenticeship requirements and limited entry to the profession. If demand remains constant, imposing restrictions on the number of physicians will increase the price of their services, even if the reason for the restriction is quality control. In addition, if entry restrictions are coupled with rules prohibiting price competition, monopoly level prices could result, even when there are many suppliers of the same service (Kessel, 1958). This is seen with the restrictions being imposed on physician assistants and nurse practitioners (Wilson, 2012). County medical associations had the power to impose sanctions on physicians if they did not cooperate, so the lack of price competition was not an unreasonable assumption. The sanctions could include loss of hospital privileges and exclusion from the medical association, for example.

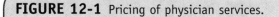

FIGURE 12-1 Pricing of physician services.

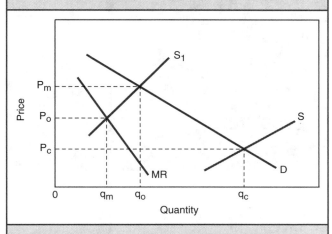

Folland, Sherman; Goodman, Allen C.; Stano, Miron, *Economics of Health and Health Care*, 5th Edition, © 2007. Reprinted/Adapted and Electronically reproduced by permission of Pearson Education, Inc., New York, New York.

In a competitive market with freedom of entry, the equilibrium price for a service would be PC and the equilibrium quantity would be QC. Restrictions on supply are shown in **Figure 12-1** as a movement from SS to S_1S_1, with a resulting competitive price of P*. If physicians' associations set prices collusively within local areas, the profit-maximizing price will approach P_m in Figure 12-1.

Policy Responses to a Shortage

Public policy in the 1960s had the goal of relieving the doctor shortage. The first piece of legislation, the Immigration Act of 1965, made it easier for internationally trained physicians to practice medicine in the United States. The second piece, the Health Professions Education Act of 1965, increased federal assistance to medical schools. These measures led to an approximate doubling in the size of physician training programs and a significant increase in the number of physicians between 1965 and 1980 (Jonas, Etzel, & Barzansky, 1991).

By 1970, returns to physician training, adjusted for hours worked, had become approximately equal to the returns to lawyers and dentists but were still higher than the returns to other professions requiring graduate degrees (Mennemeyer, 1978). However, by 1991, internal rates of return to physicians were comparable to, and in the case of primary care physicians lower than, the returns to training to business or law.

Recently, however, concerns over physician shortages have increased with the institution of the Affordable Care Act of 2010 (Christensen, 2013). With the incentives for new

insured enrollees to access primary care services, there are not enough general practitioners to meet the demand. This is an example of the maldistribution of physicians noted earlier.

Choice of Specialization

Physicians are not a homogeneous group. Very few U.S. physicians today have only the basic medical degree. Primary care physicians usually complete residencies in fields such as internal medicine or geriatrics.

The proportion of U.S. medical school graduates undertaking residencies in internal medicine declined by more than 30% between 1986 and 1994. This means that an ever-higher proportion of physicians in the primary care field had their training outside of the United States. There was a decline of 45% over the same time period in office-based primary care physicians in urban settings (Bindman, 1994). Higher earnings, greater prestige, and more regular hours attracted physicians to other specialties (McKay, 1990). However, between 1996 and 2001, the proportion of physicians in the practice of primary care stabilized and remained roughly constant. Recently, the trend is going to internal medicine in areas such as gerontology and cardiology that serve the elderly (U.S. Department of Health and Human Services, 2008).

Economic Incentives to Alter the Distribution of Physicians

Subsidies for medical training in the form of market incentives and deferred interest-bearing loans to students and subsidies to medical schools and teaching hospitals for residency training programs result in private costs of training that are much lower than the total costs to society (or social costs). Individuals' decisions about how much training to undertake are based on private costs and returns. Individuals will undertake additional training until the private marginal return on an additional unit of training is just equal to the private marginal costs. This may result in a balance of physicians trained as specialists that is not ideal from society's point of view.

As seen in earlier chapters, optimality, from the societal viewpoint, is achieved when the **marginal social benefit (MSB)** is just equal to the **marginal social cost** (MSC) of the last unit of a good or service produced. If there is a divergence between society's goals and the incentives provided by the private market, society's goals are not likely to be achieved unless the incentive structure is changed.

Public Policy to Change Incentives

Market incentives include the following actions. The U.S. government has a policy of forgiving a limited number of student loans for physicians who agree to practice medicine in underserved geographical areas under the National Health Service Corps (Cullen, Hart, Whitcomb, & Rosenblatt, 1997). Changes in Medicare's fee structure to favor primary care physicians can also be viewed as a public policy designed to alter the supply of physicians in different specialties.

Private Insurance Market Incentives

The enhanced use of primary care physicians in managed care organizations increases the opportunity for these physicians. Increased market penetration by managed care insurers over the period 1985 to 1993 was found to be associated with a narrowing of the difference between earnings of primary care physicians and specialists such as radiologists, anesthesiologists, and pathologists (Simon, Dranove, & White, 1998). Metropolitan areas with greater managed care organization penetration experienced slower rates of growth in specialists and in total number of physicians, but no change in the rate of growth in general practitioners, over the period 1987 to 1997 (Escarce, Polsky, Wozniak, & Kletke, 2000). More recently, this trend has shifted with movement toward patient-centered health systems and the view that the services from general practitioners for most health care is more feasible (van Bodegom-Vos, de Jong, Spreeuwenberg, Curfs, & Groenewegen, 2013).

THE RESULT OF CHANGING INCENTIVES

Fields Chosen by Younger Physicians

The distribution of physicians by specialty shows a different pattern if age is taken into account. By 2001, more than half of the female and more than 40% of the male physicians under the age of 35 were practicing in the fields of internal medicine, family practice, and pediatrics (AMA, 1998). For that same year, female physicians comprised about 25% of the year school student classes were approximately 40% female. This proportion rose over the next decade and now approaches more than 50% (Association of American Medical Colleges, 2002). Physicians under the age of 35 in 2001 who were trained in the United States would have been making decisions about fields beginning in approximately 1991, when Medicare payment reforms were already in place and managed care was making serious inroads into national markets. Other factors also influenced specialty decisions, including guaranteed vacations, more certain work schedules, and shorter periods of residency training (Thornton & Esposto, 2003). Overall, there is a decrease in primary care careers from 25.6% in 1999 to 21.5% in 2002 (Newton & Grayson, 2003), but this trend is changing with the implementation of the Affordable Care Act.

© Mark Winfrey/Shutterstock

PROJECTIONS ON THE SUPPLY AND DEMAND OF PHYSICIANS

By the late 1970s, it was widely believed that there had been a policy overshoot and an oversupply of physicians would soon develop. Congress, concerned about whether Medicare would continue to provide several billion dollars per year in support of residency programs, established the Council on Graduate Medical Education. This concluded that, by the year 2000, the overall physician-to-population ratio would be high. It also predicted that the specialists would be 60% higher than needed. It recommended that subsidies to hospital residency programs be reduced and more medical students be directed to the field of primary care (Weiner, 2003).

Predictions about the future supply of physicians vary. Some see a shortage looming, but this view is not universally accepted. A 2001 roundtable discussion provided a representative sample of views on this issue. According to Auerbach (2013), it is questionable whether there really is a physician shortage given current trends in medicine. For example, patient-centered homes allow less physician time than before (Bodenheimer & Smith, 2013). Moreover, the use of telemedicine gives greater efficiency to physician time, allowing more patients to be seen (Weiner, Yeh, & Blumenthal, 2013). The difference between the economists' view and the health planners' opinion is revealed in this representative sample of expert opinions.

THE MARKET FOR NURSES

In this chapter, use of the term *nurses* will refer to registered nurses (RNs). There are three different paths to achieving an RN degree. Two-year associate programs in community colleges and 3-year diploma programs in hospitals coexist with baccalaureate programs in 4-year colleges. Graduate programs in nursing, leading to a master's degree or PhD, are also available. Registered nurses, like physicians, can receive additional training in specialist areas. All nurses have some substitutability among one another or, in certain cases, with some physician services.

The main employer of RNs has traditionally been the hospital, even though by the end of the 1990s the proportion of nurses employed in hospitals had fallen to about 60% (Feldstein, 1999). The greater intensity of care within acute care hospitals increases the desired nurse-to-patient ratio and the demand for hospital nurses, but the reduction in the use of inpatient hospital services tends to reduce nurse employment in hospitals. To the extent that managed care organizations and other integrated healthcare delivery systems are able to substitute nurses for physicians in ambulatory settings, this tends to increase the demand for nurses in nonhospital settings.

The supply of nurses depends on the decisions of individuals to undertake training and to work in the profession once training is completed. Public policy is just as important in determining the training opportunities for nurses as it is for physicians. The relative rate of return to this occupation compared to other occupations that require comparable training undoubtedly affects the supply. Opportunities for women to become physicians provide an alternative for those who might otherwise enter the nursing profession. As the proportion of male RNs has remained historically under 5%, it cannot be assumed that a substitution of male for female nurses will do much to offset the increase in other professional opportunities for women. However, in recent years male nurses have become more commonplace, with the largest proportion of male nurses (41%) among nurse anesthesiologists (U.S. Census Bureau, 2013).

IS THERE A NURSING SHORTAGE?

There have been many allegations of a nurse shortage, using both the healthcare planners' and economists' definitions of shortages. The American Hospital Association complained of a nursing shortage in the 1950s and 1960s and supported these claims by noting the high vacancy rates in RN positions and the substitution of less highly trained licensed practical nurses for RNs. The demand for nurses was greater than supply at the going wage rate. From the 1940s to the early 1960s, vacancy rates for hospital nurses never fell below 13% and reached a level of 23% in 1962 (Yett, 1975).

Congress responded by passing the Nurse Training Act in 1964, which began a tradition of government subsidization of nurses' training. Using vacancy rates in hospitals as an indicator, the legislation that supported nurses' training appears to have mitigated the shortages. Vacancy rates fell to below 10% by 1971 (Feldstein, 1999).

Between 1971 and the present, there appears to have been several periods of adjustment in which high vacancy rates were followed by policy to expand nurses' training, followed by reductions in shortages. Wages have responded, for the most part, to shortages. Because the training period is so much shorter, responses to imbalances in supply and demand are more rapid than in the case of physician training.

Cyclical Shortages and Responses

Nurses' decisions about whether to enter the labor force and how many hours to work are cyclical. A very high proportion of nurses are married and are part of two-earner families. They go in and out of the labor force as employment opportunities and real wages change but also in response to the employment situation of their spouses and household economic decision making.

A recession in the early 1980s increased the labor force participation of trained nurses and reduced the vacancy rate to a record low of fewer than 5%. However, by the end of the 1980s it exceeded 12%. A decline in the participation rate of nurses when the economy improved, an increase in the demand for hospital nurses, and a decline in entrants into nurses' training in the early 1980s all contributed to the reemergence of a shortage (Feldstein, 1999). This led to the passage of the Nurse Shortage Reduction Act of 1988, which provided additional subsidies for nurses' training, and the Nurse Relief Act of 1989, which relaxed restrictions on the immigration of foreign-trained nurses. The result was a rapid increase in the supply of nurses. Vacancy rates declined again by the mid-1990s due in part to the 1992 recession that was accompanied by higher participation rates of nurses (Scanlon, 2001). This is particularly true with the increasing healthcare needs of the U.S. baby boomer population and the health reform movement that promotes preventive and primary care (American Association of Colleges of Nursing, 2014).

Wages

From the 1940s to the early 1960s, nurses' wages declined relative to other female professionals despite high vacancy rates. During that same period, nurses who were employed in nonhospital jobs experienced relative increases in wages compared with those employed in the hospital sector (Feldstein, 1999).

The situation changed with the institution of Medicare in 1965. Hospital nurses' salaries increased relative to their nonhospital colleagues, and they achieved parity with earnings in other female occupations requiring the same level of education. Price controls in the 1970s restrained nurses' wages, but they rose again as soon as the controls were removed in 1974. Wage levels were maintained throughout the 1980s

(Schumacher, 2001). Nurses' real wages increased between 1983 and 1993, followed by a temporary decline from 1993 to 1997 (Schumacher, 2002). Cost containment policies of managed care insurers have frequently been alleged to result in hospitals reducing nursing care (Spetz, 1999). However, managed care organizations' market penetration appears to have explained at most a very small proportion of the short-term real wage decline for nurses in the 1990s (Schumacher, 2001). Since 1998, the wages of hospital nurses have increased both absolutely and relative to wages for other women with comparable education levels (Hirsch & Schumacher, 2005).

THE MONOPSONISTIC MARKET FOR NURSES

Two dominant beliefs about the market for nurses have been the alleged chronic shortage of registered nurses and the sense that nurses are underpaid. The linking of shortages and low wages is counterintuitive. Because a shortage occurs when the quantity demanded is greater than the quantity supplied at a given wage, in a well-functioning competitive market a shortage should be resolved by wages increasing until equilibrium has been restored. The **monopsony** model has often been used to explain this phenomenon. A monopsonist is a monopoly or single buyer of nurses, or an employer. The market for RNs has been used as a classic example of monopsony. If there is only one hospital in the region, it has potential monopsony power over its nursing supply because there are no substitute employment opportunities in a given geographic region.

For monopsony to affect market outcomes, the supply curve of workers must be upward sloping, which means that, in order to attract more workers, the employer has to raise wages. The supply curve is an average factor cost curve from the point of view of the employer, assuming that all persons who do the same work are paid an equivalent wage. If a firm is the only one employing a given kind of worker, it is a wage setter. Therefore, it must look at the marginal costs of hiring additional workers. When the supply curve is upward sloping, the marginal factor cost curve rises more steeply than the average factor cost curve as shown in **Figure 12-2**. If the firm has to offer a higher wage to attract additional workers, it must also raise the wages of the workers it already employs.

The demand schedule for any input into production is its **marginal revenue product** (MRP) curve. The demand curve shows the maximum amount that an employer will pay for any given quantity of workers hired. A hospital will not pay more for an extra nurse than the marginal contributions to revenue. A firm will hire workers up to the quantity where the marginal factor cost (MFC) of the last worker just equals the marginal revenue product (MRP) of the last worker. This

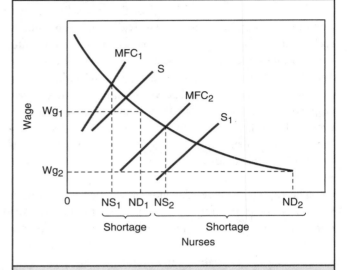

FIGURE 12-2 Increase of supply of workers under monopsony.

satisfies the profit-maximizing criterion MR = MC. In Figure 12-2, (W_{gm}, Q_m) shows the quantity of nursing help that will be employed and the wage that will be paid by the monopsonist. At (W_{gm}, Q_m), quantity demanded exceeds quantity supplied by OH. OH measures the amount of the vacancy. The monopsony model can explain the coexistence of high vacancy rates and lower-than-competitive wages of nurses due to the lack of close substitute employment opportunities.

The period from the 1940s to the mid-1960s appears to be one in which the monopsony model fits reasonably well. However, this model is less useful in explaining the trends in employment and earnings for RNs in the Medicare period. After 1965, real wages for nurses increased along with demand.

Economists have revisited the issue of monopsony in the market for nurses. Hospitals have been found to be wage setters, and the short-run supply of nurses is extremely wage inelastic (Staiger, Spetz, & Phibbs, 1999). Nurses are made to exert more effort when employers have greater market power (Currie, Farsi, & MacLeod, 2003). A study of Australian nursing markets makes a strong case for the existence of monopsony there. Australian nurses are paid about 20% less than other comparable workers in a period of high vacancy rates (Nowak & Preston, 2001). Where monopsony exists, policies to eradicate shortages by increasing the supply of workers may actually increase shortages (Lane & Gohmann, 1995). The American Nurses Association has noted the negative effects of the nurse shortage, which leads to excessive work hours and rotations to services for which training and experience are inadequate (Spetz, 2002).

A U.S. government projection of future supply and demand conditions for RNs showed quantity demanded exceeding quantity supplied by the year 2010. However, from recent reports, there are more nursing students in the pipeline than ever before (U.S. Department of Health and Human Services, 2013; RAND Corporation, 2011).

An innovative way to deal with the hospital nurse shortage is the use of contract labor. Agencies supply nurses on a short-term basis. When nurses supply their labor through these agencies, they sacrifice fringe benefits and job security for higher wages and more flexible hours (Bellemore, 1998), thus having inferior employment opportunities. In a profession dominated by married women, this trade-off may be superior to both the employer and employee. Therefore, the use of temporary RNs may be efficient for hospitals facing highly variable demand for nurses.

SUMMARY

The physician market was historically characterized by barriers to entry leading to higher-than-competitive rates of return. In the past 15 years, average hours-adjusted rates of return have been no higher for physicians as a whole than for a variety of other professionals and lower for primary care physicians. Managed care and Medicare appear to have exerted downward pressure on physicians' earnings and also changed the relative returns to different specialties. This plus the large increase in the proportion of women physicians appears to be resulting in a trend toward more primary care physicians but, as their earnings have increased, they have cut back on the number of hours worked. This results in a relatively smaller increase in primary care physician services.

Over time, the view has vacillated between perceived physician shortages and projected surpluses, but there has been a persistent geographical maldistribution of physicians as well as maldistribution among primary care physicians and specialist physicians.

The historical market for nurses appears to have been one in which the employer had monopoly power. This is the usual explanation for the combination of low wages and high vacancy rates that prevailed from the 1940s to the 1960s. The present situation reveals both high vacancy and wage rates. Projections are that the demand for nurses will outstrip the supply in the next 2 decades. Some researchers still find evidence of monopsony power. If monopsony is important, increasing the supply of nurses will not be effective in eliminating shortages and may even lead to a larger gap between supply and demand. In that situation, unionization, a minimum nursing wage, or possibly a direct wage subsidy to nurses may help to eliminate the shortages due to greater bargaining power in monopsonistic situations.

KEY WORDS

- **American Medical Association (AMA)**
- **Barriers to entry**
- **Marginal revenue product**
- **Marginal social benefit**
- **Marginal social cost**
- **Monopsony**

Questions

1. What are the economic reasons for the high ratio of specialists to general practitioners in the United States compared to other countries?

2. The AMA has often been thought to behave like a trade union in restricting the supply of physicians in order to keep earnings high. What evidence is there that the AMA has acted this way?

3. Is there a chronic shortage of nurses in the United States? Explain this from an economist's and a health planner's perspective.

4. The market for nurses has characteristics of monopsony. Outline arguments on both sides of this statement.

PROFILE: ERICA FIELD

Erica Field received her BA in economics and Latin American studies from Vassar College and, in 2003, her PhD in economics from Princeton University. She is currently an associate professor of economics and global health at Duke University. Prior to this position, she was the John L. Loeb Associate Professor of Economics at Harvard University and, during 2009 to 2010, she was an Alfred P. Sloan Research Fellow. She has also held other fellowships at institutions, such as the Institute for Advanced Study at Princeton, as well as a Fulbright scholarship.

Field's work encompasses the microeconomics of household poverty and health in developing countries and an emphasis on gender and development. She has spent much of her career using field experiments to evaluate development policy and the understanding of individual behavior. Her work is widely respected and, in 2010, Field was awarded the Elaine Bennett Prize for Research by the American Economic Association, which honors a woman economist under age 40 who has made outstanding contributions to economic research.

Data from http://econ.duke.edu/people?Uil=emf23&subpage=profile, accessed March 25, 2014.

REFERENCES

American Association of Colleges of Nursing. (2014). *Nursing shortage fact sheet*. Retrieved from www.aacn.nche.edu/media-relations/NrsgShortageFS.pdf

American Medical Association (AMA). (2013). *2013 annual report*. Chicago, IL: Author.

American Medical Association, Center for Health Policy Research. (1998). *Physician marketplace characteristics, 1997–1998*. Chicago, IL: Author.

Association of American Medical Colleges. (2002). *AAMC data book, 2002*. Washington, DC: Author.

Auerbach, D. I. (2013, December 6). Is there really a physician shortage? *The Health Care Blog*. Retrieved from www.rand.org/blog/2013/12/is-there-really-a-physician-shortage.html

Becker, G. (1965). A theory of the allocation of time. *Economic Journal, 75*(299), 493–517.

Bellemore, F. (1998). Temporary employment decisions of registered nurses. *Eastern Economic Journal, 24*(3), 265–279.

Bindman, A. B. (1994). Primary and managed care: Ingredients for health care reform. *Western Journal of Medicine, 161*(1), 78–82.

Bodenheimer, T. S., & Smith, M. D. (2013). Primary care: Proposed solutions to the physician shortage without training more physicians. *Health Affairs, 32*(11), 1881–1886.

Christensen, J. (2013, October 2). Doctor shortage, increased demand could crash health care system. *CNN*. Retrieved from www.cnn.com/2013/10/02/health/obamacare-doctor-shortage/index.html

Cooke, M., Irby, D. M., Sullivan, W., & Ludmerer, K. M. (2006). American medical education 100 years after the Flexnor Report. *New England Journal of Medicine, 355*, 1339–1344.

Cullen, T. J., Hart, L. G., Whitcomb, M. E., & Rosenblatt, R. A. (1997). The National Health Service Corps: Rural physician service and retention. *Journal of the American Board of Family Practice, 10*(4), 272–279.

Currie, J., Farsi, M., & MacLeod, W. B. (2003). *Cut to the bone? Hospital takeovers and nurse employment contracts* (NBER Working Paper No. 9428). Cambridge MA: National Bureau of Economic Research.

Duffy, T. P. (2011). The Flexnor Report—100 years later. *Yale Journal of Biology and Medicine, 84*(3), 269–278.

Escarce, J. E., Polsky, D., Wozniak, G. D., & Kletke, P. R. (2000). HMO growth and the geographical redistribution of generalist and specialist physicians, 1987–1997. *Health Services Research, 35*(4), 825–848.

Feldstein, P. J. (1999). *Health care economics* (5th ed.). Albany, NY: Delmar.

Friedman, M., & Kuznets, S. (1945). *Income from independent professional practice*. New York, NY: National Bureau of Economic Research.

Hirsch, B. T., & Schumacher, E. J. (2005). Classic or new monopsony? Searching for evidence in nursing labor markets. *Journal of Health Economics, 24*(5), 969–989.

Jonas, H. S., Etzel, S. I., & Barzansky, B. (1991). Education programs in U.S. medical schools. *Journal of the American Medical Association, 266*(7), 913–920.

Kessel, R. (1958). Price discrimination in medicine. *Journal of Law and Economics, 1*, 20–53.

Lane, J., & Gohmann, S. (1995). Shortage or surplus: Economic and noneconomic approaches to the analysis of nursing labor markets. *Southern Economic Journal, 61*(3), 644–653.

McKay, N. L. (1990). The economic determinants of specialty choice by medical residents. *Journal of Health Economics, 9*(3), 335–357.

MedScape. (2012). *MedScape physician compensation report 2012*. Retrieved from www.medscape.com/features/slideshow/compensation/2012/public

Mennemeyer, S. T. (1978). Really great returns to medical education? *Journal of Human Resources, 13*(1), 75–90.

Newton, D. A., & Grayson, M. S. (2003). Trends in career choice by US medical school graduates. *Journal of the American Medical Association, 290*(9), 1179–1182.

Nowak, M. J., & Preston, A. C. (2001). Can human capital theory explain why nurses are so poorly paid? *Australian Economic Papers, 40*(2), 232–245.

RAND Corporation. (2011, December 5). *More young people are becoming nurses; Trend may help ease future nursing shortage* [News release]. Retrieved from www.rand.org/news/ press/2011/12/05.html

Rimlinger, G. V., & Steele, H. B. (1963). An economic interpretation of the spatial distribution of physicians in the U.S. *Southern Economic Journal, 30*(1), 1–12.

Scanlon, W. J. (2001). *Nursing workforce: Recruitment and retention of nurses and nurses aides is a growing concern*. Washington, DC: U.S. Government Accountability Office.

Schumacher, E. J. (2001). The earnings and employment of nurses in an era of cost containment. *Industrial and Labor Relations Review, 55*(1), 116–132.

Schumacher, E. J. (2002). Technology, skills, and health care labor markets. *Journal of Labor Research, 23*(3), 397–415.

Simon, C. J., Dranove, D., & White, W. D. (1998). The effect of managed care on the incomes of primary care and specialty physicians. *Health Services Research, 33*(3), 549–569.

Spetz, J. (1999). The effects of managed care and prospective payment on the demand for hospital nurses: Evidence from California. *Health Services Research, 34*(5), 993–1010.

Spetz, J. (2002). The value of education in a licensed profession: The choice of associate or baccalaureate degrees in nursing. *Economics of Education Review, 21*(1), 73–85.

Staiger, D., Spetz, J., & Phibbs, C. (1999). *Is there monopsony in the labor market? Evidence from a natural experiment* (NBER Working Paper No. 7258). Cambridge, MA: National Bureau of Economic Research.

Thornton, J., & Esposto, F. (2003). How important are economic factors in choice of medical specialty? *Health Economics, 12*(1), 67–73.

Tyson, P. (2001, March 27). The Hippocratic Oath today. *Nova*. Retrieved from www.pbs.org/wgbh/nova/doctors/oath_modern.html

U.S. Census Bureau. (2013, February 25). *Male nurses becoming more commonplace, Census Bureau reports* [News release]. Retrieved from www.census.gov/newsroom/press-releases/2013/cb13-32.html

U.S. Department of Health and Human Services, Health Resources and Services Administration, Bureau of Health Professions. (2008). *The physician workforce: Projections and research into current issues affecting supply and demand.* Washington, DC: Author.

U.S. Department of Health and Human Services, Health Resources and Services Administration, Bureau of Health Professions. (2013). *The U.S. nursing workforce: Trends in supply and education.* Washington, DC: Author.

van Bodegom-Vos, L., de Jong, J. D., Spreeuwenberg, P., Curfs, E. C., & Groenewegen, P. P. (2013). Are patients' preferences for shifting services from medical specialists to general practitioners related to the type of medical intervention? *Quality Primary Care, 21*(2), 81–95.

Weiner, J. P. (2003). A shortage of physicians or a surplus of assumptions? *Health Affairs, 21*(1), 160–162.

Weiner, J. P., Yeh, S., & Blumenthal, D. (2013). The impact of health information technology and e-health on the future demand for physician services. *Health Affairs, 32*(11), 1998–2004.

Wilson, C. B. (2012, April 12). AMA supports training more M.D.s. *The Wall Street Journal.* Retrieved from www.wsj.com/articles/SB100014240527 02304356604577333956045885 0738

Yett, D. E. (1975). *An economic analysis of the hospital nursing shortage.* Lexington, MA: Lexington Books, D.C. Health Co.

CHAPTER 13

Technology Transfer in Health Care

By the end of this chapter, the student will be able to:

1. Understand the role of technology in the production of health-care services.
2. Relate the process of technological innovation.
3. Determine the efficiency of technological innovations.

INTRODUCTION

Health economists and policy analysts are particularly interested in the role of technological change in health care because of the need to assess both its benefits and it effects on the rising costs of health care. A related concern is that cost containment may impede the rate of technological change and its diffusion. In this chapter, the incentives and process of technological innovation are presented and related to the costs of health care in the United States.

TECHNOLOGY IN HEALTH CARE

Advances in health care in the second half of the 20th century raised expectations about attainable levels of health and therefore increased the demand for technologically sophisticated health care. The demand for health care was augmented by the characteristics of the U.S. health insurance system, which, from the 1940s and 1950s, imposed no cost controls and promoted the diffusion of technology. The increase in the efficacy of health care and the resulting increase in the cost of health care further augmented the demand for health insurance due to the cost of increasing technological innovations. Concern over potential medical malpractice lawsuits provided an additional incentive to use the highest technology available in order to avoid potential litigation. The combination of these factors provided a guarantee that the demand for new technology resulted in marginal improvement in health outcomes as a result of the advanced treatment.

The consensus of those who have worked to identify the factors causing the increase in the cost of health care is that technology has been the largest contributor to the upward trend in healthcare prices (Callahan, 2008; Smith, Heffler, & Freeland, 2000). Considerably less than half of the increase over time in the price of health care can be explained by the combination of expanding insurance coverage, increasing real income, supplier-induced demand, and monopoly profits to suppliers, changing demographic characteristics of the

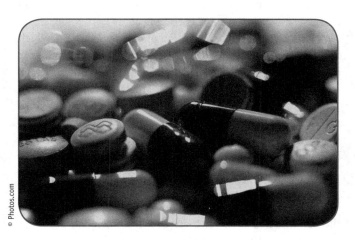

population, or the labor-intensive character of health care (Newhouse, 1993).

TECHNOLOGICAL CHANGE

Promotion of Innovation

Technological advances take place through the process of innovation. Innovation, which may be integrated with the process of discovery or invention, includes developing and marketing new products. Schumpeter (1942) viewed innovation as the driving force in a market economy. He called the process by which one product or process is replaced by a better one *creative destruction*. Schumpeter emphasized the role of profits in stimulating innovation and noted that innovation will be undertaken primarily by firms that have a good deal of market power, such as those that are oligopolies or monopolistically competitive. Such factors as professional prestige and the satisfaction derived from helping cure diseases may also be important stimuli in the process of innovation, as is government funding to support basic research.

In the United States, health research takes place within the government-funded National Institutes of Health (NIH), in universities, where much research is also funded by NIH, the National Science Foundation, and private industry and within firms. Studies show that the rate of product development is greater in firms that have more contact with academic institutions, which is particularly true with products that are radically new rather than incrementally changed (MacPherson, 2002).

Demand for products and the expectation of profits are needed for innovation to occur. Although government support for research is very important in stimulating innovation, it may not lead to a direct pipeline to commercial products. For instance, a great deal of biotechnology research originating at Oxford and Cambridge Universities has resulted in

© 4x6/iStock

commercially valuable products being developed in companies outside of the United Kingdom. Price controls on pharmaceuticals imposed by the National Health Service may have contributed to this. There is constant concern in the United States that cost-containment policies have a dampening effect on the rate of innovation in health technology (Baker & Spetz, 1999; Garber, Goldman, & Jena, 2007; Rettig, 1994).

Intellectual Property Rights

Another factor that is believed to promote innovation is patent protection for **intellectual property rights**. Patents are permits that grant exclusive ownership rights over processes or products for a specified length of time. In the United States, patents for drugs and medical devices are granted for a 20-year period, including the testing period. The lengthy testing period often reduces the effective patent life to 10 years or less. It is also possible to receive patent protection for new information on individual genes. Patents on biomedical and pharmaceutical innovations may be renewed for up to 5 years if the Food and Drug Administration has delayed the introduction of the new drug onto the market by that long of a period. However, the extension may not be granted for an effective patent life of more than 14 years (Qian, 2007).

Without patent protection, innovations would be greatly slowed unless governments were to fund product development as well as basic research processes. The incentive to innovate would be reduced because duplication makes research and development activity less profitable. The problem of imitation is particularly serious in the pharmaceutical industry where development costs are very large compared to production costs. The cost of producing the drugs is minimal compared to the extensive testing to gain government approval to market them.

The relationship between the degree of patent protection and the rate of innovation is complicated. This is illustrated by looking at differences across countries. Switzerland, which has been the location of three very profitable pharmaceutical companies, introduced patent protection for drugs only in 1977. Canada had very lax patent laws until 1987, but, since strengthening its patent protection, it has experienced a significant increase in research and development activity by attracting foreign multinational firms' research activity (McRae & Tapon, 1985; Park 2008).

U.S. Firms' Successful Innovation

The United States has been the world's leading nation in the commercialization of biotechnical knowledge, although Germany, the United Kingdom, and Canada are beginning to close the gap (Cooke, 2001). According to Grabowski and Wang (2006), the main reasons for the U.S. success appear to be:

- Existence of a large stock of human capital and research institutions
- Government support for basic research
- Well-enforced patent protection
- Historically generous insurance (third-party) payers
- Extensively subsidized employer-based private insurance for the majority of its citizens
- Physicians and hospitals that are motivated to use the highest technology available

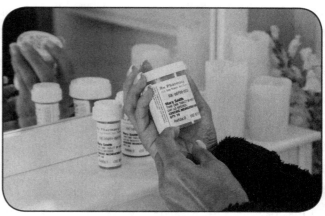

TECHNOLOGICAL DIFFUSION

The United States ranks highly in the diffusion of most medical technologies. A study comparing the United States with two other countries known for excellent health care, Canada and Germany, illustrates this (Rublee, 1994). The United States ranked highest in the diffusion of all technologies studied (Grabowski & Wang, 2006). The advantages were particularly large in the case of magnetic resonance imaging and radiation therapy. Both of these technologies require very high levels of physical and human capital investment. These examples illustrate the fact that use of advanced technologies requires complementary support in the form of well-equipped treatment centers and medical personnel with the specialized training to perform the procedures.

Factors That Promote Technological Diffusion

Economic incentives have been found to affect the rates of diffusion of new high-technology treatments. In multicountry studies of the rate with which advanced technology treatments for heart attack were adopted, higher rates of diffusion were found in countries with fee-for-service reimbursement systems. Examples of this are Japan, Korea, Australia, and France. The United States, which has a blend of fee-for-service and prospective payment systems, was found to be experiencing an immediate rate of growth in the utilization of high-technology treatments, although its stock of medical technology is still higher on a per capita basis than anywhere else in the world (McClellan et al., 2002).

MEASURING THE CONTRIBUTION OF TECHNOLOGICAL CHANGE

In empirical studies of healthcare costs, technological change has been treated as a residual that is left over as the unexplained variance after all known factors have been accounted for. This is known as the **Solow residual**. After sorting out

the effects of other factors, technological change came to be widely regarded as the chief contributor to increased healthcare expenditures in the United States (Newhouse, 1993). More recently, Cutler, McClellan, and Newhouse (1998) developed an approach that measures technological change more directly. This model can only be used to study the relationship between cost and technology change in treating specific diseases, such as coronary care. Other studies, such as that of Okunade and Murthy (2002), have also shown that technology is a major driver in aggregate healthcare costs.

Cost-Increasing Versus Cost-Saving Innovations

A cost-increasing innovation in medicine is an innovation that increases the cost of treatment for a particular disease. Where there is no incentive to contain costs, it may be more profitable for firms to develop more expensive or **cost-increasing technologies** (McGuire & Serra-Sastre, 2009). Several economists argued that, at least until the mid-1980s, both Medicare and the prevalent indemnity form of private insurance encouraged a bias toward cost-increasing (as well as quality-increasing) innovation.

In this connection, it may be useful to distinguish between process and product innovation. Process innovations often provide cost savings. For example, the institution of more expensive and more efficacious newer drugs has been shown to provide significant cost savings on nondrug expenditures that greatly outweigh the increase in the expenditures on drugs in the treatment of similar diseases (Lichtenberg, 2002). Using data from 1986 to 1998, the reduction in nondrug expenditures associated with the use of newer drugs was found to be on average 7.2 times the increase in drug expenditures. For the Medicare population, the reduction in total expenditures on nondrug aspects of treatments, including both individual out-of-pocket expenditures and Medicare's contribution, was 8.3 times the increase in drug expenditures (Lichtenberg, 2002). These are examples of unambiguous cost-savings improvements in technology.

Another form of process innovation is in health information technology. In this case, changes in clinicians' economics, more computer literacy in the general population, and, most important, changes in government policies and increased support for clinical computing suggest that the wave may break in the next decade for more use of electronic medical records in creating administrative efficiencies and increased quality of care (Berner, Detmer, & Simborg, 2005; Lau, Kuziemsky, Price, & Gardner, 2010). For example, process efficiencies were realized for preventive health reminders such as flags for vaccines and screenings (Lau et al., 2010). Further, cost savings can be seen from the buyer's perspective in the use of electronic medical records (Simborg, 2008).

An example of a cost-increasing innovation is laparoscopic cholecystectomy surgery to remove the gallbladder using a small inserted camera to direct the surgeon's instruments. It is particularly notable because of the rapid diffusion of this technique after it became available in the United States in the 1980s. By 1992, 80% of the cholecystectomies performed in the United States were laparoscopic. The technique is more frequently used in the early stages of the disease among younger, non-Medicaid patients, but it has also come to be widely used among the elderly, including the very elderly for whom it is also appropriate and effective (Walling, 1999). This technique has been shown to cut mortality rates in half for all age groups. Among the elderly, it has also greatly reduced the need for stays in skilled nursing homes.

Even if the increase in the use of gallbladder surgery had not accompanied the development of the laparoscopic technique, the innovation, defined narrowly, is more expensive. Operating room costs are much higher for laparoscopic than for open surgery. Moreover, equipment, supplies, and anesthesiology charges are all higher. Even though hospital stays are shorter, total surgeon and hospital charges are higher than for open surgery and they outbalance savings in hospitalization costs.

Certain stages in the development of medical treatments may tend to involve initially higher costs followed by lower costs. Therefore, it depends at which point in the life cycle of the innovation that the costs are measured. Scientific discoveries often have life cycles that lead to first- and second-generation technological improvements. These two stages have been called halfway technologies and high technology by Weisbrod (1991). Halfway technologies are usually more expensive than cures and are cost increasing when compared to no treatment or watching and waiting during certain disease stages. Compare the early treatments for polio mellitus, a life-threatening disease well into the 1950s in high-income countries. The iron lung was an expensive machine that kept the paralyzed alive but who required intensive care. Contrast this with the second-generation innovation, the Salk and Sabine vaccines, which prevented the disease and were inexpensive and noninvasive. Here, the development of vaccines replaces expensive combinations of machinery and drugs.

Productive Efficiency

Studies of alternative technologies used in the treatment of specific diseases often compare treatment methods in terms of their productive efficiency. **Productive efficiency** compacts the quantities of inputs used to produce a given output. Comparing production functions without reference to prices of inputs is a fairly standard way of making intercountry comparisons of the use of various medical technologies. For example, Bailey and Garber (1997) compared the United States, Germany, and the United Kingdom in the treatments for diabetes, gallstones, breast cancer, and lung cancer. The United States was found to be more productively efficient than Germany in the treatment of each of the diseases except for diabetes, which requires long-term therapies and little high technology.

The lack of capacity of capital equipment imposed by the British National Health Service budget limited the use of laparoscopic surgery. In Germany as well, these techniques were less prevalent than in the United States. This resulted in more time and resources to achieve better or worse outcomes. Productive efficiency is therefore not independent of previous decisions made in several counties about how much to allocate to developing capital capacity and technology (Retzlaff-Roberts, Chang, & Rubin, 2004).

In the treatment of breast cancer, the United States and the United Kingdom were both unambiguously more productive than Germany. The United States achieved a 9% better outcome using 38% fewer inputs, and the United Kingdom achieved a 6% better outcome using 53% fewer resources. Compared to the United Kingdom, the United States used 15% more inputs to achieve a 3% better outcome (Bailey & Garber, 1997).

SUMMARY

The United States still leads the world in the introduction of healthcare technology in spite of cost-containment policies on the part of government and private managed care insurers. In the best-case scenario, cost containment will tip the balance toward cost-saving technologies but will not significantly reduce the rate of innovation.

KEY WORDS

- **Cost-increasing technology**
- **Intellectual property rights**
- **Productive efficiency**
- **Solow residual**

Questions

1. How would you characterize the effect of the U.S. health insurance system on healthcare technology changes from 1960 to 1990?

2. How may the way in which providers are reimbursed affect the diffusion of technology?

PROFILE: DAVID CUTLER

David Cutler received his AB in economics from Harvard University in 1987 and a PhD in economics from MIT in 1991. He is currently the Otto Eckstein Professor of Applied Economics at Harvard University. He has a joint appointment in the economics department, the Kennedy School of Government, and the School of Public Health. Previously, he served in the Clinton and Obama administrations.

Cutler's work spans many topic areas, but he is best known for his book *Your Money or Your Life: Strong Medicine for America's Health Care System*, an introduction to the U.S. healthcare system. Cutler believes that the U.S. healthcare system receives a big bang for its buck in that, even though U.S. health care is expensive, people place a high value on the health benefits.

Cutler's work and mentorship of students has earned him international acclaim. He has been an advisor on numerous presidential campaigns and has held positions at the National Institutes of Health and the National Academy of Sciences.

Data from Harvard University. (2015). Biography: David M. Cutler. Retrieved March 31, 2014, from http://scholar.harvard.edu/cutler/biocv.

REFERENCES

Bailey, M. N., & Garber, A. M. (1997). Health care productivity. *Brookings Papers on Economic Activity: Microeconomics, 143–202.*

Baker, L., & Spetz, J. (1999). *Managed care and medical technology growth* (NBER Working Paper No. 6894). Cambridge, MA: National Bureau of Economic Research.

Berner, E. S., Detmer, D. E., & Simborg, D. (2005). Will the wave finally break? A brief view of the adoption of electronic medical records in the United States. *Journal of the American Medical Informatics Association, 12*(1), 3–7.

Callahan, D. (2008). Health care costs and medical technology. In The Hastings Center, *From birth to death and bench to clinic: The Hastings Center bioethics briefing book for journalists, policymakers, and campaigns* (pp. 79–82). Garrison, NY: The Hastings Center.

Cooke, P. (2001). Biotechnology clusters in the UK: Lessons from localization in the commercialization of science. *Small Business Economics, 17*(1–2), 43–59.

Cutler, D., McClellan, M., & Newhouse, J. (1998). *The costs and benefits of intensive treatment for cardiovascular disease* (NBER Working Paper No. 6514). Cambridge, MA: National Bureau of Economic Research.

Garber, A., Goldman, D. P., & Jena, A. B. (2007). The promise of health care cost containment. *Health Affairs, 26*(6), 1545–1547.

Grabowski, H. G., & Wang, Y. R. (2006). The quantity and quality of worldwide new drug introductions, 1982–2003. *Health Affairs, 25*(2), 452–460.

Lau, F., Kuziemsky, C., Price, M., & Gardner, J. (2010). A review on systematic reviews of health information system studies. *Journal of the American Medical Informatics Association, 17*(6), 637–645.

Lichtenberg, F. (2002). *Benefits and costs of newer drugs: An update* (NBER Working Paper No. 8996). Cambridge, MA: National Bureau of Economic Research.

MacPherson, A. (2002). The contribution of academic-industry interaction to product innovation: The case of New York State's medical devices sector. *Papers in Regional Science, 81*(1), 121–129.

McClellan, M. B., Every, N., Garber, A. M., Heidenreich, P., Hlatky, M., Kessler, D. P., . . . Saynina, O. (2002). Technological change in heart attack care in the United States. In M. B. McClellan & D. P. Kessler (Eds.), *Technological change in health care: A global analysis of heart attack* (pp. 21–54). Ann Arbor: University of Michigan Press.

McGuire, A., & Serra-Sastre, V. (2009). What do we know about the role of health care technology in driving health care expenditure growth? In J. Costa-Font, C. Courbage, & A. McGuire (Eds.), *The economics of new health technologies: Incentives, organization, and financing* (pp. 3–18). New York, NY: Oxford University Press.

McRae, J. J., & Tapon, F. (1985). Some empirical evidence on post-patent barriers in the Canadian pharmaceutical industry. *Journal of Health Economics, 4*(1), 43–61.

Newhouse, J. P. (1993). *Free for all? Lessons from the RAND health insurance experiment.* Cambridge, MA: Harvard University Press.

Okunade, A. A., & Murthy, V. N. R. (2002). Technology as a "major driver" of health care costs: A cointegration analysis of the Newhouse conjecture. *Journal of Health Economics, 21*(1), 147–159.

Park, W. G. (2008). International patent protection: 1960–2005. *Research Policy, 37*(4), 761–766.

Qian, Y. (2007). Do national patent laws stimulate domestic innovation in a global patenting environment? A cross-country analysis of pharmaceutical patent protection, 1978–2002. *The Review of Economics and Statistics, 89*(3), 436–453.

Rettig, R. A. (1994). Medical innovation duels cost containment. *Health Affairs, 13*(3), 7–27.

Retzlaff-Roberts, D., Chang, C. F., & Rubin, R. M. (2004). Technical efficiency in the use of health care resources: A comparison of OECD countries. *Health Policy, 69*(1), 55–72.

Rublee, D. A. (1994). Medical technology in Canada, Germany, and the United States: An update. *Health Affairs, 13*(4), 113–117.

Schumpeter, J. R. (1942). *Capitalism, socialism, and democracy.* New York, NY: Harper & Brothers.

Simborg, D. W. (2008). Promoting electronic health record adoption: Is it the correct focus? *Journal of the American Medical Informatics Association, 15*(2), 127–129.

Smith, S. D., Heffler, S. K., & Freeland, M. S. (2000). *The impact of technological change on health care cost spending: An evaluation of the literature.* Washington, DC: Health Care Financing Administration.

Walling, A. D. (1999). Laparoscopic cholecystectomy vs. open surgery in the elderly. *American Family Physician, 59*(8), 2322–2323.

Weisbrod, B. A. (1991). The health care quadrilemma: An essay on technological change, insurance, quality of care, and cost containment. *Journal of Economic Literature, 29*(2), 523–552.

PART V

Evaluating the Healthcare System

CHAPTER **14**

Economic Evaluation Methods

LEARNING OBJECTIVES

By the end of this chapter, the student will be able to:

1. Understand the role of economic evaluations in health care.
2. Describe the types of economic evaluations and their uses.
3. Determine the components of a complete economic evaluation.
4. Develop an economic evaluation design.

INTRODUCTION

Economic evaluations involve the quantification of changes in health resource utilization due to the introduction of new courses of action. Policymakers are increasingly turning to such analyses to acquire information before making decisions about alternatives in health care (Sculpher et al., 2005; Stoddart, 1982). Such analyses are used by insurers to determine which services to pay for, and government policy analysts use technology assessments to shed light on the economics of new interventions and courses of action (Tengs et al., 1995). Economic evaluations are used to make systematic decisions concerning the allocation of resources in the market. It provides insights into how resources ought to be allocated. This chapter includes an overview of the methodology; an introduction to the main components and issues surrounding cost-minimization analysis, cost-effectiveness analysis, cost-utility analysis, and cost-benefit analysis; and guidelines for the use of economic evaluations.

WHAT DO ECONOMIC EVALUATIONS ADDRESS?[1]

Economic evaluations answer the following questions in order to provide an objective set of criteria for making choices among alternatives given scarce resources:

1. *Are health services worth doing given limited resources?* For example, a health department may ask, "Should everyone get a flu shot each year, given that shortages of vaccine can exist?" Or clinicians may ask, "Should the blood pressure be checked for every adult who walks into the office, given the time constraints of the standard office visit?"
2. *Are we satisfied with the way health resources are utilized among the different courses of action chosen?* For example, a hospital administrator may ask, "Should each and every new diagnostic instrument really be a good purchase?" Or an insurer may ask, "Should people request that they receive annual checkups?"

The Purpose of an Economic Evaluation

The purpose of an economic evaluation is to compare alternative courses of action that are solutions to the same problem. Without systematic analysis, it is difficult to clearly identify the alternative uses for resources and the opportunity cost of employing one alternative over another in solving a problem.

---

[1] There is a growing literature on economic evaluation in health care. Studies have been conducted by economists, medical researchers, clinicians, and multidisciplinary teams based on one or more of these types of expertise. Although the studies vary in quality, several good introductions to health economic evaluations already exist (Drummond, Sculpher, Torrance, O'Brien, & Stoddart, 1997; Gold, Siegel, Russell, & Weinstein, 1996; Jacobs & Rapoport, 2002; Stoddart, 1982). All of these give the reader a basic interpretation of the nature of economic evaluation and an appreciation of the decision making required at all levels. This chapter is a supplement to such sources, and the reader is encouraged to explore these other materials as needed.

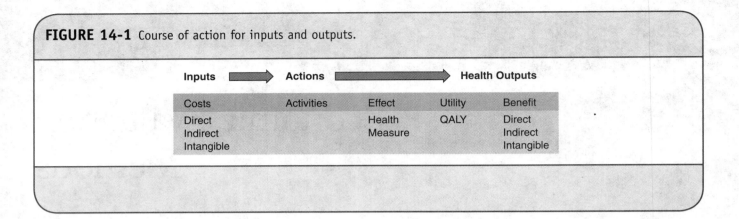

FIGURE 14-1 Course of action for inputs and outputs.

For example, a health department may need to evaluate the efficiency of a diabetes prevention program and a bicycle helmet initiative in reducing the number of disability days in a population (Messonnier, Corso, Teutsch, Haddix, & Harris, 1999). It can also determine if the course of action is worthwhile—that is, whether to address the problem—and whether the changes are worth the cost (Scheffler & Paringer, 1980).

Economic evaluations provide an objective way to determine resource allocations from an individual, community, or societal viewpoint. There are two general viewpoints to an economic evaluation: private and societal. The private perspective is focused on the individual, an organization, or a set of organizations. A healthcare organization may be interested in the cost benefit of a palliative care program versus traditional medical protocols. In this case, the firm is not interested in the transfer payments that may result by participation because these are not paying for resources being utilized. Instead, the firm is concerned with its own direct and indirect costs of the courses of action and their associated outputs. The societal view includes all persons so that the opportunity cost of the various courses of action can be taken into account. In terms of a palliative care intervention, this would include all direct and indirect costs of the courses of action and the transfer payments that may be involved as well because they reflect the opportunity costs of pursuing one course of action versus another for the population as a whole.

Economic evaluations link the alternative courses of actions' inputs and outputs and provide a comparative analysis of alternative courses of action in terms of the value of both their inputs and outputs. Without such an analysis, it is difficult to objectively justify the value for the money invested in an alternative. The real cost of any alternative is not measured by the budgetary allocations but by the health output achieved through some other alternative that has been foregone by committing resources or inputs to the alternative in question. This cost is the opportunity cost of the alternatives considered and is compared to the alternative's benefits (see **Figure 14-1** and **Table 14-1**).

TYPES OF ECONOMIC ANALYSES

The identification and measurement of costs is similar across the economic evaluation methods and are discussed later in the chapter. However, the type of output from the alternative courses of action can vary significantly across the methodologies. Four types of evaluation methods illustrate this concept. A summary of the various types is provided in **Table 14-2**.

Cost-Minimization Analysis

In this case, outputs of the courses of action are identical (or at least assumed to be so), and costs only are considered. For example, a comparison of the common output of interest is the number of successful procedures at a day surgery center versus performing the procedures at a hospital's outpatient center (Evans & Robinson, 1980). In this example, an identical number of procedures performed may be found but possibly at different costs. The principle decision rule is focused on the costs per procedure successfully performed, where the least cost course of action is determined to be the efficient choice.

Cost-Effectiveness Analysis

In this case, the output of the courses of action is common across alternatives, but the alternatives have varying degrees of success in achieving the output. An example would be the comparison of different diabetes prevention programs (Elixhauser, 1990; Gray et al., 2000) or colon cancer screenings (Lansdorp-Vogelaar, Knudsen, & Brenner, 2011; Lieberman, 1995). The decision rule is based on the cost per unit of output,

TABLE 14-1 Types of Outputs of a Course of Action

Outputs: Changes in physical, social, or emotional role function			
Health: Changes in natural units (e.g., reduction in disability days, reduction in blood glucose levels)	**Utility:** Changes in the quality of life of patients and their families (e.g., quality-adjust life years or healthy years)	**Benefits:** Changes in resources utilized	
		Direct	1. Organizing and operating services within the health sector for original or unrelated conditions 2. Related activities of patients and their families (e.g., savings in expenditures or leisure time input)
		Indirect	Savings in patients' or families' lost work time

Data from O'Brien, B. (1995). Principles of economic evaluation for health care programs. *J Rheumatol, 22*:1399–1402; Drummond, M. F., et al., (1997). *Economic Evaluations of Health Care Programmes*, Oxford, England: Oxford University Press.

or output per unit of costs. The decision maker selects the course of action that yields the most output per dollar spent, or the least cost per output. The latter decision is used when the decision maker is working within a given budget. This implies that there is a single, common effect that is constrained, and

the alternatives are within the same range of scale. This analysis can be conducted considering any courses of action with a common output. The worth of the courses of action is assumed to be positive. Here, it is assumed that the courses of action have value for the population and are efficacious.

TABLE 14-2 Summary of Economic Evaluation Methods

Method	Measure of Costs of Courses of Action	Identification of Outputs	Measurement of Outputs
Cost-minimization analysis	Dollars	Identical across alternatives	None
Cost-effectiveness analysis	Dollars	Single, common output among alternatives, achieved in varying degrees	Natural units (e.g., disability days reduced or reduction in blood glucose levels)
Cost-utility analysis	Dollars	Single or multiple outputs, not necessarily common across alternatives, and achieved in varying degrees	Healthy days or QALYs
Cost-benefit analysis	Dollars	Single or multiple outputs, not necessarily common across alternatives, and achieved in varying degrees	Dollars

Data from O'Brien, B. (1995). Principles of economic evaluation for health care programs. *J Rheumatol, 22*:1399–1402; Drummond, M. F., et al., (1997). *Economic Evaluations of Health Care Programmes*, Oxford, England: Oxford University Press.

The outputs can be health effects directly or measures that show improvements in health status. For instance, one can compare a prevention program versus a chronic care program in terms of disability days saved per dollar invested in each program (Hatzriandreu, Koplan, Weinstein, Caspersen, & Warner, 1988; Tengs et al., 1995). In cost-effectiveness analysis, there is a dominant dimension of success that is considered. If there is an equivalent level of effectiveness, it is best to perform a cost-minimization analysis. Also, it is important to be open to the possibility of using more sophisticated analyses, such as cost-benefit analysis, if there is more than one dimension of effectiveness.

In conducting a cost-effectiveness analysis, several data issues should be addressed. First, the analyst must assure that there is a random allocation of patients to groups. Second, if the investigation is examining existing literature, it is important to see how studies relate to provider expertise and patient case load in question. Third, a sensitivity analysis, discussed later in the chapter, can eliminate the need for clinical trials (especially in extreme effectiveness issues). However, if a clinical trial is used, the investigator must assure that the analysis of the clinical trial does not cause any deviation of normal working practices (Drummond et al., 1997). Fourth, it is more meaningful if the results of the cost-effectiveness analysis are compared to some standard for the problem being investigated (Doubilet, Weinstein, & McNeil, 1986; Laupacis, Feeny, Detsky, & Tugwell, 1992).

Cost-Utility Analysis

This is often considered a special case of cost-effectiveness analysis, where the output of the courses of action is valued commonly across alternatives, but the alternatives have varying degrees of success in achieving the value of the improvement in the output. In this case, both the output and the worth of the courses of action are measured. An example of such an analysis is the improvement in the **quality-adjusted life years (QALYs)** due to a diabetes intervention versus usual care. This technique is preferred by many economists because it incorporates the utility of the output (Torrance & Feeney, 1989), or in other words, the preferences of the patients or the population considered.

Utility is the value or worth of a specific health state and can be measured by the preferences of persons for any set of health states. Utility of the health output is different than the health output itself. It brings in quality-of-life adjustments for treatment output while providing a common denominator for comparing the costs and outputs of different alternatives. The measure for utility is seen in the measures of health

days or QALYs. Here, the length of time of the health state is adjusted through a utility scale of 0–1, with 0 being worst value of the health state (Sintonen, 1981; Williams, 1981). The decision rule is to choose the alternative with the lowest cost per healthy day equivalent or QALY.

Willingness to pay for an additional QALY has strict methodological underpinnings (Bobinac, Van Exel, Rutten, & Brouwer, 2010; King, Tsevat, Lave, & Roberts, 2005) and can be determined from community-based surveys (Hirth, Chernew, Miller, Fendrick, & Weissert, 2000; O'Brien & Viramontes, 1993; Olsen & Donaldson, 1998). However, these surveys must follow procedures similar to those for contingent valuation studies discussed later in the chapter (Gold et al., 1996).

Cost-Benefit Analysis

In this case, the output of the courses of action may not be a single common effect, or it may be multiple effects that may or may not be common to the alternatives. For example, one could compare a health promotion program for youths with a chronic care intervention with the elderly on a variety of output dimensions. A cost-effectiveness analysis could be performed on multiple effects to determine a decision rule where an alternative is superior on all or a majority of dimensions or base a primary effect to study the comparison.

Alternatively, a method to combine multiple effects into one common valuation could be developed. Here, the measure of value is the dollar, translating effects into the dollar value of benefits of life years gained, improved productivity, more convenience, and so on. This comparison of dollar costs, or dollar benefits, is cost-benefit analysis. This results in a ratio of dollar costs to dollar benefits, or the sum of net social benefits, where net social benefits = social benefits – social costs. The decision rule is to choose the course of action that has the greatest net social benefits (Drummond, 1981). Benefits will be large enough so that those who gain could theoretically compensate the losers, and everyone is made better off. This is known as he Preto Principle. The preferred method is to maximize net benefits rather than benefits-to-costs ratio because the ratio can be misleading depending on how benefits and costs are categorized.

In this method, the absolute benefit is determined, which is the value of the resources used compared to the value of the resources saved or created. The implicit assumption is that the courses of action are compared to a do-nothing alternative. However, in health care, because there are usually costs involved in do-nothing states, this is not typically done in practice. The valuation of the benefits can be conducted through the human capital method or the contingent valuation framework. The instrument depends on the purpose of the evaluation.

The human capital method places a value on the opportunity cost of lost time, such as lost wages or the value of replacement workers for duties without a wage (Viscusi, 1978). For example, if a person is in the labor force and needs to take time off from work due to disability, then the value of the loss of work would be measured in the wage rate. If the person is out of the labor force and has a disability that reduces the level of productivity, then the value of the loss is the replacement worker to complete the tasks no longer accomplished by the person in question. In many ways, this approach is debatable among economists because wages underestimate the total loss of time, particularly leisure time. Also, the approach favors the employed rather than those out of the labor market, which leads to inequities in compensation.

Contingent valuation is what a person would hypothetically pay if he or she could achieve the benefits from specific interventions. In other words, it is the willingness to pay for improved care (Donaldson, 1999; Shogren, Shin, Hayes, & Kliebenstein, 1994). Because this is a hypothetical approach, surveys obtaining the value of the preferences must be clearly defined with the following characteristics:

- They must clearly state the characteristics of the alternative.
- They must identify other goods and services that are competing for the person's household budget.
- They must explain that spending would be reduced on other goods or services if more is spent on the alternative in question.
- They must explain that the cost of the alternative would be seen with an increased tax or price.
- There must be a follow-up survey to obtain the rationale for respondents' valuations of the alternatives.

Because the Pareto principle is satisfied hypothetically, cost-benefit analysis traditionally does not account for income redistribution. Redistribution takes the form of taxes and transfers and can be criticized as inefficient. In practice, such as welfare reform plans, redistributional effects have been explicit, where the most general procedure is to classify the benefits and costs on a person-by-person or group-by-group basis. The redistribution depends on the relative weights applied to benefit distribution, and redistributional criteria may override efficiency criteria because projects are usually constrained so that the poor cannot be made worse off.

Cost

Costs are the value of the resources used for any particular course of action. The type and scope of costs depend on the analysis viewpoint (i.e., society, government, patient, employer, program agency). When in doubt, it is best to go to the broadest, or societal, viewpoint. In any viewpoint, the costs include the direct and indirect costs of the course of action considered. Direct costs are the actual expenses incurred by participating in the alternative. This includes the medical expenses, transportation costs, and other training costs that can be part of the alternative. Indirect costs are the productivity losses associated with the course of action, which reflect the opportunity costs of using one alternative and foregoing another (Jacobs & Fassbender, 1998; Luce & Elixhauser, 1990; Olsen, 1994). For example, this could include the waiting time for appointments, as well as transportation time as part of the participation in a course of action. In the private perspective, transfer costs are also included because they reflect changes in payments for individuals, providers, or organizations. From the societal view, direct and indirect costs are included but not transfer costs because these are not resources used. A summary of costs is shown in **Table 14-3**.

If the magnitude is small, then the study can merely identify it. Overall, economic costs go beyond simply listing expenditures because opportunity costs must be reflected, such as the need to consider other nonmarketed resources (e.g., leisure time, donated space). Costs can be estimated in a variety of ways. For example, values are imputed for nonmarket items. Leisure time may be measured by earnings lost by the corresponding wage rate.

Discounting

Discounting accounts for the differential timing of costs and outputs of particular courses of action under consideration over multiple periods of time. People place a higher value on benefits in the present period than in future periods. The discount rate reflects this social rate of time preference and expresses this preference for the present over the future. Therefore, all costs are discounted to their present value.

The discount rate is equal to the social rate of time preference, which denotes that people prefer their benefits now rather than in the future. Empirically, this rate is equal to the interest rate on a risk-free asset, such as government treasury bills. Discounting nonmonetary benefits has been controversial, especially for prevention or health education

TABLE 14-3 Summary of Types of Costs Considered in an Economic Evaluation

Direct Costs	1. Organizing and operating costs related to the course of action (e.g., capital costs, supplies, labor, equipment, utilities) 2. Costs borne by patients and their families (e.g., out-of-pocket expenses, patient and family input into course of action, psychological costs)
Indirect Costs	Time lost from work due to participation in course of action or to illness related to course of action
External/Societal Costs	Costs borne externally to the health sector and patients and their families

Data from O'Brien, B. (1995). Principles of economic evaluation for health care programs. *J Rheumatol, 22*:1399–1402; Drummond, M. F., et al., (1997). *Economic Evaluations of Health Care Programmes*, Oxford, England: Oxford University Press.

programs (Viscusi, 1995). Specifically, the approach diminishes the influence of health promotion programs that have a longer time horizon until outputs are recognized to their fullest but favors those programs that have a more immediate result.

Sensitivity Analysis

Over time, this technique has become virtually mandatory in economic evaluations, and improvements in the technique have occurred with more statistically inclined economists working on the method.

Sensitivity analysis is a means to determine the robustness of the evaluation recommendations under circumstances where the estimates are controversial or uncertain (Briggs & Sculpher, 1995; Briggs, Sculpher, & Buxton, 1994). It clearly identifies uncertain or controversial estimates in the study and presents an exposition of the ways in which different assumptions influence the study results. In terms of when to use this analysis, consider estimates that are subject to debate due to new variables being used (i.e., value of life scales), variations in data collection or measurement (i.e., per diem costs), and controversy in value judgments (i.e., choice of discount rate).

There are many ways to perform this analysis based on the type of uncertainty in the model (Saltelli et al., 2008). The most basic approach is to set upper, expected, and lower range of evaluation estimates based on varying the parameters in question. These estimates can be obtained from empirical evidence from other research, current practice in the literature, and judgments from decision makers in the study.

The course of action that is dominant under most or all of the scenarios would be the one chosen. This analysis also allows the analyst and audience to understand which conditions would make the course of action inefficient relative to other alternatives. It may be necessary to specify a threshold

set of study result estimates above or below which a course of action may no longer be efficient.

ASSESSMENT OF AN ECONOMIC EVALUATION

A sound economic evaluation has the components seen in a good empirical research study. These are outlined in **Table 14-4**. While these questions are not raised to create hypercritical users of economic evaluations, they do provide a means to quickly identify the strengths and weaknesses of the economic evaluation. It is highly unlikely that every economic evaluation would include all of the components noted in Table 14-4. However, even with weaknesses in a study, the reader may find that the method of the evaluation considered compares well with alternative approaches to the same problem.

A more thorough explanation of the questions follows.

1. *Was a well-defined and operational question formed?* In answering this question, the reader would determine if there is a comparison of alternatives, a description of the viewpoint of the analysis, and whether both costs and outputs of the alternatives are considered.

2. *Was a complete description of the alternative courses of action provided?* In answering this question, the study should address the *To whom?, The what?, The where?,* and *The frequency?* questions and whether a do-nothing alternative was considered.

3. *Was there evidence of program effectiveness?* In answering this question, the reader must determine how effectiveness is established. For example, was the effectiveness derived from current literature, and how strong is this determination from the literature?

4. *Were all important costs and outputs for each course of action identified?* In answering this question, the program description and analysis viewpoint should provide enough evidence that the appropriate costs and outputs are included. For example, a study may be considered

TABLE 14-4 Critical Questions When Reviewing an Economic Evaluation

1.	Was a well-defined and operational question formed?
2.	Was a complete description of the alternative courses of action provided?
3.	Was there evidence of program effectiveness?
4.	Were all important costs and outputs for each course of action identified?
5.	Were costs and outputs measured accurately?
6.	Were costs and outputs valued credibly?
7.	Were costs and outputs adjusted for differential timing?
8.	Was an incremental analysis of costs and outputs performed?
9.	Was a sensitivity analysis performed?
10.	Did the presentation of the findings include all issues of concern to the users of the analysis?

Data from O'Brien, B. (1995). Principles of economic evaluation for health care programs. *J Rheumatol, 22*:1399–1402; Drummond, M. F., et al., (1997). *Economic Evaluations of Health Care Programmes*, Oxford, England: Oxford University Press.

where a reduction in the highway speed limit decreases traffic-related deaths and injuries but also includes a higher wage for the transportation workers. It is also important that the outcomes of interest be identified clearly for the reader to judge the appropriateness of the economic evaluation method being used. The reader needs to know whether the outputs are health effects (appropriate for cost-effectiveness analysis), changes in the quality of life of the participants (appropriate for cost-utility analysis), or the overall value of the outcome created (appropriate for cost-benefit analysis).

5. *Were costs and outputs measured accurately?* For example, the measurement of operating costs of a particular course of action may include such things as 500 examinations, 100 hours of physician time, 200 hours of nursing time, rental for 1,000 square feet of clinic space, and so on. Costs borne by the participants may be measured by medicines purchased, time lost from work or leisure, and travel time to the treatment location.

6. *Were costs and outputs valued credibly?* For example, it should be remembered that costs are a valuation of the resources depleted by a particular course of action. Costs are usually valued in local currency based on the prevailing process of resources and can be taken from operating budgets. All current and future program costs are measured in constant dollars of some base year in order to put the values in real terms.

7. *Were costs and outputs adjusted for differential timing?* Different courses of action may have different time profiles of costs and outputs, but the comparison of the alternatives must be made at one point in time and the

timing among programs must be taken into account. For example, the main benefits of an influenza vaccine program are immediate, while the benefits of a colorectal screening program are not identified until well into future periods. In order to compare the different timing of the courses of action considered, the reader should determine if discounting is used as described earlier.

8. *Was an incremental analysis of costs and outputs performed?* For a more meaningful comparison across courses of action, the reader should be able to determine the additional costs that one course of action imposes over another compared to the additional outputs (i.e., health effects, utilities, or benefits) it yields. In practice, the influence of most courses of action adds to both costs and outputs, especially compared to no course of action being taken.

9. *Was a sensitivity analysis performed?* Every evaluation will have some degree of uncertainty or methodological controversy. For example, "What if a discount rate of 6% were used rather than 3%?" Or, "What if the rate for childhood vaccinations is 10% lower than considered in the analysis?" Evaluators will often rework the analysis by employing different assumptions or estimates in order to test the sensitivity of the conclusions of the analysis to such changes. If large variations in the assumptions or parameters yield little variations in the results of the study, then the reader would have more confidence in the original results.

10. *Did the presentation of the findings include all issues of concern to the users of the analysis?* A good study should begin to help the user interpret the results in

the context of his or her own particular situation. For example, many users of these analyses are interested in the bottom line, such as whether to purchase a new magnetic resonance imaging (MRI) machine. The analysis can be presented in such a way that it is explicit about the viewpoint being considered and by identifying how particular costs and benefits may vary by location. For example, the purchase of a new MRI machine may vary depending on whether the MRI will be a replacement unit in an existing imaging center or one that will be part of a newly converted center.

SUMMARY

This chapter provided the reader with an introduction to the nature of economic evaluation and the main types of economic evaluations, as well as the elements of a sound

economic evaluation. The complexity of the analysis must match the breadth of the questions posed. In determining the type of economic evaluation techniques, cost-minimization analysis and cost-effectiveness analysis assume that the courses of action considered are worth considering, while cost-benefit analysis and cost-utility analysis determine the value of the alternative through mechanisms for preference revelation.

Different approaches can be used together for complicated problems, and at times a cost-benefit analysis is performed of the economic evaluation itself because these studies are costly to perform.

KEY WORDS

- **Quality-adjusted life year (QALY)**
- **Willingness to pay**

Questions

1. You are asked to compare the outputs and costs of two cardiac interventions that affect the severity of the illness and the patient's survival rate. Which evaluation method would you use and why?

2. You are asked to evaluate three medical interventions that reduce the number of deaths due to congestive heart failure. Among these interventions, there are no influences on the patient's quality of life. Which evaluation method would you use and why?

3. You are asked whether a new drug to combat congestive heart failure symptoms should be used. Which evaluation method would you use and why?

4. How would you account for the differential timing and costs between a health promotion intervention and a treatment regime? What are the pros and cons of using this technique?

5. In practice, the social rate of time preference is measured as the interest rate on a risk-free asset. Is this interest rate appropriate? Why or why not?

PROFILE: NANCY STOKEY

Nancy Stokey received her BA in economics from the University of Pennsylvania in 1972 and her PhD in economics from Harvard University in 1978 under the advisement of Nobel Laureate Kenneth Arrow. Stokey is the Frederick Henry Prince Distinguished Service Professor of economics at the University of Chicago. She is the editor or co-editor of numerous journals such as *Econometrica* and the *Journal of Economic Theory*.

Stokey's work encompasses topics in growth and development with applications to games and economic behavior. Her work is widely praised and has led to such honors in service as vice president of the American Economic Association from 1996 to 1997, election into the National Academy of Sciences in 2004, and selection into the 2004 Copenhagen Consensus, a venue where some of the leading world economists gather to solve world challenges.

Data from University of Chicago faculty profiles, Retrieved from uchicago.edu. Accessed June 10, 2014.

REFERENCES

Bobinac, A., Van Exel, N. J. A., Rutten, F. F. H., & Brouwer, W. B. F. (2010). Willingness to pay for a quality-adjusted life-year: The individual perspective. *Value in Health, 13*(8), 1046–1055.

Briggs, A., & Sculpher, M. (1995). Sensitivity analysis in economic evaluation: A review of published studies. *Health Economics, 4*(5), 355–371.

Briggs, A., Sculpher, M., & Buxton, M. (1994). Uncertainty in the economic evaluation of health care technologies: The role of sensitivity analysis. *Health Economics, 3*(2), 95–104.

Donaldson, C. (1999). Valuing benefits of publicly-provided health care: Does "ability to pay" preclude the use of "willingness to pay"? *Social Science and Medicine, 49*(4), 551–563.

Doubilet, P., Weinstein, M. C., & McNeil, B. J. (1986). Use and misuse of the term "cost-effective" in medicine. *New England Journal of Medicine, 314*, 253–256.

Drummond, M. F. (1981). Welfare economics and cost benefit analysis in health care. *Scottish Journal of Political Economy, 28*(2), 125–145.

Drummond, M. F., Sculpher, M. J., Torrance, G. W., O'Brien, B. J., & Stoddart, G. L. (1997). *Methods for the economic evaluation of health care programmes* (2nd ed.). New York, NY: Oxford University Press.

Elixhauser, A. (1990). The cost effectiveness of preventive care for diabetes mellitus. *Diabetes Spectrum, 2*(6), 349–353.

Evans, R. G., & Robinson, G. C. (1980). Surgical day care: Measurements of the economic payoff. *Canadian Medical Association Journal, 123*(9), 873–880.

Gold, M. R., Siegel, J. E., Russell, L. B., & Weinstein, M. C. (Eds.). (1996). *Cost-effectiveness in health and medicine.* New York, NY: Oxford University Press.

Gray, A., Raikou, M., McGuire, A., Feen, P., Stevens, R., & Cull, C. (2000). Cost effectiveness of an intensive blood glucose control policy in patients with type 2 diabetes: Economic analysis alongside randomized controlled trial (UKPDS 41). *BMJ Clinical Research, 320*(7246), 1373–1378.

Hatziandreu, E. I., Koplan, J. P., Weinstein, M. C., Caspersen, C. J., & Warner, K. E. (1988). A cost-effectiveness analysis of exercise as health promotion. *American Journal of Public Health, 78*(11), 1417–1421.

Hirth, R. A., Chernew, M. E., Miller, E., Fendrick, A. M., & Weissert, W. G. (2000). Willingness to pay for a quality-adjusted life year: In search of a standard. *Medical Decision Making, 20*(3), 332–342.

Jacobs, P., & Fassbender, K. (1998). The measurement of indirect costs in the health economics evaluation literature: A review. *International Journal of Technology Assessment in Health Care, 14*(4), 799–808.

Jacobs, P., & Rapoport, J. (2002). *The economics of health and medical care* (5th ed.). Gaithersburg, MD: Aspen.

King, J. T., Tsevat, J., Lave, J. R., & Roberts, M. S. (2005). Willingness to pay for a quality-adjusted life year: Implications for societal health care resource allocation. *Medical Decision Making, 25*(6), 667–677.

Lansdorp-Vogelaar, I., Knudsen, A. B., & Brenner, H. (2011). Cost-effectiveness of colorectal cancer screening. *Epidemiological Reviews, 33*(1), 88–100.

Laupacis, A., Feeny, D., Detsky, A. S., & Tugwell, P. X. (1992). How attractive does a new technology have to be to warrant adoption and utilization? Tentative guidelines for using clinical and economic evaluations. *Canadian Medical Association Journal, 146*(4), 473–481.

Lieberman, D. A. (1995). Cost-effectiveness model for colon cancer screening. *Gastroenterology, 109*(6), 1781–1790.

Luce, B. R., & Elixhauser, A. (1990). Estimating costs in economic evaluations of medical technologies. *International Journal of Technology Assessment in Health Care, 6*(1), 57–75.

Messonnier, M. L., Corso, P. S., Teutsch, S., Haddix, A. C., & Harris, J. R. (1999). An ounce of prevention . . . what are the returns? *American Journal of Preventive Medicine, 16*(3), 248–263.

O'Brien, B. (1995). Principles of economic evaluation for health care programs. *Journal of Rheumatology, 22*(7), 1399–1402.

O'Brien, B., & Viramontes, J. L. (1993). Willingness to pay: A valid and reliable measure of health state preference? *Medical Decision Making, 14*(3), 289–297.

Olsen, J. A. (1994). Productivity gains: Should they count in health care evaluations? *Scottish Journal of Political Economy, 41*(1), 69–84.

Olsen, J. A., & Donaldson, C. (1998). Helicopters, hearts and hips: Using willingness to pay to set priorities for public sector health care programmes. *Social Science and Medicine, 46*(1), 1–12.

Saltelli, A., Ratto, M., Andres, T., Campolongo, F., Cariboni, J., Gatelli, D., . . . Tarantola, S. (2008). *Global sensitivity analysis: The primer.* West Sussex, England: John Wiley & Sons.

Scheffler, R. M., & Paringer, L. (1980). A review of the economic evidence on prevention. *Medical Care, 18*(5), 473–484.

Sculpher, M. J., Pang, F. S., Manca, A., Drummond, M. F., Golder, S., Urdahl, H., . . . Eastwood, A. (2005). Generalisability in economic evaluation studies in health care: A review and case studies. *Health Technology Assessment, 8*(49), 3–5.

Shogren, J. F., Shin, S. Y., Hayes, D. J., & Kliebenstein, J. B. (1994). Resolving differences in willingness to pay and willingness to accept. *American Economic Review, 84*(1), 255–270.

Sintonen, H. (1981). An approach to measuring and valuing health states. *Social Science and Medicine, 15*(2), 55–65.

Stoddart, G. L. (1982). Economic evaluation methods and health policy. *Evaluation and the Health Professions, 5*(4), 393–414.

Tengs, T. O., Adams, M. E., Pliskin, J. S., Safran, D. G., Siegel, J. E., Weinstein, M. C., & Graham, J. D. (1995). Five-hundred life-saving interventions and their cost-effectiveness. *Risk Analysis, 15*(3), 369–390.

Torrance, G. W., & Feeny, D. (1989). Utilities and quality-adjusted life years. *International Journal of Technology Assessment in Health Care, 5*(4), 559–575.

Viscusi, W. K. (1978). Labor market valuations of life and limb: Empirical evidence and policy implications. *Public Policy, 26*(3), 359–386.

Viscusi, W. K. (1995). Discounting health effects for medical decisions. In F. Sloan (Ed.), *Valuing health care: Costs, benefits, and effectiveness of pharmaceuticals and other medical technologies* (pp. 123–145). New York, NY: Cambridge University Press.

Williams, A. H. (1981). Welfare economics and health status measurement. In J. van der Gaag & M. Perlman (Eds.), *Health, economics, and health economics* (pp. 271–281). New York, NY: North-Holland.

CHAPTER **15**

Comparing Healthcare Systems

INTRODUCTION

A healthcare system consists of organizational units and processes by which a society determines the choices concerning the production, consumption, and distribution of healthcare services. The structure of a health system is important because it answers basic questions such as what to produce and who should receive the services produced. At one extreme, the systems may be totally centralized by the government and the government makes these choices, in another extreme, the choices can be made by the market, through the interaction of consumers and producers of healthcare services. This chapter discusses the predominant types of healthcare systems in the world.

ELEMENTS OF A HEALTHCARE SYSTEM

From a societal point of view, it is difficult to determine whether a centralized or decentralized health system is superior. A normative statement of that kind involves value judgments and trade-offs. A centralized authority with complete control may be more capable of distributing services more uniformly and have a greater ability to exploit economies of

scale and scope in supplying goods and services and purchasing healthcare inputs.

Alternatively, a healthcare system that is decentralized, such as the marketplace or a system of local governments, may provide more alternatives and innovations but result in diseconomies of scale and scope and lack of coordination. Determining the best structure for a healthcare system involves quantifying the value society places on several alternatives and sometimes competing outcomes, such as choice, innovation, uniformity, and production efficiency. Indeed, alternative systems throughout the world exist because people place different values on each of the various outcomes (Reinhardt, 1997). Reflecting the trade-offs involved, most health systems today are neither purely centralized nor decentralized but are mixed economies.

Types of Systems

No two healthcare systems are identical, although many share characteristics that allow for the development of typologies that are useful in analysis of any particular system. It must be noted that while typologies are useful in that they allow for a simplification of complex reality and focus on the most important aspects, they must always be viewed as a heuristic tool, not a full representation of reality. The specific configuration of any health system depends on a multitude of factors such as politics, culture, demographics, historical events, and social structures inherent to a specific country. Societal goals and priorities develop over time and shape all social institutions and values, which themselves are fluid and changeable and allow various topologies to succeed or fail.

Despite widespread variation among the healthcare systems of developed nations, at root they represent variants or combinations of a limited number of types. Typologies here can be useful in simplifying a variety of cross-cutting dimensions, but one must be cautious in interpreting them because they represent ideal types of instructional characteristics. Real-world healthcare systems are considerably more complex.

For initial comparative purposes, then, several models that have been used to classify healthcare systems are introduced here. The first classification scheme centers on the dimension of the degree of government involvement in funding and provision of health care. At one extreme is the potential of a completely free market system with no government intervention. At the other extreme is a tax-supported government monopoly of provision and funding of all healthcare services. Although in reality neither extreme exists, along the continuum are three models that together represent the core types of healthcare systems operating across developed countries.

As illustrated in **Figure 15-1**, the private insurance or consumer sovereignty model is that with the least state involvement in the direct funding or provision of healthcare services. This type is characterized by the purchase of private health insurance financed by employers and/or individual contributions that are task oriented. The basic assumption of this approach is that funding and provision of care is best left to market forces. These types are most clearly represented by the United States and, until recently by Australia, but many systems contain some elements of this type.

The second basic type of health system with state involvement is the social insurance (Bismarck) model. Although there is significant variation as to organization, this type is based on a concept of social solidarity and characterized effectively by a universal insurance coverage generally within the framework of social security. As a rule, this compulsory health insurance is funded by a combination of employer and individual contributions through nonprofit insurance funds, often regulated and subsidized by the state. The provision of services tends to be private, often on a fee-for-service basis, although there may be some public ownership of factors of production and delivery. Germany, Japan, and the Netherlands are viewed as examples of this type. Singapore, with its compulsory MediSave program, is a variation on the theme of social insurance.

The third type, and the one that might approach the government monopoly in its pure form, is the National Health Service (Beveridge) model. This model is characterized by universal coverage funded out of general taxation. Although this model is most identified by the United Kingdon, New Zealand created the first National Health Service (NHS) in the 1938 Social Security Act, which promised all citizens open-ended access to all of the healthcare services they needed free at the point of use. The provision of health services is solely under the auspices of the state, which either owns or controls the factors of production or delivery. Although they have all moved away from the pure model to varying degrees, the United Kingdom, Sweden, and New Zealand are examples of the NHS model.

Financing Methods Across Countries

Because the time and amount of medical treatment costs are uncertain from an individual consumer's perspective, third-party payers, such as private insurance, and the government play a major role in the healthcare economy.

In addition, third-party payers are responsible for managing the financing risk of purchasing medical services. A third-party payer can face a much lower level of risk than an individual consumer because it can pool its risk among various subscribers by operating on a large scale. The law

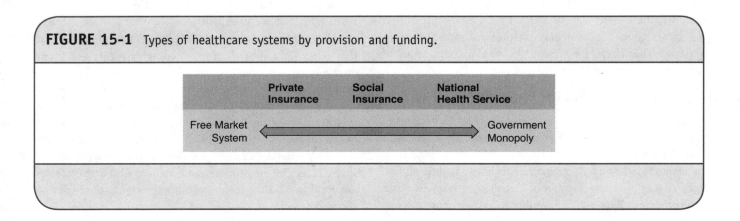

FIGURE 15-1 Types of healthcare systems by provision and funding.

of large numbers states that, while individual events may be random and unpredictable, the average outcome of many similar events across a large population can be predicted fairly accurately. For example, an insurance firm can predict the appendectomy rate by judging from past experiences involving a large number of people, while an individual may not be able to predict the risk of appendicitis. A risk-averse consumer is made better off by making a certain present payment to an insurer for coverage against an unforeseen medical event rather than facing the possibility of paying some unknown medical costs that can be potentially devastating to household income.

Third parties make the healthcare system much more complex because the source of third-party financing and the method of reimbursement must be worked into the model. If the third-party payer is a private insurance company, the consumer pays a premium in exchange for some amount of medical coverage. As part of the health insurance plan, the consumer may be responsible for paying a deductible and a copayment or coinsurance. The deductible provision requires the consumer to pay the first $X of medical expenses, after which the insurer is responsible for reimbursement. With a coinsurance provision, the consumer pays a fixed percentage of the expense at each medical visit. The copayment is the fixed amount of money the consumer pays at each medical visit.

When a government agency or public insurance company acts as a third-party payer, the financing of medical care insurance usually comes from taxes. Premiums and taxes differ in the way risk is treated and the voluntary nature of the payment (Bodenheimer & Grumbach, 1992). Premiums are voluntary and are paid according to the risk category of the insured. Taxes are mandatory and are paid regardless of the risk category.

Some alternative methods of financing can be ascertained by examining the different methods used in Canada, Germany, and the United Kingdom, as well as other major countries (Blank & Burau, 2004; Raffel, 1997; Thomson, Osborn, Squires, & Jun, 2012). These countries are chosen because many features of the U.S. financing system have been derived from these countries.

Canada has a compulsory national health insurance (NHI) program administered by each of the 10 provinces. Each province has its own unique type of administration. The NHI provides first dollar coverage with no limits on the amount of medical care received during a consumer's lifetime. Each province finances the program through taxes. In addition, the Canadian government provides up to 40% cost sharing and makes hospital construction grants available to the provinces (Schabloski, 2008). Private insurance is

available for some forms of "frill" or optional health services, but not services covered under the NHI. Because the public sector is responsible for the NHI, there are no marketing costs, no allocation of profits, and no determination of who to cover.

The Socialized Health Insurance Program in Germany is based on government-mandated financing by employers and employees. The premiums of unemployed individuals and their dependents are paid by former employers or come from public sources (e.g., public pension funds). **Sickness funds**, which are private nonprofit companies, are responsible for collecting funds and reimbursing healthcare providers and hospitals. Statutory medical benefits are comprehensive, and there are small copayments for some services.

Mechanic (1995) and others refer to the healthcare system in the United Kingdom as a public contracting model because the government contracts with various providers of healthcare services on behalf of the people. The United Kingdom healthcare system, under the auspices of the NHS, offers universal health insurance coverage financed through taxation. The NHS provides **global budgets** to district health authorities. Each district health authority (DHA) is responsible for assessing and prioritizing the healthcare needs of more than 300,000 people (Schabloski, 2008) and then purchasing the necessary healthcare services for public and private healthcare providers. Hospital services are provided by nongovernment trusts, which compete with themselves and with private hospitals for DHA contracts. Community-based primary care providers also contract with DHAs. In addition, general practitioner fund holders apply for budgets from the DHAs and, with the budgets, service a group of more than 5,000 patients by providing primary care and purchasing elective surgery outpatient therapy and specialty nursing services (Schabloski, 2008).

SUMMARY OF VARIOUS HEALTHCARE SYSTEMS

The essential features of the Canadian healthcare system are national insurance, free choice of healthcare provider, private production of medical services, and regulated global budgets and fees for healthcare providers. The dominating features of the German healthcare system include socialized health insurance financed through sickness funds, negotiated payments to healthcare providers, free choice of provider, and private production of healthcare services. In the case of the United Kingdom, the distinguishing characteristics include restrictions on the choice of provider, public contracting of medical services, global budgets for hospitals, fixed salaries for hospital-based physicians, and capitation payments to general practitioners. The pluralistic healthcare system in the United States contains a system of private production but relies more heavily on a fee-for-service method relative to other systems. In addition, healthcare providers are reimbursed by many types of payers, including the government and private insurance firms—in contrast to the **single payer system** of Canada, Germany, and the United Kingdom (World Health Organization, 2000).

PERFORMANCE OF THE U.S. HEALTHCARE SYSTEM

An aggregate assessment of the U.S. healthcare economy is performed and compared to the performance of a select group of healthcare systems around the world.

Overall Assessment

Prices and expenditures on various medical services continue to rise but more slowly in recent years. The transition to managed care delivery or other restrictive delivery models has helped to promote some cost savings in various medical care markets but has also resulted in some rationing of care. Choices of physicians, hospital admissions, and selection of pharmaceutical products have all been greatly limited by the movement of supply side controls in the healthcare system. Whether managed care organizations have been able to curb the excesses brought on by unlimited fee-for-service plans of the past or have unnecessarily denied care remains a heated issue and an area for future research.

It also seems that competition in the healthcare sector may have created its own beginnings of destruction. For example, cherry picking and redlining of benefits in the private insurance industry take place because of competition. Quantity-setting behavior in the physician services industry and medical arms race in the hospital industry are a result of competition.

© Dean Mitchell/Shutterstock

The discussion turns now to how the U.S. healthcare system compares to others around the world. It is interesting and informative to understand how the United States compares to other countries in terms of healthcare expenditures, utilization of medical care, and healthcare outcomes.

Lifestyle and environmental factors play an important role in determining the health status and demand for medical care. People may try to compensate for risky lifestyle behaviors, such as poor diet or lack of exercise, by consuming healthcare services. This would cause the demand for health care to increase and result in growth in overall healthcare expenditures.

Information on medical utilization indicates that perhaps the high medical care spending in the United States occurs in a relatively large amount of inpatient and physician office visits. Focusing on overall expenditures, the United States spent 17.9% of the gross domestic product (GDP) on health care in 2012, while France spent 11.7%, Germany spent 11.3%, and the United Kingdom spent 9.4% (The World Bank, 2013). An examination of the medical utilization data suggest just the opposite, however (Thomson, Osborn, Squires, & Jun, 2013). In particular, in 2011, the United States had only 125 hospital discharges per 1,000 populations, compared to 244 in Germany and 169 in France during that time. Only Japan (111 discharges per 1,000) and Canada (82 per 1,000) had lower rates than the United States.

A similar profile is seen for physician visits. In 2011, per capita visits in the United States were only 4.1, while Canada had 7.4, France had 6.8, Germany had 9.7, and the United Kingdom had 5.0. Therefore, medical utilization does not explain the high aggregate expenditures in the United States.

Comparatively high healthcare expenditures with lower utilization rates lead many analysts to believe that U.S. medical prices must be significantly higher than in other countries. Others argue that the underlying cause may be due to differing quality in health care across countries. Specifically, the quality of medical care may be higher in the United States, thus accounting for the higher prices. Although anecdotal evidence suggests that waiting times are lower in the United States than in other countries, true quality indicators are difficult to derive due to measurement errors.

In summary, approximately 13% of the U.S. population is without health insurance coverage throughout the year as of 2014 (Newport, 2014). In contrast, nearly universal coverage exists in the other countries studied. The U.S. government is responsible for financing about 45% of all healthcare spending. The comparable figure for other countries is approximately 90%. Healthcare spending as a fraction of the GDP is higher, medical utilization is lower, lifestyle is poorer, and infant mortality rates are higher in the United States relative to the other countries considered. Many analysts believe that these findings are a result of the lack of universal coverage in health insurance in the United States and that the government plays a more dominant role in the delivery of health care in other countries. Many analysts also believe that the United States would have similar statistics to other counties if universal coverage and greater government involvement existed in the health economy.

Medical Technology in Canada, Germany, the United Kingdom, and the United States

The availability of technology has a profound effect on healthcare costs and the availability of medical care. Technologies such as drugs, medical devices, and procedures may offer cost savings or higher-quality services.

Four stages are associated with the development and diffusion of medical technology. According to the National Science Foundation, the first stage, basic research, is defined as "original investigation for the advancement of scientific knowledge without specific commercial objectives." (NSF, p. 38). Basic research produces new medical knowledge about areas in biomedical sciences, for example. In the second stage, applied research, the basic knowledge is applied to yield solutions for the prevention, treatment, or curing of diseases. At the clinical investigation and testing stage, news medical technologies are tested on human subjects. The benefits and safety of the technologies are tested at this point. The final stage, diffusion or imitation, involves the commercial introduction, adoption, and spreading of medical technologies (Cooper & Zmud, 1990).

Health policy analysts have expressed concern that the unconstrained healthcare markets result in medical technologies that offer low benefits at high costs (Aaron, 1991). As a result, many countries have implemented policies to either directly or indirectly control the adoption and diffusion of medical technologies to contain costs (Bodenheimer, 2005). Although diffusion of technology takes place more slowly in more tightly budgeted systems, the use of innovative technologies in those systems tends to catch up over time to that in the United States.

For example, hospital budgets are limited in Canada and the United Kingdom partly to indirectly control the proliferation of expensive medical technologies. It is argued that limited budgets create a financial incentive for hospital administrators to economize on medical technologies, offering low benefits at high costs. At the other extreme, the adoption and diffusion of technology are determined more by market forces in the United States. Germany, on the other hand, has taken a middle position between the two extremes,

with some limited control over the proliferation of new medical technologies (Rublee, 1989).

Reinhart, Hussey, and Anderson (2002) provide some evidence on the relative availability of different medical technologies in several countries. Many implications can be drawn from their study. First, given the greater reliance on market forces, the data show a greater availability of medical technology in the United States than in the three other countries. For example, the United States has nearly 50% more magnetic resonance imagers (MRIs) per million people than the United Kingdom and more than four times more MRIs than Canada. In addition, only Germany had more CT scanners per million people than the United States. There is also a much greater prevalence of coronary artery bypass procedures, coronary angioplasty procedures, and patients undergoing dialysis in the United States than in the other three counties. Second, the data suggest that, to some degree, the relative availability of medical technologies in Germany tends to fall somewhere between the United States and the other two countries. Besides having the most CT scanners, Germany has the second greatest number of MRIs and persons undergoing dialysis and coronary angioplasty. Germany, however, is last among the four countries in terms of coronary bypass procedures.

Third, it is difficult to conclude from the available information whether medical technologies are overprovided in the United States or underprovided in the other three countries. In fact, a different level of medical technology could be optimal for each country because of differing social values (Rublee, 1994). Cost-benefit analysis, cost-effectiveness studies, or outcomes research would be necessary to draw definitive conclusions on this issue. Finally, the availability of medical technology in itself indicates little about the overall effectiveness of the healthcare system. To determine overall

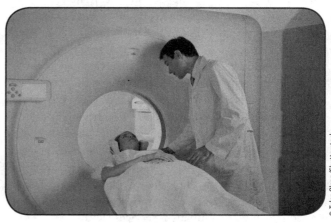

© Tyler Olson/Shutterstock

healthcare system effectiveness, a host of factors must also be considered, including the quantity and quality of other medical inputs.

The Case of Singapore

The pressure to contain rising medical costs has brought considerable attention to Singapore's healthcare system due to its reliance on **medical savings accounts**. In 2012, Singapore spent 4.7% percent of the GDP on health care. This is far lower than the 17.9% that the United States spends (The World Bank, 2013). Some attribute the ability of Singapore to control healthcare spending on the cost containment incentives that arise with medical savings accounts.

According to Barr (2001), the Singapore health system is composed of three basic institutional arrangements. The MediSave program is a compulsory savings plan that forms the basis for the individual savings accounts. The contribution rates range from 6% to 8% of monthly income and are shared between the employee and employer. Self-employed individuals must pay the entire amount, and caps are placed on monthly contributions, which prohibit more affluent individuals from accumulating unreasonably high savings balances. MediSave accounts are used primarily to finance inpatient hospital care, and strict payment schedules are in place to protect accounts from being depleted too quickly.

To protect individuals from the financial burden of a major illness, a catastrophic illness insurance plan, call MediShield, is available. This insurance plan is optional and pays for 80% of hospital expenses after a rather substantial deductible has been met. The third institutional component is the MediFund, which is an endowment established by the government to finance the healthcare needs of the poor.

Barr (2001) contends that the ability of the Singapore healthcare system to contain costs can only partially explain the implementation of medical savings accounts. Strict government controls on inputs and prices, along with the rationing of medical care, have played an even greater role in controlling costs. Other explanations include a relatively young population and the existence of several traditional Chinese medical practitioners who are not funded under the government-sponsored healthcare programs. Abeysinghe, Himani, and Lim (2010) have concluded more recently that Singapore has developed a unique healthcare model that has produced outstanding health outcomes per dollar spent. However, this system is highly dependent on income levels despite the substantial government subsidies and heavy reliance on inpatient treatment. This style of healthcare delivery does not follow current trends in models for medicine, which are more focused on outpatient services worldwide.

Consumer Satisfaction with the Healthcare System in Canada, Germany, the United Kingdom, and the United States

People in various nations count on their governments to choose and support the healthcare system that best promotes efficiency and equity given their historical background, cultural system, and political belief. One question is whether people in these countries are satisfied with their current healthcare system. In an attempt to answer this question, public opinion polls have tried to estimate the degree of consumer satisfaction with the present healthcare system in several nations.

Blendon, Kim, and Benson (2001) cited various opinion polls involving interviews of random samples of households in a variety of countries, including Canada, Germany, the United Kingdom, and the United States. The households were asked if they were satisfied with the present healthcare system in their respective countries. Several findings from these polls are worth noting.

In terms of overall satisfaction, the German system was superior but only in a slight margin relative to that in the United Kingdom. Fifty-eight percent of the German households surveyed were satisfied with their system compared to 57% in the United Kingdom. Germany has a healthcare system characterized by a universal social insurance program. The comparable rates for Canada and the United States are 46% and 40%, respectively, suggesting that U.S. residents are least satisfied with their current healthcare system.

However, if the poll results are indicative only of those households considered to be poor, the relative ranking changes, with the United Kingdom on top with a 67% satisfaction rate and the rate for Germany falling to 52%. Among the poor, the U.S. healthcare system fares a bit better, with 47% of the poor satisfied with their healthcare system relative to 40% of the poor in Canada.

If the poll results were confined to the elderly, the poll ranking changes once again. The United Kingdom healthcare system is superior, with 69% of the elderly satisfied with their healthcare system, and the United States ranking second with 61% of satisfied households. This could possibly be due to the fact that the elderly have Medicare, a universal health insurance plan for this demographic group. Canada fared the worst, with only 48% satisfied with their healthcare system.

Public opinion polls may not accurately reflect the success or failure of a healthcare system or provide a complete representation of the quality of life in a nation. For example, low education and income levels may cause individuals to be generally dissatisfied with their environment. How people feel about the operation of the healthcare system relative to the functioning of the overall economic system may provide a more accurate indicator of public satisfaction. In addition, unknown to the public, the structure of the healthcare system may not account for the poor performance of the medical sector. The poor performance of a medical care system may be due to inadequate or inefficient allocation of income, resources, or adverse lifestyles. Moreover, from a general welfare perspective, individuals may be very satisfied with other aspects of the economy but dissatisfied with aspects of the health economy. These trade-offs may not be seen in opinion polls solely focusing on the health economy. These aspects should be considered when assessing the overall quality of healthcare systems.

A more recent study by Jankauskiene and Jankauskaite (2011) of 10 European countries found that, overall, the best quality and healthcare access countries are Austria, Denmark, and Germany, and the worst are in Eastern European nations. These findings are consistent with the opinion poll conducted by Blendon and colleagues (2001) but focused on a different set of countries.

According to a Gallup Poll, about 13% of the U.S. adult population remains uninsured, and these people are half as likely as those with insurance to say they are satisfied with the way the healthcare system is working for them (Newport, 2014). However, approximately 30% of Americans without insurance are satisfied, and almost as many of those with insurance are dissatisfied, indicating that there is more involved in satisfaction than having insurance. Of those with insurance, more Americans with government-paid insurance are satisfied with the way the system is working than is true for those with private plans. The differing satisfaction levels between those with insurance and those without, and between those with federal and those with private plans, however, indicate that the way this coverage is provided is clearly related to healthcare satisfaction.

Americans' high level of satisfaction with how the healthcare system is treating them suggests that health care is not in a crisis state for most Americans. Further, some Americans who are dissatisfied with the way the healthcare system is treating them may be expressing their displeasure with particular doctors, hospitals, billing issues, or medical procedures—aspects that have little to do with the broader issue of how healthcare coverage is provided. These findings are slightly more pessimistic than the poll performed earlier by Blendon and colleagues (2001) but show that there is still need for improvement in the U.S. system.

SUMMARY

Every healthcare system must answer four basic questions concerning the allocation of medical resources and the distribution of medical care services. Some systems rely on centralized decision making, whereas others answer the basic questions through decentralized processes. Healthcare systems are complex largely because third-party payers are involved.

Important elements that make up a healthcare system are the financing, reimbursement, and production methods and the degree of choice over the healthcare provider. Medical care is financed by out-of-pocket payments, premiums, and/or taxes. Medical care providers are reimbursed on a fixed or variable basis. The production of medical care may take place in a for-profit, nonprofit, or public setting, and medial care providers may operate in dependent or large group practices. Choice of provider may be limited. All of these features are important because they influence one operation and performance of the healthcare sector. The U.S. healthcare system is very pluralistic. For instance, considerable variation exists in the financing, reimbursement, and production of medical care.

KEY WORDS

- **Global budgets**
- **Medical savings accounts**
- **Sickness funds**
- **Single payer system**

Questions

1. Identify four basic healthcare systems discussed in the chapter.

2. What are the advantages and disadvantages of a single payer system?

3. What are the chief areas of efficiency and inefficiency in the German healthcare system?

PROFILE: SUSAN DENTZER

Susan Dentzer is a renowned policy analyst and expert. She was one of the first women to attend Dartmouth College, receiving a BA in English in 1977. She is currently the senior health policy advisor for the Robert Wood Johnson Foundation and editor in chief of *Health Affairs*. Her work in policy and health has led to many honors and influential positions such as election into the Institute of Medicine and the Council on Foreign Relations. Her previous work included positions as a correspondent for *NewsHour with Jim Lehrer, U.S. News & World Report*, and *Newsweek*.

Data from Robert Wood Johnsons Foundation. Accessed June 10, 2014; "Dentzer leaving post at *Health Affairs*" in *Modern Healthcare*. Accessed June 10, 2014.

REFERENCES

Aaron, H. J. (1991). *Serious and unstable condition: Financing America's health care*. Washington, DC: The Brookings Institution.

Abeysinghe, T., Himani, M., & Lim, J. (2010). *Singapore's healthcare financing: Some challenges*. Retrieved from https://courses.nus.edu.sg/course/ecstabey/Singapore%20health%20chapter-earlier%20version.pdf

Barr, M. D. (2001). Medical savings accounts in Singapore: A critical inquiry. *Journal of Health Politics, Policy and Law, 26*(4), 709–726.

Blank, R. H., & Burau, V. (2004). *Comparative health policy*. New York, NY: Palgrave Macmillan.

Blendon, R. J., Kim, M., & Benson, J. M. (2001). The public versus the World Health Organization on health system performance. *Health Affairs, 20*(3), 10–20.

Bodenheimer, T. (2005). High and rising health care costs. Part 2: Technologic innovation. *Annals of Internal Medicine, 142*(11), 932–937.

Bodenheimer, T., & Grumbach, K. (1992). Financing universal health insurance: Taxes, premiums, and the lessons of social insurance. *Journal of Health Politics, Policy and Law, 17*(3), 439–462.

Cooper, R. B., & Zmud, R. W. (1990). Information technology implementation research: A technological diffusion approach. *Management Science, 36*(2), 123–139.

Jankauskiene, D., & Jankauskaite, I. (2011). Access and quality of health care system by opinion of patients in ten European countries. *Management in Health, 15*(3), 1–13.

Mechanic, D. (1995). The Americanization of the British National Health Service. *Health Affairs, 14*(2), 51–67.

Newport, F. (2014, June 16). Most Americans remain satisfied with health-care system. *Gallup*. Retrieved from www.gallup.com/poll/171680/americans-remain-satisfied-healthcare-system.aspx

Raffel, M. W. (Ed.). (1997). *Health care and reform in industrialized countries*. University Park, PA: Pennsylvania State University Press.

Reinhardt, U. E. (1997). Economics. *Journal of the American Medical Association, 277*(23), 1850–1851.

Reinhardt, U. E., Hussey, P. S., & Anderson, G. F. (2002). Cross-national comparisons of health systems using OECD data, 1999. *Health Affairs, 21*(3), 169–181.

Rublee, D. A. (1989). Medical technology in Canada, Germany, and the United States. *Health Affairs, 8*(3), 178–181.

Rublee, D. A. (1994). Medical technology in Canada, Germany, and the United States: An update. *Health Affairs, 13*(4), 113–117.

Schabloski, A. K. (2008). *Health care systems around the world*. Washington, DC: Insure the Uninsured Project.

Thomson, S., Osborn, R., Squires, D., & Jun, M. (Eds.). (2012). *International profiles of health care systems, 2012*. New York, NY: The Commonwealth Fund.

Thomson, S., Osborn, R., Squires, D., & Jun, M. (Eds.). (2013). *International profiles of health care systems, 2013*. New York, NY: The Commonwealth Fund.

The World Bank. (2013). *Health expenditure, total (% of GDP)*. Retrieved from http://data.world bank.org/indicator/SH.XPD.TOTL.ZS/

World Health Organization. (2000). *The world health report 2000—Health systems: Improving performance*. Geneva, Switzerland: Author.

CHAPTER **16**

International Health System Issues and Reforms

INTRODUCTION

Across the world, countries are trying to cope with limited healthcare resources in the prevention and treatment of conditions such as obesity, chronic disease, and addictions. This dilemma is seen in both the developed and developing world. This chapter explores the common issues faced across countries, building capacity across countries and the context and principles around universal coverage reform models that are currently under way globally.

COMMON HEALTH ISSUES ACROSS COUNTRIES

Regardless of economic status, nearly every country is faced with growing problems with noncommunicable or chronic diseases and complications due to obesity. While a growing proportion of populations worldwide are facing heart disease, stroke, cancer, and diabetes that require concerted global efforts, most countries do not have affordable, cost-effective, and feasible interventions (Beaglehole, Bonita, Horton, et al., 2011). In developing countries, much of this lack of resources to fight **noncommunicable disease** is due to the historical allocation of healthcare services to infectious disease.

A study by Alwan and colleagues (2010) found that 64% of total deaths in 23 countries were due to noncommunicable disease in people aged 70 years or younger, with tobacco use and obesity being prime drivers of mortality. The study also concluded that surveillance and interventions to reduce the incidence and prevalence of chronic disease were inadequate in most countries. Those with complex chronic conditions were most troublesome due to deficits in post-hospital discharge planning and the use of multiple providers for a variety of illnesses (Schoen, Osborn, How, Doty, & Peugh, 2009). Further, with growing aging populations worldwide, there is a significant burden of disease with the increased frailty of the population (Ward, Parikh, & Workman, 2011). Given these issues, *The Lancet* NCD Action Group set out to prioritize healthcare interventions globally to meet this crisis in chronic disease through actions such as improved diet and physical activity, reduction in alcohol and smoking, and the use of technology to monitor patients and the system (Beaglehole, Bonita, Alleyne, et al., 2011).

Obesity has also become a growing **pandemic** across most countries. Much of this is due to the overconsumption of affordable, readily available processed foods. However, the profile of those most likely to become obese varies between developing and developed countries. For example, those in low-income countries who tend to be obese are more likely to be middle-aged women from wealthy urban environments, while for those in higher-income countries, obesity can cross all socioeconomic boundaries (Swinburn et al., 2011). Focusing on developing countries, as well as disadvantaged groups in developed countries, the major public health initiatives to combat obesity include education and incentives to eat more nutritious and less caloric foods (Popkin, Adair, & Ng, 2012) as well as creating infrastructure to combat the pandemic of physical inactivity through safe walking and exercising areas (Kohl et al., 2012). However, these measures and interventions can fall short in areas where there are **food deserts**, or locations where healthier foods are not available.

Health disparities are common concern across countries as well. Cotlear and colleagues (2014) found that continued segregation in Latin America has led to perceptions that there is segregation in health care despite improvements in life expectancy and advances in the view of the right to health. Kulzhanov and Rechel (2007) identified many health reform initiatives in Kazakhstan in the mid-1990s, but there has been inconsistent progress in outcomes in attaining universal coverage and uniform health outcomes for all.

Satisfaction with Health Systems

With the growing need for health services to address increasing chronic conditions, satisfaction with the healthcare system is a major tension in reform efforts. Affordability and effectiveness are key, as well as waiting times in measuring satisfaction and discontent, respectively. A study initiated by The Commonwealth Fund and conducted by Papanicolas, Cylus, and Smith (2013) found that, among 11 countries surveyed, respondents from the United Kingdom were most discontented with the system, with expenditures of 9.4% of the gross domestic product (GDP) in 2012, while 25.4% of U.S. respondents felt that a major overhaul of the system was needed, with expenditures of 17.9% of the GDP in 2012 (The World Bank, 2013). Given this survey and controlling for socioeconomic differences among respondents, there was no consistent association between satisfaction and patient experiences across the countries surveyed regardless of expenditures on health care in the economies considered.

Those with chronic conditions often find that care is poorly coordinated regardless of the healthcare system (Schoen et al., 2011). Specifically, those in Switzerland and the United Kingdom reported the greatest satisfaction with care coordination, while those in the United States were more likely to find billing problems and care being foregone because of costs. With more complicated patient populations worldwide, there is a greater need for **medical homes** or central providers to coordinate care and provide interventions for complex populations.

Insurance coverage models have a great effect on access to care and satisfaction with the health system as seen in a study of 11 countries by Schoen and colleagues (2010). In this analysis, there was significant variation in access, costs, and problems due to the type of insurance market or model

employed. For example, those in the United States were more likely to have higher cost burdens and more administrative problems with insurers. Germans also experienced administrative problems but had much lower out-of-pocket costs of care. In general, the U.S. system was in the greatest need of reform, especially concerning the health disparities related to socioeconomic status and financial access to care.

From the supply side, providers across many countries found that there was spotty success in the use of health information technology in treating complicated patient populations (Schoen et al., 2012). A high percentage of primary care providers across 10 countries determined that it was difficult to get medical information from specialists in many cases. In the United States in particular, providers were more apt to grapple with problems with third-party payers or insurers in reimbursing services rendered. Therefore, from both patient and provider perspectives, it appears that common issues in satisfaction are seen in that more administrative overhead or longer waiting time for treatment leads to greater levels of dissatisfaction with the healthcare system considered.

SCALING UP INTERNATIONAL HEALTH

In the mid-1990s to early 2000s, there was a major focus on disease-specific initiatives in the delivery of health services globally. Currently, there is a greater and more concerted movement toward strengthening health systems overall. Much of the interest in **health system strengthening**, or health system development, is from international organizations, even though the systems are nation specific. Scott and Jha (2014) noted that, globally, increases in health care have led to poorer health outcomes and that universal access is a goal across countries. A study by Hafner and Shiffman (2013) found that there was a growing concern that global health initiatives were too taxing to the health systems and that, without the appropriate infrastructure, the initiatives may not achieve their organizational objectives. However, the concept of health system strengthening is vague at best and there may not be the resources or the willingness to sustain the agenda of building the health systems. This unwillingness may be due to global financial crises and the history of policy swings in regard to the importance of international health.

The most common connotation of scaling up of international health is the expansion of international health interventions, but it can also imply the expansion of financial, human, and capital resources to increase healthcare coverage of the populations considered (Mangham & Hanson, 2010). This increase in coverage usually implies geographic reach of the services considered. The decrease in HIV/AIDS mortality can be seen as a successful example of an increase in scaled-up health care internationally, where such a case had strong leadership, effective management, reasonable financial resources and stakeholder ownership, and technological infrastructure (Frenk, 2010a; Gilson & Schneider, 2010; Medlin, Chowdhurry, Jamison, & Measham, 2006). However, over the long term, there must be a concerted commitment to maintaining the delivery of interventions to improve population health (Hanson, Ranson, Oliveira-Cruz, & Mills, 2003). This can be particularly challenging in developed countries with competing needs between national priorities and international goals.

REFORM MODELS

There are no perfect healthcare systems because every intervention or reform entails a trade-off in cost, quality, and access to care (Naylor & Naylor, 2012). For many, the view of the health economy, regardless of country, is that the system is a "black box" that is far too complicated to fully comprehend or change, and that if change was to be considered, the funds would simply go into a "black hole" because no infusion of funds would be sufficient (Frenk, 2010b). These views, however, are slowly being diffused across the world as interventions are being devised, applied, and evaluated, and many systems have achieved efficient ways of attaining improved health outcomes for their populations.

Reform efforts and system changes need several components for successful outcomes. These are effective and visionary leadership, shared goals systems thinking rather than the simple achievement of individual goals, and the appropriate use of technology in delivering interventions (Frenk, 2010b). However, even with these features in reform efforts, evaluation is key for determining whether additional resources or changes are needed in the dynamic social and political environments in which the interventions take place.

Context

Politics plays an important role in reform efforts. For example, a movement toward **universal coverage** (or universal access to health care) relies on political and social processes to promote interventions that improve equity, enhance access, and create large pools for financial risks (Savedoff, de Ferranti, Smith, & Fan, 2012). This allows for the benefits to be concentrated among those deemed to be deserving of the interventions or policy changes while diffusing the costs of the reform in the form of general taxes, for example, which have relatively small effects on the population at large.

Further, the methods for reform over time, regardless of the system, are more likely based on reactions to previous or concurrent paradigms than on collective or progressive accumulations of insights about a problem in the system or condition in the population (van Olmen, Marchal, Van Damme, Kegels, & Hill, 2012). In addition, there is usually very little political analysis of the reforms attempted or implemented, so there is little understanding as to whether the initiatives are acceptable to most or all of the actors involved.

Many of the recent incentives for reforming international health systems were based on *The World Health Report 2000* (World Health Organization, 2000). In this volume, the view of health systems was expanded to ask the following questions (Murray & Frenk, 2000):

- What is included as part of the health system?
- What are the goals of the health system?
- What are the functions of the health system?
- How can we assess health system performance?
- What is the relationship between the function and outcomes of the health system?

These questions are classic features of an evaluation design for assessing health system performance. While the report focused on and resulted in debates mainly on empirical measurement issues in assessment, the rationale behind the assessment is that accountability does not occur only from resource management but also in the attainment of health outcomes in the populations served (Frenk, 2010b). This view has led to the evaluation of reforms and interventions in health systems as a top priority across countries.

Universal Coverage

The World Health Report 2010 (World Health Organization, 2010) set the stage for considering financing issues for universal coverage in health systems worldwide. In this report, it was determined that universal coverage is resource intense and requires efficient use of inputs because it needs to assure that a core set of services is available to all in the society.

In an assessment of three core components of universal coverage in nine countries conducted by Chisholm and Evans (2010), there were notable differences among countries in terms of depth of coverage (i.e., proportion of population covered), breadth of coverage (i.e., range of services covered in plans offered), and height of coverage (i.e., proportion of costs covered by out-of-pocket expenditures). For example, Cuba and Sri Lanka have the deepest and longest established universal coverage plans, but the breadth and height of coverage across countries are difficult to compare because there are usually no defined benefit packages. Only Chile and Thailand have easily discernable packages, but most have established primary care packages in place. In general, however, the highest-performing low- to middle-income countries considered are those with the most established efforts at delivering universal coverage to their populations.

In a robust review of universal coverage internationally, Moreno-Serra and Smith (2012) noted that broader coverage (i.e., movements to universal coverage) led to better access to services and better health outcomes, especially for those in lower socioeconomic strata. However, variations exist in data collection and interpretation among countries as well as the political and social contexts that surround system reforms that may confound the results of such evaluations of universal or other healthcare or health insurance coverage models. In any international assessment effort, more comparable information is needed to unequivocally determine which systems are truly superior in the delivery of health services and their associated health outcomes.

SUMMARY

Across the world, societies are grappling with similar health conditions, such as the reduction of incidence and prevalence of infectious disease, only to see a surge in the number and types of chronic conditions that occur that are associated with increasingly aged or overweight populations. Given these pressures on healthcare system resources and population health, countries have been actively working on system reforms to more efficiently and equitably utilize services to improve population health status. Regardless of the system, basic features must be attained for a successful reform effort, such as effective leadership, appropriate technology, adequate institutional support, and systems-level thinking. One example of reform being considered is the movement toward universal coverage, which appears to be successful in varying degrees in attaining health goals, but better empirical evidence needs to be gathered globally to completely understand the effects of such a reform.

KEY WORDS

- **Food desert**
- **Health system strengthening**
- **Medical home**
- **Noncommunicable disease**
- **Pandemic**
- **Universal coverage**

Questions

1. Why is obesity such a problem in so many countries worldwide?

2. What are some of the challenges to scaling up international health and how can they be addressed?

3. Why is it so difficult to determine which country has the best health system? Describe the empirical issues related to evaluation of the systems as well as possible ways to overcome these difficulties.

PROFILE: NANCY FOLBRE

Nancy Folbre was born in 1952 and earned a BA in philosophy from the University of Texas in 1971, an MA in Latin American studies from the University of Texas in 1973, and a PhD in economics from the University of Massachusetts Amherst in 1979. Her work encompasses feminist economics with a research agenda on economics and economics of care.

Folbre is a notable economist who has had numerous fellowship opportunities in academia and research, including a postdoctoral research fellowship offered by the Yale University Economic Growth Center from 1979 to 1980 and being named the Charlotte Perkin Gilman Fellow at the American Academy of Political and Social Science in 2004. She also served the profession as president of the International Association of

Feminist Economists in 2002 and has served as associate editor of the *Feminist Economics* journal since 1995. In 2004, she was named a member of the National Academy of Science Panel, which investigated the models for nonmarket accounts.

Folbre has authored six books and numerous articles that focus on the economics of the family and caregiving. She is on the economics faculty at the University of Massachusetts Amherst.

Data from "Nancy Folbre Bio." Retrieved from apps.olin.wustl.edu/macarthur/bio/folbre.htm). Accessed July 10, 2014; University of Massachusetts Retrieved from people.umass.edu/folbre/folbre/. Accessed July 10, 2014.

REFERENCES

Alwan, A., MacLean, D. R., Riley, L. M., d'Espaignet, E. T., Mathers, C. D., Stevens, G. A., & Bettcher, D. (2010). Monitoring and surveillance of chronic non-communicable diseases: Progress and capacity in high-burden countries. *The Lancet, 376*(9755), 1861–1868.

Beaglehole, R., Bonita, R., Alleyne, G., Horton, R., Li, L., Lincoln, P., . . . Stuckler, D. (2011). UN high-level meeting on non-communicable diseases: Addressing four questions. *The Lancet, 378*(9789), 449–455.

Beaglehole, R., Bonita, R., Horton, R., Adams, C., Alleyne, G., Asaria, P., . . . Watt, J. (2011). Priority actions for the non-communicable disease crisis. *The Lancet, 377*(9775), 1438–1447.

Chisholm, D., & Evans, D. B. (2010). *Improving health system efficiency as a means of moving towards universal coverage* (World Health Report Background Paper, 28). Geneva, Switzerland: World Health Organization.

Cotlear, D., Gomez-Dantes, O., Knaul, F. M., Atun, R., Barreto, I. C. H. C., Cetrángolo, O., . . . Sáenz, R. (2014). Overcoming social segregation in health care in Latin America. *The Lancet, 385*(9974), 1248–1259.

Frenk, J. (2010a). The global health system: Strengthening national health systems as the next step for global progress. *PLoS Medicine, 7*(1). doi:10.1371/journal.pmed.1000089

Frenk, J. (2010b). *The World Health Report 2000*: Expanding the horizon of health system performance. *Health Policy and Planning, 25*(5), 343–345.

Gilson, L., & Schneider, H. (2010). Managing scaling up: What are the key issues? *Health Policy and Planning, 25*(2), 97–98.

Hafner, T., & Shiffman, J. (2013). The emergence of global attention to health systems strengthening. *Health Policy and Planning, 28*(1), 41–50.

Hanson, K., Ranson, M. K., Oliveira-Cruz, V., & Mills, A. (2003). Expanding access to priority health interventions: A framework for understanding the constraints to scaling-up. *Journal of International Development, 15*(1), 1–14.

Kohl, H. W., III, Craig, C. L., Lambert, E. V., Inoue, S., Alkandari, J. R., Leetongin, G., & Kahlmeier, S. (2012). The pandemic of physical inactivity: Global action for public health. *The Lancet, 380*(9838), 294–305.

Kulzhanov, M., & Rechel, B. (2007). Kazakhstan: Health system review. *Health Systems in Transition, 9*(7), 1–158.

Mangham, L. J., & Hanson, K. (2010). Scaling up in international health: What are the key issues? *Health Policy and Planning, 25*(2), 85–96.

Medlin, C. A., Chowdhury, M., Jamison, D. T., & Measham, A. R. (2006). Improving the health of populations: Lessons of experience. In D. T. Jamison, J. G. Breman, A. R. Measham, G. Alleyne, M. Claeson, D. B. Evans, . . . P. Musgrove (Eds.), *Disease control priorities in developing countries* (2nd ed., pp. 165–179). New York, NY: Oxford University Press.

Moreno-Serra, R., & Smith, P. C. (2012). Does progress towards universal health coverage improve population health? *The Lancet, 380*(9845), 917–923.

Murray, C. J., & Frenk, J. (2000). A framework for assessing performance of health systems. *Bulletin of the World Health Organization, 78*(6), 717–731.

Naylor, C. D., & Naylor, K. T. (2012). Seven provocative principles for health care reform. *Journal of the American Medical Association, 307*(9), 919–920.

Papanicolas, I., Cylus, J., & Smith, P. C. (2013). An analysis of survey data form 11 countries finds that "satisfaction" with health system performance means many things. *Health Affairs, 32*(4), 734–742.

Popkin, B. M., Adair, L. S., & Ng, W. (2012). Global nutrition and the pandemic of obesity in developing countries. *Nutrition Reviews, 70*(1), 3–21.

Savedoff, W. D., de Ferranti, D., Smith, A. L., & Fan, V. (2012). Political and economic aspects of the transition to universal health coverage. *The Lancet, 380*(9845), 924–932.

Schoen, C., Osborn, R., How, S. K. H., Doty, M. M., & Peugh, J. (2009). In chronic condition: Experiences of patients with complex health care needs, in eight countries, 2008. *Health Affairs, 28*(1), w1–w16.

Schoen, C., Osborne, R., Squires, D., Doty, M. M., Pierson, R., & Applebaum, S. (2010). How health insurance design affects access to care and costs, by income, in eleven countries. *Health Affairs, 29*(12), 2323–2334.

Schoen, C., Osborn, R., Squires, D., Doty, M., Pierson, R., & Applebaum, S.

(2011). New 2011 survey of patients with complex care needs in eleven countries finds that care is often poorly coordinated. *Health Affairs, 30*(12), 2437–2448.

Schoen, C., Osborn, R., Squires, D., Doty, M., Rasmussen, P., Pierson, R., & Applebaum, S. (2012). A survey of primary care doctors in ten countries shows progress in use of health information technology, less in other areas. *Health Affairs, 31*(12), 2805–2816.

Scott, K. W., & Jha, A. K. (2014). Putting quality on the global health agenda. *New England Journal of Medicine, 371*, 3–5.

Swinburn, B. A., Sacks, G., Hall, K. D., McPherson, K., Finegood, D. T., Moodie, M. L., & Gortmaker, S. L. (2011). The global obesity epidemic: Shaped by global drivers and local environments. *The Lancet, 378*(9793), 804–814.

van Olmen, J., Marchal, B., Van Damme, W., Kegels, G., & Hill, P. S. (2012). Health systems framework in their political context: Framing divergent agendas. *BMC Public Health, 12,* 774.

Ward, S. A., Parikh, S., & Workman, B. (2011). Health perspectives: International epidemiology of ageing. *Best Practice and Research Clinical Anesthesiology, 25*(3), 305–317.

The World Bank. (2013). *Health expenditure, total (% of GDP)*. Retrieved from http://data.world bank.org/indicator/SH.XPD.TOTL.ZS/

World Health Organization. (2000). *The world health report 2000—Health systems: Improving performance*. Geneva, Switzerland: Author.

World Health Organization. (2010). *The world health report 2010—Health systems financing: The path to universal coverage*. Geneva, Switzerland: Author.

CHAPTER **17**

National and State Healthcare Reform

INTRODUCTION

As society ages, the incidence and prevalence of chronic diseases, such as diabetes, coronary artery disease, and arthritis, increases dramatically. Continued improvement of life-extending technologies, such as mechanical ventilation, artificial resuscitation, and minimally invasive surgeries, can also be expected.

However, using these technologies on sicker patients leads to escalating costs and more tensions in society related to who deserves the resources. Quality and access are important considerations, but the overriding concern is the cost of health care because more healthcare expenditures implies that less resources will go to another sector of the economy. This chapter explores the history of and methods for healthcare reform, the types of reforms at the national and state levels, and the advantages and disadvantages of reform strategies.

THE HISTORY OF AND METHODS FOR REFORM

Since nearly the beginning of the 20th century, there has been some formal movement or piece of legislation brought forth that would help to modify the healthcare system to improve access to and quality of care or to control costs of

care. These issues have remained the same to politicians, policy analysts, and the public at large, but the debates rose to a new level of intensity at the turn of the 21st century when significant healthcare legislation to improve access to care was enacted. Among the main catalysts for the reform success were the escalating costs coupled with the declining proportion of those with insurance coverage, leading to the increased concern about the healthcare system.

To understand the incentives and goals of the reform movements, it is necessary to explore the reasons underlying the need for reform. Some analysts and politicians focus on the poor and the elderly as the deserving segments of society for reform goals, while others note the growing proportion of uninsured who are denied the care, or have discontinuous care, that is needed to improve or maintain health (The Commonwealth Fund, 2015). In either case, the lack of access to quality care can lead to other losses in society such as increased use of social services or welfare aid due to the inability to maintain income or wealth because of poor health. Many Americans are afraid to change jobs for fear of being without insurance coverage. This fear and potential to lose insurance leads to job-lock. Because of increasing healthcare costs, most workers are also feeling the rise of insurance premiums through larger payroll deductions, where nominal and real wages decline over time and result in less buying power for goods and services.

Further, with annual health insurance premiums rising each year due to escalating drug and other technologically based costs, employee health benefits are often eating into significant shares of firms' profits. Therefore, firms cannot afford to offer health insurance benefits, and a growing perception is that these benefits would be better viewed as a public good under government responsibility.

The Goals of Reform

The challenge facing analysts, politicians, and individuals is one of attempting to satisfy unlimited demands given limited resources in the economy. Because of this, healthcare choices must be placed in the context of competing with other goals considered important by society such as national defense and education, for example. In establishing spending priorities among all sectors of the economy, improvements in health and medical care have a significant advantage over goals placed in other sectors. The needs of this sector can be dramatized in the policy arena and in public awareness by recounting specific individual cases where human welfare is involved. These personalized examples can easily shift priorities toward the health sector due to society's value for human life.

Two concerns must be addressed when developing and implementing policies to reform the healthcare system: access to care and costs of care.

Access to Care

Expanded access requires additional funding due to the fact that people enter the system previously having no, or uncoordinated, care. This results in large amounts of health care consumed as people gain access to affordable care, thus shifting the demand for care to the right. On the supply side, increases in personnel and services used also create increases in the costs of health care, thus shifting the supply of care to the left due to increased supply and labor costs. This results in an increase in overall expenditures in equilibrium. Although the private healthcare market cannot sustain large increases in access to care, the public is wary of any policy changes that require large tax increases to implement the reforms. This has led to more incremental reforms or phasing in of access over several years, creating delays in coverage for deserving groups such as the poor or disabled.

One model for universal coverage is the **single payer system** in the Canadian Medicare system. This model has a universal benefits package and limits the choices for "frill" services available to those who can pay for additional care. Extra coverage for such services as private hospital rooms can be purchased by individuals.

Alternatively, expanding coverage to marginal "deserving" or disenfranchised groups is a different form of attempting to attain universal coverage. For example, market-based insurance reforms such as the Affordable Care Act provide small business owners, their employees, and dependents access to group health insurance purchasing cooperatives that offer group insurance at affordable rates when private insurance plans are either physically or financially unattainable. This incremental reform geared to enhancing **social welfare** can easily lead to a multi-tiered system of coverage rather than more equal coverage across everyone in society.

Costs of Care

In defining a benefits package, opinions vary on how services should be prioritized, whether it is on principles of evidence-based medicine or economic evaluations. For example, one group may focus on providing all essential preventive, acute, and catastrophic care, while another group may decide that only catastrophic care should be considered (Arnold & Austin, 2009).

Once a society decides what should be covered, the financing decision remains. Most publicly provided healthcare systems have some form of collective funding through a combination of taxes and insurance premiums. However, inevitably, expanding access and providing even moderately comprehensive benefits will cause costs to rise dramatically in the short term due to the increased access issues previously described. Perceptions of the increase depend on whether the costs are borne out of pocket directly for individuals in society or through general taxes, thus broadening the burden of the spending increase among members of society.

FEDERAL REFORM ALTERNATIVES

Three alternative strategies are routinely proposed at the federal and state levels to increase financial access to health care: the single payer option, **mandated insurance coverage** secured through place of employment or individually, and expanded use of **market incentives** such as health insurance purchasing cooperatives to encourage and enable individuals to purchase insurance. Each approach is outlined briefly next.

Single Payer National Health Insurance

Proponents of universal health insurance coverage prefer the single payer national insurance program (Messerli, 2013). Among the benefits include the elimination of administrative waste in duplicate billings and procedures and the ability for persons with preexisting conditions to be covered by insurance. In this model, everyone participates under a single plan, administered and financed under the government or some quasi-government entity.

The main advantage of the single payer system is in its administrative simplicity, which leads to improved efficiency and cost control (Messerli, 2013). The only paper trail is between the government payer and the provider of care.

Another advantage is that everyone in society is covered, regardless of ability to pay or employment because coverage is not linked to jobs.

Critics believe that the single payer system provides more power over and control of healthcare resources to the government. Further, a single payer system results in a higher tax burden because the direct effect of personal insurance premium changes are eliminated by the more generalized tax base (Messerli, 2013) and individuals lose the responsibility to control expenditures. Therefore, the benefits and costs of the model are spread over an entire society.

Employer-Based Health Insurance

Once the venerable insurance for the vast majority of Americans, employer-sponsored insurance had a substantial decline from 1999/2000 to 2010/2011 (Sonier, Fried, Au-Yeung, & Auringer, 2013). The percentage decline was more than 10%, from 69.7% to 59.5%, while public coverage increased by 3.1%. Although the percent covered declined significantly, the percent of workers eligible for coverage at firms that offered insurance remained relatively constant. The take-up rate of coverage fell to 76.3%, while the greatest decline in offer of insurance was among small firms, with 56.3% of these firms offering insurance in 2010/2011. Major drivers of the decrease in take-up rates and offers of insurance was due to the costs of insurance for both the insured and the firm. Premium costs doubled for individuals, from $2,490 to $5,081, and family premiums rose 125%, from $6,415 to $14,447. Employee contributions increased to 20.8% of the total premiums paid for employer-based insurance. With these significant increases in employer-based insurance coupled with decreases in offers of insurance, this model of financial access to care is becoming less influential in the healthcare sector.

Employer-Mandated Health Insurance

Historically, proponents of employer mandates have used this market-based principle to support the plan to provide insurance coverage to all working Americans and their dependents. This would have been reasonable up until the latter part of the 20th century. However, given the trends just described, this approach is less viable. In this model, a common way of implementing an employer mandate is when employers would be required to purchase a basic healthcare package for their employees as defined by lawmakers. If employers chose not to do this, they could pay for a government-sponsored health plan through a new tax used to fund the insurance that the workers and their dependents require (Eibner, 2008). The Affordable Care Act includes such a mandate for U.S. firms with 50 or more full-time equivalent employees. Currently, fewer than 1% of all American businesses would be subject to a tax due to no insurance offered based on data presented in a study conducted by Semro (2013). However, even though in most larger firms the majority of workers are offered insurance, the issue is whether the availability of government-sponsored insurance alternatives would create an incentive for firms to drop insurance coverage and simply pay a tax that could be much lower than the premiums being paid for the employer-based insurance. This would be an example of **public sector crowd out**.

Individual Mandates

Instead of an employer mandate, an individual mandate could be employed. Under the Affordable Care Act, the paradox of rising healthcare expenditures coupled with lower life expectancies is attempting to be addressed through a massive financial overhaul of the U.S. healthcare economy (Dolan & Mokhtari, 2013). It is a legal requirement that individuals carry their own insurance protection regardless of employment status, in much the same way that people obtain automobile insurance for all registered vehicles or homeowners and renters secure insurance plans. Here, Americans would need to purchase insurance or pay a tax if they fall above a particular income floor. This type of mandate has the same goal as the employer mandate and single payer options: getting more people into the insurance pool in order to lower the health insurance costs overall. Proponents consider this mandate a "moral" and "economic imperative" (Manning & Edmundson, 2012). Those with preexisting conditions no longer need to worry about purchasing coverage, and fewer would rely on emergency room care as primary or routine care options. This is the rationale behind the individual mandate in the Affordable Care Act. The Congressional Budget Office (2010) concludes that this mandate under the Affordable Care Act would save $39 billion in uncompensated care alone, which is compatible with economic growth.

Critics of the Affordable Care Act approach believe that, while in principle this method may work, the implementation is too weak in that the tax for noncompliance is only a fraction of the cost of an insurance policy (Matthews, 2009). Overall, however, the progress toward increased coverage has been positive under the Affordable Care Act (Blumenthal & Collins, 2014).

Market-Based Alternatives

The United States uses the market mechanism to allocate healthcare resources to a large extent. However, in this model, the number of uninsured Americans has risen from

37 million in 2000 to 50 million in 2010 (The Commonwealth Fund, 2015). This does not concern advocates of the market approach because they see this as a failure of the government to correct market imperfections.

Problems with the traditional market approach that were seen before the enactment of the Affordable Care Act are that the market limits insurance availability because individuals and small businesses are fed into small pools for underwriting purposes. These small pools make premiums significantly higher because of the high costs of administering the small groups and are subject to large increases in premiums in the event of a single catastrophic loss within the pool. Another problem is that insurance is denied to certain vulnerable groups—those in job transitions and those with preexisting or catastrophic conditions. The traditional insurance market would not allow insurance to be portable for these groups of people.

A market solution to this problem must include measures to make it easier to form larger risk pools, concentrating purchasing power and lowering costs. Specifically, **health insurance purchasing cooperatives**, used to enhance access to and lower the cost of insurance to individuals and small groups, is included in the Affordable Care Act.

Market-based approaches are built around the assumption that individual decisions are better than collective decisions. The market approach would provide more power to the individual, whereas the single payer alternative would give more power to the government. The real debate is between those who feel that individuals can gather enough information to correct perceptions of health risks to be responsible for making medical care decisions and those who believe that the medical care system and risk perception are too complex for individual decision making.

INIDIVIDUAL STATE INITIATIVES

State healthcare costs are at an unprecedented level, and great tension exists in many states for reform. In 2009, U.S. healthcare expenditures per capita were $6,815, while in Massachusetts costs were $9,278 and in Vermont costs were $7,635 (Kaiser Family Foundation, 2009a). The expenses for these two states created an incentive to pass legislation to control costs and increase access to quality care. These cases are outlined next.

Commonwealth Care Health Insurance Program

In 2006, Massachusetts passed a healthcare reform package that provided near universal coverage for state residents. This package included the expansion of government-sponsored programs and the creation of a health insurance exchange

(Kaiser Family Foundation, 2012). Major successes of this legislation include the following:

- Within 1 year of implementation, the number of uninsured dropped dramatically. By 2010, the rate of uninsured was 6.3%, while the national average was 18.4%.
- Since the reform, more adults received preventive care services, and the supply of primary care providers is growing due to government incentives to provide medical school loan repayment for work in underserved areas.
- As of 2012, the expenditures on health care still are 15% higher than the national average, and the state has the highest individual insurance premiums in the country. To address this, legislation was proposed to provide comprehensive provider payment reform. This increase in expenditures was not unforeseen as the initial goals were to provide financial access to care for residents and to control future costs.
- The Affordable Care Act was modeled on the Commonwealth Health Care Insurance Program, but several differences remain between the federal and state reforms that require interagency coordination and the creation of new information technology programs.

This reform model greatly informed the Affordable Care Act components and is continuing to show signs of improvement in access to affordable, quality care. Cost control will eventually be realized, and more residents coordinate care early on rather than wait for acute or chronic conditions to manifest.

Green Mountain Care

In Vermont, the legislature enacted a plan in 2011 to create a single payer system. This plan created the Green Mountain Care Board to improve cost control and the health insurance exchange to provide universal insurance coverage. This plan works in concert with the Affordable Care Act parameters to provide affordable health care to Vermonters. As this plan is being implemented, savings are estimated at $281 billion over the first 3 years, even with enhancements to coverage and a decrease in personal out-of-pocket expenditures. The plan also institutes a uniform payment structure to eliminate fee negotiations between insurers and providers and lower administrative costs. This plan will be fully operational in providing universal coverage to Vermonters in 2017 (Spaulding & Lunge, 2013).

Other State Initiatives

The Centers for Medicare and Medicaid Services are currently partnering with several states in the State Innovation Models (SIM) Initiative, established in 2012, to reform delivery and payment methods in their states' health economies. Currently, there are 6 model-testing states, 3 model-pretesting states, and 16 model-design states. Findings follow for the six model-testing states (Silow-Carroll & Lamphere, 2013).

SIM is authorized under the Affordable Care Act and coordinates the pilot projects that focus on the financial alignment of provider and payment incentives to provide accessible high-value health care. The six model-testing states received $33 million to $45 million over 42 months to implement their plans. These states include Arkansas, Maine, Massachusetts, Minnesota, Oregon, and Vermont. Findings of the model implementation are as follows:

- States need strong leadership from officials. The states with the most success in their pilot projects had the longest history of reform efforts.
- States need collaboration between multiple payers and providers. The success of the reforms need stakeholder engagement from areas in points, goals, and strategies.
- Successful implementation requires good information foundations. Success depends on provider and payer access to reliable, targeted, and efficiently produced data on cost and quality of care.
- Success depends on state government policy levers to ensure adequate supply and distribution of a well-trained and diverse workforce.
- Success depends on early consensus on scope and goals of projects among all stakeholders.

These pilot projects are diverse, but those that are successful include these features and need ample time to prepare for reforms in order to hire staff and secure vendors.

FEDERAL REFORM HISTORY

Federal healthcare reform efforts are not a new phenomenon. Since the early 1900s, proposals to reform health care have been considered. Since the 1930s, opinion polls concluded that the general public was supportive of guaranteed access to health care for all but stopped short when there were costs associated with this benefit for society. These findings continued throughout the 20th century. Discussed next is a brief history of the major federal reform efforts (Kaiser Family Foundation, 2009b).

Socialized medicine was first seen in 1915, when Roosevelt's Bull Moose Party campaigned for health insurance for industry. Further, in the 1920s, progressive reformers called for compulsory insurance. Although these efforts were ineffectual, there was significant opposition to the term *socialized health care*.

During the time of the New Deal from 1934 to 1939, President Roosevelt addressed old age and unemployment issues as well as medical care and health insurance. His Committee on Economic Security worked in private, and the recommendations were never made public due to the more pressing need to pass the Social Security bill.

During the Fair Deal from 1943 to 1950, Roosevelt wanted to press for health insurance at the conclusion of World War II. Upon Roosevelt's death 3 months after the war, President Truman continued to push for legislation for access to medical care under the Fair Deal Package. However, with the fear of communism growing in Germany and China in the late 1940s, the public was concerned about greater government control over the U.S. economy. Further, private employer-based insurance was growing at this time.

During the Great Society from 1960 to 1965, reformers focused on the elderly and poor as the deserving population segments for healthcare programs. The major pieces of legislation that were enacted during this time were two entitlement programs: Medicare for the elderly and Medicaid for long-term care for the poor. In these programs, there were no provisions for cost control with the elderly in need of services such as eyeglasses, prescriptions drug coverage, and long-term care. In 1965, Medicaid and Medicare were incorporated into the Social Security Act and signed by President Johnson, with Truman in attendance. These massive programs were successfully enacted through the political skill of Johnson and a supportive Democratic majority in Congress.

Other national health insurance proposals from 1970 to 1974 were offered by Senator Ted Kennedy, who put forth a single payer plan, and President Nixon, who countered with his own market-based insurance model that would include the replacement of Medicaid with another program that would cover the poor and uninsured. Several splinter groups also developed at this time, creating more complexity in the legislative process. While there was general support for healthcare reform in the legislative arena, the numerous complex bills and the scandal of Watergate and resignation of President Nixon led to the defeat of national insurance efforts.

In the cost containment era from 1976 to 1979, President Carter was more concerned with containing costs due to high inflation and a sluggish economy overall (known as a period of stagflation) and pledged to consider national health insurance once the economy stabilized. Senator Kennedy grew impatient with the delay and drafted yet another reform proposal for Congress to consider. Carter released a proposal soon after Kennedy presented his, which included the stipulation that businesses provide a minimum benefits package and include coverage for the poor and aged. The economy was so unstable with inflation, recession, and uncontrolled healthcare costs that reforms were essentially tabled. However, the groundwork for the 1983 Medicare Prospective Payment System was laid that changed the financial payments Medicare made to hospitals from a fee-for-service-based system to a predetermined rate per episode of care.

The Health Security Act under consideration from 1992 to 1994 was developed while the public was concerned about losing medical benefits and being unable to afford health care. President Clinton favored the managed competition approach to cost containment and quality initiatives and proposed a plan that called for universal coverage, employer and individual mandates, private insurer competition, and government regulations for cost control. The concept of health purchasing alliances was created, where insurers and providers in the private healthcare markets would compete for business. The proposal was defeated due to its complexity and split along party lines in Congress. However, even though this bill did not come to fruition, the Children's Health Insurance Program was enacted in 1997 with bipartisan support, which is an enhancement to Medicaid for low-income children who would otherwise not qualify for government insurance.

The Affordable Care Act was developed in 2009 under the Obama administration and adopted the individual mandate as a central component to provide universal coverage to Americans. The act was signed in 2010, and the mandate took effect in 2014. The question of whether an individual mandate was constitutional was reviewed by the Supreme Court in *National Federation of Independent Business v. Sebelius* and the act was upheld in a 5 to 4 vote.

Even with the Affordable Care Act implementation in 2010, the Congressional Budget Office (2010) estimated that more than 20 million people will remain without insurance.

Further, it was concluded that the uninsured are forced to subsidize the insured patients (Uninsured billed unfairly [Editorial], 2010). Finally, because cost control is not an initial goal of the act, it could add up to higher costs for society overall (Levey & Oliphant, 2009).

The history of health reform at the federal level has a long and rich past and include many fears of socialized medicine. However, national health insurance reform in the form of the Affordable Care Act strives for universal coverage and improvements in prevention and health information technology. However, all proposals and policies have unintended consequences, with increases in access leading to cost control issues.

SUMMARY

Healthcare reform is, historically, a complicated and daunting challenge for federal and state policymakers. People want change but often are concerned with the role of government and their costs in the reform. This chapter includes several examples and findings of state reform efforts, focusing mostly on strong government interventions. The federal reform history includes employer and individual mandates as well as single payer and market-based reform models. Most proposals had difficult timing or too much mystique in the development process to come to fruition. However, the Affordable Care Act is one piece of recent legislation that had the political window to be enacted and is currently folding into the fabric of the healthcare economy.

KEY WORDS

- **Health insurance purchasing cooperatives**
- **Mandated insurance coverage**
- **Market incentives**
- **Public sector crowd out**
- **Single payer system**
- **Social welfare**

Questions

1. What are the respective roles of the federal and state governments in providing health services?

2. Is death an enemy that should be fought off at all costs or is it a condition of life that is to be accepted? How does the way this question is answered affect the kind of healthcare system that we might embrace?

3. In what sense do Americans have a right to medical care? In what sense is access to medical care not a right?

PROFILE: THOMAS C. SCHELLING

Thomas C. Schelling was born in 1921 in Oakland, California, and traveled in his early years as the son of a naval officer. He graduated from the University of California, Berkeley, in 1944 with a degree in economics, and then pursued a PhD in economics from Harvard University. He spent years abroad and in Washington working on negotiations with European governments, mostly on military issues. In 1953, he joined the faculty at Yale University and began his work on bargaining and conflict resolution, which was the area that was recognized by the Nobel committee later in his life.

Schelling's work encompasses a variety of topics related to game theory and bargaining behavior, which include such areas as military strategy, environmental policy, health policy, tobacco and drug policy, and the military draft. He has received many honors for his work, including his post as president of the American Economic Association (1991) and now Distinguished Fellow of the association, and election into the National Academy of Sciences, the Institute of Medicine, and the American Academy of Arts and Sciences. In 2005, he was awarded the Sveriges Riksbank Prize in Economic Sciences in Memory of Alfred Nobel for his work on further understanding competitive and cooperative game theory.

Schelling held numerous positions in his career, notably as a guest of the RAND Corporation and then as a faculty member at Harvard University in the Department of Economics and the Center for International Affairs, where he stayed for 31 years. He is currently a Distinguished University Professor of Economics in the Department of Economics in the School of Public Policy at the University of Maryland, a position he has held since his retirement from Harvard University in 1990.

Data from University of Maryland Department of Economics. Retrieved from econ.umd.edu/facultyprofiles. Accessed June 10, 2014; "Thomas C. Schelling – Biographical." Nobelproze.org. Nobel Media AB 2013. Accessed June 10, 2014.

REFERENCES

Arnold, S. B., & Austin, B. J. (2009). *Health care benefits—Creating the optimal design.* Princeton, NJ: Robert Wood Johnson Foundation.

Blumenthal, D., & Collins, S. R. (2014). Health care coverage under the Affordable Care Act—A progress report. *New England Journal of Medicine, 371*, 275–281.

The Commonwealth Fund. (2015). *Health care delivery system reform.* Retrieved from www .commonwealthfund.org/grants-and-fellowships/ programs/health-care-delivery-system-reform

Congressional Budget Office. (2010). *H.R. 4872, Reconciliation Act of 2010 (Final health care legislation).* Retrieved from www.cbo.gov/publication/21351

Dolan, E. M., & Mokhtari, M. M. (2013). The Patient Protection and Affordable Care Act (ACA): Pros and cons. *Journal of Family and Economic Issues, 34*(1), 1–2.

Eibner, C. (2008). *Is the economic burden of providing health insurance greater for small firms than for large firms?* Santa Monica, CA: RAND Corporation.

Kaiser Family Foundation. (2009a). *Health care expenditures per capita by state of residence.* Retrieved from http://kff.org/other/state-indicator/ health-spending-per-capita/

Kaiser Family Foundation. (2009b). *National health insurance—A brief history of reform efforts in the U.S.* Retrieved from https://kaiser familyfoundation.files.wordpress.com/2013/01/7871.pdf

Kaiser Family Foundation. (2012). *Massachusetts health care reform: Six years later.* Retrieved from https://kaiserfamilyfoundation.files.wordpress .com/2013/01/8311.pdf

Levey, N. N., & Oliphant, J. (2009, September 24). Mandate minus price controls may increase healthcare costs. *Los Angeles Times.* Retrieved from http://articles.latimes.com/2009/sep/24/nation/ na-healthcare-affordability24

Manning, J., & Edmundson, P. (2012, July 6). The individual mandate benefits us all. *Boston Business Journal.* Retrieved from www.bizjournals.com/ boston/print-edition/2012/07/06/the-individual-mandate-benefits-us-all .html?page=all

Matthews, K. (2009, February 15). Individual health insurance mandates—Pros and cons. *Policy Prescriptions.* Retrieved from www.policyprescriptions .org/individual-health-insurance-mandates-pros-cons/

Messerli, J. (2013). *Should the government provide free universal health care for all Americans?* Retrieved from www.balancedpolitics.org/ universal_health_care.htm

Semro, R. (2013, July 12). The role of the "employer mandate" in the Affordable Care Act. *Huffington Post.* Retrieved from www.huffingtonpost .com/bob-semro/the-role-of-the-employer-mandate_b_3575041 .html

Silow-Carroll, S., & Lamphere, J. (2013). *State innovation models: Early experiences and challenges of an initiative to advance broad health system reform.* New York, NY: The Commonwealth Fund.

Sonier, J., Fried, B., Au-Yeung, C., & Auringer, B. (2013). *State-level trends in employer-sponsored health insurance.* Princeton, NJ: Robert Wood Johnson Foundation.

Spaulding J., & Lunge, R. (2013). *Health care reform financing plan: In accordance with Act 48, Section 9.* Retrieved from http://hcr.vermont.gov/ sites/hcr/files/2013/Health%20Care%20Reform%20Financing%20 Plan_typos%26formatting%20corrected_012913.pdf

Uninsured billed unfairly [Editorial]. (2004, July 1). *USA Today.* Retrieved from http://usatoday30.usatoday.com/news/opinion/editorials/ 2004-07-01our-view_x.htm

Public Policy and Health Economics

INTRODUCTION

The fundamental difference between the approach to the provision of health care in the United States and most other industrialized nations is that the United States is more market oriented, and insurance coverage is less inclusive. When health insurance is offered to workers as part of their compensation package it is a trade-off for higher cash wages. In most states, employers are not required to offer health insurance to employees, and it is dependent on the labor regulations between workers and employers. In this chapter, a discussion of the basic benefits and problems of this system is included, with recommendations for greater efficiency.

THE MARKET-BASED SYSTEM

All societies ration scarce resources. Therefore, the question is what basis should be used to ration access to health care. A market-based system relies more heavily on the price mechanism as a rationing device. The U.S. healthcare system is a mixture of a market system and a system in which services are allocated on the other bases. For example, **Medicaid**, an insurance program for low-income families managed by both the state and federal governments, and the joint federal and state **Children's Health Insurance Program** for families who have incomes that are too high for them to be considered for Medicaid but who cannot afford private health insurance, do not use the price mechanism to allocate healthcare resources. **Medicare**, a federal government-sponsored insurance program primarily for seniors, relies less on it because services are so heavily subsidized.

Demand Versus Need

The greater reliance in the United States on the market and rationing by price and affordability rather than by government control is paralleled by an approach in healthcare economics that focuses on supply and demand. Thomas Rice is critical of a demand-driven system (Rice, 1998; Rice & Unruh, 2009). He questions the concept of consumer **sovereignty**, or the power of consumers to determine which goods and services are produced, in a situation where demand determines the direction of technology development in health care. These criticisms rely on the assumption that nonmarket-based methods can and should be used to prioritize the resources that a society decides to devote to health care and to determine the way in which they are distributed among the population.

Evaluating Efficiency Versus Equity

Critiques of a healthcare system usually subject it to two criteria: one concern is efficiency and the other has to do with fairness, or **equity**. In most economic decisions, there is some degree of trade-off between the two criteria (Okun, 1975). For example, pricing insurance using experience rating is more efficient than broad-based community rating because it relates the marginal cost of insuring the individual to the price of the insurance policy. However, risk sharing through community rating is thought to be more equitable because consumers are not penalized for poor health.

In the case of health care, equity and efficiency may also be complementary. It is widely believed that the social costs of health care for the uninsured are higher than for the insured, given that our society often does not refuse to provide health care to the sick, even if they cannot pay. It is argued that the uninsured do not receive health care until illnesses are more advanced and that this results in higher treatment costs than if they had access to preventive care or earlier treatment. Moreover, people without health insurance tend to overuse hospital emergency rooms, often as primary or routine venues for care, which are more expensive than physician office visits for nonemergency cases. This is due to the fact that emergency departments do not turn people away based on ability to pay.

A good deal of research has provided estimates of the incremental costs associated with insuring the uninsured. A study by Long and Marquis (1994) provides an estimate of $28.6 billion (adjusted to 2001 dollars). Adjusting for increases in the number of uninsured between 1993 to 2001 raised the estimate to $35 billion (Institute of Medicine, 2003). A study by Miller, Banthin, and Moeller (2004) provides 2002 estimates ranging from $44.9 billion to $57.4 billion, if the spending of the currently uninsured mirrors that of the privately insured. Assuming that the healthcare utilization and spending are comparable to those of the Medicaid population, the range is from $35.1 to $38.1 billion (Miller et al., 2004). Both sets of estimates deduct the value of in-kind uncompensated care that this group would receive if uninsured. In 2012, 47 million nonelderly Americans were uninsured (Kaiser Health News, 2013). Among the insured, the uninsured burden is felt deeply: An average family pays an extra $1,017 in premiums per year to pay for the healthcare costs of the uninsured (Kaiser Health News, 2009).

The health status of the community also has public good aspects because poor health is associated with lower labor force participation and increased poverty and homelessness. Poorer health status is also associated with increased risks of spreading communicable diseases to other community members. As seen from the economic evaluation methods, the reduction in these indirect social costs that would be accomplished by insuring the uninsured should be subtracted from the increase in direct healthcare costs.

The Rising Cost of Health Care

Increases in healthcare costs are an international problem. Cutler (2002) noted that social insurance systems were originally more concerned with equity and provided the most of what people wanted without a great deal of concern with efficiency. Today, this is no longer possible. The common problem facing all industrialized nations is how to pay for the level of health care that their citizens want. Given the dramatic improvements in medical technology, people everywhere have rising expectations about what can be done to improve their health. Public healthcare systems are finding it necessary to cut back on coverage by limiting emergency care and/or requiring higher copayments for services in order to curb utilization. With this trend, satisfaction with health systems is lower in most countries than it was a decade ago (Blendon et al., 2002; Papanicolas, Cylus, & Smith, 2013; Papanicolas, Kringos, Klazinga, & Smith, 2013).

Technology Change and the Cost of Health Care

Several economists have demonstrated that the largest contributor to rising healthcare costs is technological advances. Therefore, it is important to develop strategies to identify particular components of healthcare expenditures that have low marginal benefits (Cutler & Richardson, 1999).

Technological change shifts the production function for health in favor of more health care versus other inputs. This has been the story of U.S. health care during much of the second half of the 20th century. Therefore, there is no mystery about why the total amount of medical spending is rising. Medical care absorbed 17.9% of the U.S. gross domestic product (GDP) in 2013 (The World Bank, 2013).

The Role of Market Imperfections

The contribution of market imperfections to the cost of health care has been a constant concern in economics. Critic have often associated a combination of **fee-for-service** payment and the lack of price competition with monopoly rents to providers. Fee-for-service charges for each service received by the patient separately and provides an incentive for providers of care to offer more treatments because payment is dependent on the quantity rather than the quality of care. The healthcare market does not consist of small, perfectly competitive firms subject to long-run zero profit competitive equilibrium. Instead, the markets for goods and services provided by physicians, hospitals, and pharmaceuticals are at best **monopolistically competitive**. Monopolistically competitive markets have a few dominant firms and many small firms with little market power. However, price competition has increased greatly and was introduced largely because of the active role of third-party payers, both private and public. Managed care has also provided a mechanism for negotiating fees with hospitals, physicians, and pharmaceutical manufacturers.

Imperfect Information

Problems associated with imperfect information occur not only in the insurance markets but also in the provision of health care. Integrated delivery systems may contribute to this because managed care subscribers often have little knowledge of the costs of the different services that they consume. Further, providers have imperfect information concerning the effectiveness and side effects of treatment on a given individual. One way to improve efficiency is for health plans to provide information about the costs of particular services. This is likely to be more helpful in decisions about **nonacute care** (Baker, Birnbaum, Geppert, Mishol, & Moyneur, 2003), where the decision to receive care is more discretionary.

Another area of imperfect information that affects both costs and quality of care is the lack of systemization of patients' medical records. There is also a lack of formally articulated instructions from patients about their desires for end-of-life treatment. A nontrivial proportion of total U.S. healthcare expenditures is devoted to keeping very sick terminally ill people alive by artificial means that are frequently counter to their wishes, which can no longer be expressed. In 2011, of the $554 billion spent on Medicare services, 28% of it, or $170 billion, was spent on the last 6 months of life (Kaiser Health News, 2013). End-of-life care is more often used to prolong life during the grieving process of families than it is used as palliative care.

Inefficiency of Insurance Markets

Advocates of a single payer system often point to the costs of administering an insurance system that consists of insurance contracts with such a confusing array of technicalities about coverage. A system of multiple insurers is administratively more expensive than a single payer system. However, it provides more choice to consumers as well as more problems of adverse selection. It is unclear whether streamlining and standardizing insurance coverage, which would require additional regulatory costs and limit consumers' options, would bring about a net improvement in social welfare.

A lower deductible on an insurance policy is inefficient when its marginal cost is greater than the marginal benefit of additional coverage. The load or loading fee is a much higher proportion of the insurance premium in low deductible policies. This is one of the reasons why some economists have advocated for a combination of high deductible insurance policies (usually called *catastrophic coverage*) and personal **medical savings accounts** (Eichener, McClellan, & Wise, 1996; Jensen, 2000). This way, costs of care are internalized by the consumers of care rather than the third-party payer, such as the private government insurer.

Experience rating is a well-known form of achieving greater efficiency in insurance markets. **Price discrimination**, which is the process of selling the same product at different prices to different buyers based on some characteristic of the buyers in order to maximize profits, is based on differences in the costs of insuring different individuals. This promotes efficiency in that it relates marginal costs and price of insurance. It is a common practice in the homeowners, life insurance, and automobiles insurance markets. Experience rating also removes the incentive to cream skim, the practice whereby insurance companies select out healthier clients.

The argument for community rating is that risk sharing among community members is more equitable. It is thought to be unfair to charge people more for insurance because they experience unavoidable bouts of illness or deterioration of health. Because the purpose of insurance is to pool risks, experience rating, if carried to an extreme, undermines the goal of insurance because the insured pool becomes drastically smaller.

Finally, there is considerable evidence that medical malpractice law in many states does not promote higher-quality care but contributes marginally to the costs of medical practice and encourages the practice of defensive medicine (Bendix, 2013).

RECOMMENDATIONS FOR IMPROVING THE EFFICIENCY OF THE U.S. HEALTHCARE SYSTEM

Critics maintain that there are few financial incentives for hospitals and integrated healthcare delivery systems to reorganize so as to reduce medical errors by monitoring overuse or misuse of medical treatments (Becher & Chassin, 2001). Drawing from an analogy of the U.S. auto industry, critics have suggested that the absence of competition of the kind that Toyota provided for U.S. automakers has resulted in a lack of quality improvements in medicine (Coye, 2001). Physician groups within leading medical schools of public health have, however, been devoting considerable effort to designing ways of reorganizing clinical settings so as to provide more fail-safe checks on potential medical errors (Bates & Gawande, 2000). Their point of view is that human error is inevitable. Failure to report such errors is due to fears of individual **tort** liability. Tort is a wrongful act that leads to civil legal liability. If the system could provide checks so that errors could be detected before damage is done to patients, and if the institutions, not the individuals, were the focus of responsibility of medical errors, the organizations can be greatly improved to reduce medical errors (Weiner, Shortell, & Alexander, 1997).

Information technology can be used in a variety of healthcare systems to improve performance and efficiency. This includes compiling patients' medical records, monitoring safety procedures in clinical settings, and disseminating information to doctors about new technologies and biopharmaceutical products (Girosi, Meili, & Scoville, 2005).

It is technically possible to provide to patients their medical histories in electronic record format, with password protection of the kind that is used for computerized financial information. Concerns about privacy and the reluctance of the medical profession to provide this kind of record-keeping have prevented this system from being employed (Clinton, 2004) until the policy incentives put into place in a broad scale by the Affordable Care Act (Point-of-Care Partners, 2012).

In the past decade, there have been strong advocates of reporting systems that provide consumers with statistics on treatment outcomes. Some medical delivery systems, health associations, and government agencies have been established to perform this kind of monitoring. The Centers for Medicare and Medicaid Services was instrumental in developing more programs in this area. Such programs may appear to have no downside, but critics of this innovation argue that it can lead to providers attempting to avoid treating the most difficult cases, or even to the falsification of records. Any system of reporting health outcomes of treatments must be carefully designed to adjust for severity of illness of the patient pool treated. A review of the literature determined that many computerized clinical decision support systems do indeed improve system performance, but the effect on patient outcomes remains inconclusive (Garg et al., 2005).

A program that has served as a model is the Cardiac Surgery Reporting System in New York State. It has collected and published hospital and surgeon data on adjusted death rates following coronary artery bypass graft (CABG) surgery since 1989. It is operated by the New York State Health Department and is guided by an advisory committee. It has been effective in causing cardiac units to restrict operating privileges of surgeons whose patients have high mortality rates. Since this reporting system was instituted, New York has had the lowest risk-adjusted mortality rates following CABG surgery and the most rapid rate of decline in mortality rates following cardiac surgery (Becher & Chassin, 2001).

Many states have already engaged in legal reforms affecting medical malpractice law. Reforms that appear to have reduced the extent of the practice of defensive medicine include limiting the proportion of damage awards that attorneys can claim as fees, paying damages over the lifetime of the injured rather than in one lump sum, and establishing statewide pools to pay for serious medical errors, even when they are not a result of negligence or incompetence. Even with these reforms, the type and strength of tort law changes have a small but significant effect on malpractice claims (Waters, Budetti, Claxton, & Lundy, 2007).

One reason why the cost of health care in the United States is higher than in other countries is that, on average, Americans are less healthy. The proportion of low birth weight babies is much higher than in many comparable countries. The rate of obesity is higher. For the elderly, most of the healthcare expenditures are on cardiac disorders or cancers. This view of improved health maintenance and conditioning has been underscored in the legislation of the Affordable Care Act of 2010, with its emphasis on disease prevention (Koh & Sebelius, 2010).

Healthier lifestyles might also be encouraged by giving insurance discounts for healthy behavior. However, this form of price discrimination is difficult to implement in a system that is dominated by group insurance, where community rating is applied over the entire group.

Further, if it became routine practice for adults to establish healthcare powers of attorney combined with written instructions for end-of-life treatment, this could reduce the per capita cost of health care as well as provide utility to patients and their families. However, given the technological challenges in health science, it becomes increasingly difficult to specify what constitutes irreversible medical states.

The role of public health is vitally important in controlling healthcare costs. The United States has failed to maintain vaccination programs for children at a level it once achieved. The private market failed to provide enough flu vaccine in 2004, and the public sector has not been able to obtain an adequate supply in many of the years since. Further, the emergence of multiple disease-resistant strains of communicable diseases such as tuberculosis require a major public health effort. Prevention programs must be in place, and infected people need to be located, treated, and monitored. Research being conducted at the Centers for Disease Control and Prevention must be maintained or expanded. The possibility of international crises such as the SARS scare in 2002 and 2003 and threats of bioterrorism provide additional reasons for enhancing public health in the United States (Koh & Sebelius, 2010).

Further, greater use of public health nurses and paramedical workers could raise the level of health in underserved communities and provide savings by reducing the use of hospital emergency rooms. This is one lesson to be learned from developing nations, where health workers are widely used to promote community health.

SUMMARY

The proportion of the GDP devoted to health care in the United States and other high-income countries is likely to continue to rise with improving medical technology, the shifting of the age distribution of the population, increases in longevity, and the fact that health care tends to be a superior good. However, if cost effectiveness is taken into consideration, the trends in healthcare costs are much less alarming.

Although there are many types of market failures in the production and consumption of health care, the rising costs of health care do not at present appear to be primarily the result of market failure. Market failures in the production and delivery of health care have been somewhat offset by the countervailing power of third-party payers.

Technology, rather than market failure, appears to be the main cause of the increase in healthcare costs. Countries that have succeeded in controlling healthcare costs to a greater extent than the United States have done so largely through direct price controls and/or limiting the diffusion of technology. However, there are several inefficiencies in the system that should be overcome with the help of the high level of information technology available. Programs to improve the overall health status of the population could also reduce the proportion of GDP devoted to health care.

KEY WORDS

- **Children's Health Insurance Program**
- **Equity**
- **Fee-for-service**
- **Medicaid**
- **Medical savings accounts**
- **Medicare**
- **Monopolistically competitive**
- **Nonacute care**
- **Price discrimination**
- **Sovereignty**
- **Tort**

Questions

1. Approximately how much would it cost to insure the currently uninsured? Explain which costs are included and excluded in the estimates.

2. It has been said that employer-based insurance is obsolete. Give an argument on each side of the question.

3. Describe the advantages and drawbacks of health information technology in improving quality and efficiency in health care.

PROFILE: VERNON L. SMITH

Vernon L. Smith was born in 1927 of modest means and just prior to the Great Depression. He spent his first years in college at CalTech, where he majored in physics, switched to electrical engineering, and stumbled on economics in his senior year. He graduated with an engineering degree and went on to earn an MA in economics from the University of Kansas. He pursued a PhD in economics at Harvard University and completed those studies in 1955.

Smith's work encompassed experimental economics with early research on price and investment theory. He was guided by numerous Nobel Laureates at Harvard and beyond and has authored or coauthored more than 250 articles and books on capital theory, finance, natural resource economics, and experimental economics. He received many accolades for his work, including the Sveriges Riksbank Prize in Economic Sciences in Memory of Alfred Nobel in 2002.

Smith holds joint appointments with the Argyros School of Business and Economics and the School of Law at Chapman University, and he is creating a new Economic Science Institute at Chapman.

Data from http://www.chapman.edu/research-and-institutions/economic-science-institute/about-us/vernon-smith-personal/vernon_about.aspx. Accessed March 13, 2015.

REFERENCES

Baker, L., Birnbaum, H., Geppert, J., Mishol, D., & Moyneur, E. (2003). The relationship between technology availability and health care spending. *Health Affairs*. doi:10.1377/hlthaff.w3.537

Bates, D. W., & Gawande, A. A. (2000). Error in medicine: What have we learned? *Annals of Internal Medicine, 132*(9), 763–767.

Becher, E. C., & Chassin, M. R. (2001). Improving the quality of health care: Who will lead? *Health Affairs, 20*(5), 164–179.

Bendix, J. (2013, August 12). Report: Healthcare costs not driven by malpractice awards. *Medical Economics*. Retrieved from http://medicaleconomics.modernmedicine.com/medical-economics/content/tags/defensive-medicine/report-healthcare-costs-not-driven-malpractice-awa?page=full

Blendon, R. J., Schoen, C., DesRoches, C. M., Osborn, R., Scoles, K. L., & Zapert, K. (2002). Inequalities in health care: A five-country survey. *Health Affairs, 21*(3), 182–191.

Clinton, H. R. (2004, April 18). Now can we talk about medical care? *The New York Times*. Retrieved from www.nytimes.com/2004/04/18/magazine/now-can-we-talk-about-health-care.html

Coye, M. J. (2001). No Toyotas in health care: Why medical care has not evolved to meet patients' needs. *Health Affairs, 20*(6), 44–56.

Cutler, D. M. (2002). Equity, efficiency, and market fundamentals: The dynamics of international medical care reform. *Journal of Economic Literature, 40*(3), 881–906.

Cutler, D. M., & Richardson, E. (1999). *Your money and your life: The value of health and what affects it* (NBER Working Paper No. 6895). Cambridge, MA: National Bureau of Economic Research.

Eichener, M. J., McClellan, M. B., & Wise, D. A. (1996). *Insurance or self-insurance? Variation, persistence, and individual health accounts* (NBER Working Paper No. 5640). Cambridge, MA: National Bureau of Economic Research.

Garg, A. X., Adhikari, N. K., McDonald, H., Rosas-Arellano, M. P., Beyene, J., Sam, J., . . . Haynes, R. B. (2005). Effects of computerized clinical decision support systems on practitioner performance and patient outcomes: A systematic review. *Journal of the American Medical Association, 293*(10), 1223–1238.

Girosi, F., Meili, R. C., & Scoville, R. (2005). *Extrapolating evidence of health information technology savings and costs*. Santa Monica, CA: RAND Corporation.

Institute of Medicine. (2003). *Hidden costs, value lost: Uninsurance in America*. Washington, DC: National Academies Press.

Jensen, G. A. (2000). Making room for medical savings accounts in the U.S. health care system. In R. D. Feldman (Ed.), *American health care: Government, market processes, and the public interest* (pp. 119–144). New Brunswick, NJ: Transaction Press.

Kaiser Family Foundation. (2014). *Key facts about the uninsured population*. Retrieved from http://kff.org/uninsured/fact-sheet/key-facts-about-the-uninsured-population/

Kaiser Health News. (2009). *Study: Insured paying higher "hidden tax" for uninsured health care*. Retrieved from http://kaiserhealthnews.org/morning-breakout/hidden-tax/

Kaiser Health News. (2013). *End-of-life care: A challenge in terms of costs and quality*. Retrieved from http://khn.org/morning-breakout/end-of-life-care-17/

Koh, H. K., & Sebelius, K. G. (2010). Promoting prevention through the Affordable Care Act. *New England Journal of Medicine, 363*, 1296–1299.

Long, S. H., & Marquis, M. S. (1994). The uninsured "access gap" and the cost of universal coverage. *Health Affairs, 13*(2), 211–220.

Miller, E., Banthin, J. S., & Moeller, J. F. (2004). *Covering the uninsured: Estimates of the impact on total health expenditures for 2002* (AHRQ Working Paper No. 04007). Rockville, MD: Agency for Healthcare Research and Quality.

Okun, A. M. (1975). *Equality and efficiency: The big tradeoff*. Washington, DC: Brookings Institution Press.

Papanicolas, I., Cylus, J., & Smith, P. C. (2013). An analysis of survey data from eleven countries finds that "satisfaction" with health system performance means many things. *Health Affairs, 32*(4), 734–742.

Papanicolas, I., Kringos, D., Klazinga, N. S., & Smith, P. C. (2013). Health system performance comparison: New directions in research and policy. *Health Policy, 112*(1–2), 1–162.

Point-of-Care Partners. (2012). *Health plans and health information technology: Six areas of opportunity under the Affordable Care Act.* Coral Springs, FL: Author.

Rice, T. (1998). Can markets give us the health system we want? In M. A. Peterson (Ed.), *Healthy markets? The new competition in medical care* (pp. 27–65). Durham, NC: Duke University Press.

Rice, T., & Unruh, L. (2009). *The economics of health reconsidered* (3rd ed.). Chicago, IL: Health Administration Press.

Waters, T. M., Budetti, P. P., Claxton, G., & Lundy, J. P. (2007). Impact of state tort reforms on physician malpractice payments. *Health Affairs, 26*(2), 500–509.

Weiner, B. J., Shortell, S. M., & Alexander, J. (1997). Promoting clinical involvement in hospital quality improvement efforts: The effects of top management, board, and physician leadership. *Health Services Research, 32*(4), 491–510.

The World Bank. (2013). *Health expenditure, total (% of GDP).* Retrieved from http://data.world bank.org/indicator/SH.XPD.TOTL.ZS/

Glossary

Absolute Advantage—The ability of a given amount of resources to produce more of some goods or services in one industry or organization than in another one.

Abuse (Health Care)—Excessive, unnecessary, or improper treatment, including failure to provide medically necessary care.

Access—The potential and actual entry of a population into the healthcare delivery system (U.S. Congress, 1988).

Accountability—A duty to provide the evidence necessary to establish confidence that the activity for which one is responsible is performed and described in a way that reflects transparently the activity that has been performed to all concerned.

Accountable Care Organization (ACO)—A group of doctors, hospitals, and other healthcare providers who come together voluntarily to give coordinated high-quality care to their Medicare patients (Centers for Medicare and Medicaid Services, 2015).

Accountable Care Plan—A form of health plan proposed in the 1990s as part of the managed competition approach to health care, accountable for meeting federal requirements for providing a defined set of standardized services.

Accreditation—A process performed by a nongovernment agency to evaluate an institution or education program to determine if a set of standards has been met.

Activities of Daily Living (ADL)—Activities that are typically done for oneself, such as eating, dressing, teeth brushing, and so on.

Acuity—The level or severity of an illness.

Acute Care—Inpatient diagnostic and short-term treatment of patients.

Adjusted Community Rate—A term used in Medicare risk contracts to indicate the premium to be charged for providing exactly the same Medicare-covered benefits to a community-rated group, adjusted to allow for greater intensity and frequency of utilization by Medicare recipients.

Administered Price—A price set by the seller or payer instead of by impersonal market forces.

Admission—Formal acceptance of a patient by a hospital or other healthcare institution in order to provide care to that patient.

Adverse Drug Event—Harm (illness or injury) resulting from the use or administration of a drug or medication.

Adverse Selection—The systematic selection by high-risk consumers of insurance plans with greater degrees of coverage. The insurers who offer these plans end up with insureds who incur greater than normal costs.

Advocacy—An attempt to persuade regarding the rightness of a cause or point of view regarding an issue.

Affiliation—The number of arrangements among providers outlining relationships and individual responsibilities.

Agency (Agent)—A group or individual who has been the delegated authority to make decisions and perform activities on behalf of those doing the delegating. Physicians are often said to act as agents for their patients, indicating that physicians make decisions about treatments based on their knowledge.

Aggregate Demand—Total desired purchases by all buyers of goods or services produced.

Aggregate Supply—Total desired sales by all producers of goods or services.

Algorithm—A set of rules for carrying out a process or the calculation of a statistic.

Allocative Efficiency—No reorganization of production or consumption could make one person better off without making someone else worse off.

All-Payer System—A system of reimbursing providers in which all separate insurers coordinate to set uniform payment policies. Individual providers will then receive the same reimbursement from different insurers for cases with similar characteristics.

Alternate Level of Care (ALC)—A level of care other than the appropriate one, such as that given to a nonacute treatment patient occupying an acute care bed.

Ambulatory Care—Care rendered to individuals under their own cognizance any time when they are not resident in an institution.

Ambulatory Care Groups (ACGs)—A case-mix classification system incorporating related ambulatory care visits, based on ICD-9-CM diagnostic codes and patient age and gender (Starfield, Weiner, Mumford, & Steinwachs, 1991).

Ambulatory Visit Groups (AVGs)—A classification system by which ambulatory care visits with associated procedures are classified into similar resource-using groups based on diagnosis, procedure, age, and gender.

Ancillary Services—Hospital services other than room and board (nursing services are included as part of room and board).

Antikickback Statute—Federal legislation making it a felony for an individual to receive or offer a bribe, or kickback, in exchange for a referral from another person in any federally financed healthcare program.

Antitrust—Laws seeking to prevent monopolies or unfair competition in a market, or other activities that unreasonably restrain trade.

Any Willing Provider—State laws requiring a managed care organization to grant participation to any provider who is legally qualified as a practitioner and who is willing to become a member of the organization.

Apache III—A system designed to predict risk of dying in a hospital, generally used to measure the severity of illness of intensive care unit patients.

Appropriateness of Care—The degree to which tests, medications, procedures, education, and other healthcare services are clearly indicated, adequate, not excessive, and provided in the setting most appropriate to meet the needs of the patient.

Area Wage Adjustment—Part of the prospective payment formula allowing for differences in wage scales in different parts of the country.

Assignment of Benefits—A voluntary action by an insured beneficiary to have insurance benefits paid directly to the provider of services.

Asymmetric Information—An imbalance of information between buyers and sellers of a service, by which one group is better informed than the other.

Atypical Patients—Patients who exhibit patterns of care different from typical cases, either because they do not complete a full and successful course of treatment in a single institution or because their length of stay exceeds the statistical trim point.

Autonomy—The right of an individual to make decisions for his or her health or life.

Availability—The supply of services, generally in relation to the demand for services.

Average Adjusted Per Capita Cost (AAPCC)—An estimate of the average cost incurred by Medicare per beneficiary in the fee-for-service system, adjusted by county for geographic cost differences related to age, gender, disability status, Medicaid eligibility, and institutional status.

Average Cost (AC)—The unit cost for a selected volume of output; total cost divided by total quantity of output. The average cost is equal to the average variable cost plus the average fixed cost.

Average Fixed Cost (AFC)—The unit fixed cost for a specific volume of output. The average fixed cost is equal to the total fixed cost divided by the volume of output.

Average Length of Stay—See LENGTH OF STAY.

Average Product (AP)—Total product divided by number of units used in its production.

Average Revenue (AR)—Total revenue divided by number of units (quantity) sold.

Average Variable Cost (AVC)—The unit variable cost for a specific volume of output; total variable cost divided by quantity of output.

Baby Boomers—Individuals born in the United States from 1946 to 1964.

Balance Billing—A practice of physicians to charge patients the difference between their charges and the amount paid by the insurance company for the service.

Balanced Budget Act of 1997 (BBA)—A federal law enacting many changes in health care, including the creation of the Children's Health Insurance Program, as well as changes designed to extend the Medicare Trust Fund's financial life and create the Medicare+Choice program.

Basis of Payment—The unit of output in terms for which the provider is paid. This can be used for per day of care, per service provided, per case, or per person (capitation).

Bed Capacity—The number of patients a hospital can house.

Bed Days—The number of days in a period that beds are available. In a year, bed days are the number of regularly maintained available beds multiplied by 365.

Behavioral Health—An umbrella term including mental health and substance abuse; used to distinguish between services provided for physical health.

Benchmark—A reference point for each element being monitored; used to compare performance or outcomes of an institution or a provider against the defined measure or best practice.

Benefit—Money, care, or other services that an individual is entitled to receive because of insurance coverage, or the compensation of labor that is additional to wages (health insurance, life insurance, pension rights, etc.).

Benefit Cost—The relationship between the dollar effect of an intervention and its opportunity cost. It can be expressed as a ratio (benefits divided by costs) or as a net value (benefits minus costs).

Biased Selection—The deliberate choice, by a provider or insurer, of a group of patients (insureds) with preselected characteristics associated with low utilization of health care.

Break-Even Point—The volume of activity where revenues and expenses are equal.

Budget Neutrality—A requirement that payment under a new system cannot be larger or smaller than under the previous system.

Bundling—Grouping goods and services together into a package for delivery or payment.

Burden—With reference to a tax, the reduction in real income resulting from the tax (Due, 1957).

Cafeteria Plan—A plan that allows employees to choose from a menu of different healthcare coverage and provider options.

Capacity—A measure of the output that can be reached when existing resources are fully and efficiently used; output corresponds to the firm's minimum short-run average total cost.

Capital—Human, physical, and financial means of production, usually long-term assets that are primarily fixed and not bought and sold in the course of operations.

Capitalist Economy—When capital is predominately owned privately rather than by the state.

Capitation—A payment system in which the entity financially responsible for the patients' healthcare services receives a fixed periodic sum for each patient (per capita) that covers the costs of utilization by the patient. The sum can be adjusted for specific patient characteristics, such as age and gender.

Cartel—An organization of producers who agree to act as a single seller in order to maximize joint profits.

Case Management—A collection of organized activities to identify high-cost patients as early as possible, locate and assess alternative treatment methods, and manage healthcare benefits for these patients in a cost-effective manner (Scheffler, Sullivan, & Ko, 1991). Sometimes used interchangeably with *care management* and *disease management*.

Case Mix—Grouping of patients according to characteristics (age, gender, diagnoses, treatments, severity of illness, etc.) and then determining the proportion of the total falling into each group.

Case-Mix Groups (CMGs)—A Canadian system for classifying hospital inpatients into groups using similar quantities of resources according to selected patient characteristics such as diagnosis, procedure, age, and comorbidity. CMGs are maintained by the Canadian Institute for Health Information.

Case-Mix Index—An index or measure of the average level of resource requirements for a group of cases sorted and weighted according to type of case. The weights represent the estimated resource use for each type of case.

Census—The number of patients in a hospital at a given point in time.

Change Agent—An individual whose efforts facilitate change in an organization.

Change in Demand—An increase or decrease in the quantity demanded at each possible price of the good or service, represented by a shift in the entire demand curve.

Change in Quantity Demanded—An increase or decrease in the specific quantity bought at a specified price, represented by a movement along a given demand curve.

Change in Quantity Supplied—An increase or decrease in the specific quantity sold at a specified price, represented by a movement along a given supply curve.

Change in Supply—An increase or decrease in the quantity supplied at each possible price of the goods or services, represented by a shift in the entire supply curve.

Charges—A price set for a product by the supplier. Charges may not equal cash received because some payers may receive a discount or fail to pay.

Charity Care—Healthcare services provided free of charge to those who do not have the ability to pay for care.

Cherry Picking—A practice by insurers of selling policies only to low-risk individuals; also called *cream skimming*.

Chronic—An illness that lasts a long time and usually without prospect of immediate change for either improvement or deterioration.

Churning—A practice of discharging a patient from the hospital and readmitting the patient for what is really a single episode of care in order to increase payment.

Cognitive Services—The activities of a health professional other than the performance of a procedure.

Coinsurance—A system of provider payment in which the patient is responsible for a portion or percentage of the payment, and the insurer or third party is responsible for the rest.

Collusion—Overt or covert, explicit or tacit, agreement among suppliers to act jointly in their common interests.

Community Care—Care provided in a noninstitutional setting, including in the home or in the patient's "neighborhood."

Community Rating—A method of setting insurance premiums for healthcare coverage. In this method, all insureds in the group pay the same premium, regardless of their risk-related characteristics, such as age or health problems.

Comorbidity—A disease or condition that is present at the same time as the principal disease or condition of the patient.

Comparative Advantage—The ability of one supplier to produce goods or services at a lower cost than other suppliers.

Competition—A state of competition exists in a market if no single firm or consumer is large enough to influence the market price. This state usually occurs if there are many buyers and sellers in the market.

Competitive Price—The price at which demand and supply are in equilibrium in a competitive market.

Complements—Two goods or services that are consumed together, such as surgeons' services and operating room services. The economic relevance of complementarity is that a change in the direct price of a complement will cause a shift in the demand curve of the other service.

Complex Adaptive System—A collection of individual components possessing the freedom to act in ways that are not always predictable and whose actions are interconnected.

Complications—Adverse patient conditions that arise during the process of medical care.

Concentration (Market)—The extent to which market activity is confined to a limited number of firms.

Concierge Physician Practice—An arrangement between a healthcare provider and a patient in which the patient pays a retainer fee to the provider and, in return, is provided a special class of care and services; also called *boutique medicine*.

Concurrent Review— A process of ongoing review while the patient is undergoing treatment in the hospital and of certifying the length of stay that is appropriate for the approved admission (Scheffler et al., 1991).

Conspiracy of Silence—An alleged tacit agreement among health professionals not to testify against one another in malpractice lawsuits.

Consumer-Driven Health Plan—An option designed to influence consumer behavior, typically offering a cost-sharing health plan in conjunction with discretionary healthcare dollars (a high-deductible health plan combined with a health savings account).

Consumerism—A view that health care should be directly driven by consumer interest.

Consumer's Surplus—The difference between what an individual is willing to pay for a given quantity of goods or services and what is actually paid. This is equal to the area under the demand curve between no consumption and that specified quantity minus the amount paid for all of the units (price times quantity).

Consumption—The use of goods or services to satisfy current wants.

Contingent Valuation—The valuation that a person would place on a service if he or she had the option of having it available.

Continuum of Care—The entire spectrum of specialized health, rehabilitative, and residential services available to the frail and chronically ill. The services focus on the social, residential, rehabilitative, and supportive needs of individuals, as well as needs that are essentially medical in nature (Burwell, & Crown, 1994).

Conversion Factor—The dollar amount for one base unit in the relative value scale or the diagnosis-related group.

Copayments—Out-of-pocket payments for health services made by users at the time a service is rendered.

Core Services—In Canada, health services that must be available to every resident of a province (Government of Saskatchewan, 1993). See also INSURED SERVICES. In U.S. hospitals, the set of services that must be provided by if they are to be eligible for registration with the American Hospital Association.

Cost—The expense incurred in producing goods and services. See also OPPORTUNITY COST and MONEY COST.

Cost Curve—The relationship between cost and volume of output. It can be specified in terms of total costs, average or unit costs, and marginal costs. See also LONG-RUN COST CURVE and SHORT-RUN COST CURVE.

Cost Effectiveness—The relationship between the additional cost and the additional health outcome (expressed in physical terms) of one intervention compared with another.

Cost Function—A behavioral relationship between cost (viewed from a marginal, average, or total perspective) and the variables that influence cost, including volume of output, quality of output, input prices, and variables affecting organizational efficiency. See also COST CURVE, LONG-RUN COST CURVE, and SHORT-RUN COST CURVE.

Cost Sharing—The joint payment or sharing of a price by the consumer and the payer (insurer).

Cost Shifting—The charging of different prices for differentially insured patients, usually including the subsidization of care for another group of patients for which the costs are not covered and for nonpaying patients.

Cost Utility—The relationship between the additional cost and the additional health outcome (expressed in terms of a utility index) of one intervention compared with another.

Critical Access Hospital (CAH) Program—Medicare's Rural Hospital Flexibility Program designed to assist rural communities to preserve access to primary care and emergency services by paying rural hospitals on a cost-plus basis and having different operating requirements for these hospitals, providing the hospitals meet certain conditions.

Critical Care—See INTENSIVE CARE.

Current Procedural Terminology (CPT)—A classification of procedures and services, primarily for physicians, widely used for coding in billing and payment for physician services.

Customary, Prevailing, Reasonable Charge (CPR)—The charge that is the lowest of the following: the actual charge made for the service, the provider's customary (usual) charge for the service, or the fee prevailing in the community for the service.

Day Procedure Groups (DPGs)—A classification system for ambulatory patients in which patients are assigned to classes according to principle procedures that use similar resources. The DPG system was developed from New York State's PAS (Products of Ambulatory Surgery) system and is used by the Canadian Institute for Health Information.

Deductible—A fixed amount that a consumer must spend out of pocket before insurance coverage begins. For example, if the deductible is $200, the individual must pay for the first $200 of medical expenditures out of pocket before the insurance company begins to pay its share of the remaining costs.

Defensive Medicine—A provision of services, mainly diagnostic services, in anticipation of defending against a possible lawsuit alleging malpractice.

Defined Benefit—A type of health insurance in which specific benefits are promised to the purchaser (employee).

Defined Contribution—A type of health insurance in which the purchaser (employee) of the insurance is provided a specific amount for the insurance premium.

Demand—Consumer willingness to purchase alternative quantities of services at various specified prices, represented by the position of the demand curve.

Demand Curve (Schedule)—A schedule indicating the quantities of a service that an individual or group is willing to purchase at different prices for that service, all other factors (income, tastes, other prices) held constant.

Derived Demand—A good or service that is desired or wanted, not for its own sake, but for its contribution to another good or service. For example, the demand for a physician visit is derived from a demand for better health, not for the direct utility of a physician visit.

Diagnosis—A determination of the specific physical ailment of an individual.

Diagnosis-Related Groups (DRGs)—A system of classifying hospital inpatients into groups using similar quantities of resources according to selected characteristics, such as diagnoses, procedure, age, and any complications or comorbidities. DRGs were used for hospital reimbursement in the U.S. Medicare system (Fetter, 1992). See INTERNATIONAL CLASSIFICATION OF DISEASES, INJURIES, AND CAUSES OF DEATH, TENTH REVISION, CLINICAL MODIFICATION (ICD-10-CM) for the current classification system.

Diminishing Marginal Rate of Substitution—The marginal rate of substitution changes systematically as the amount of two goods or services being consumed varies.

Direct Cost—In social cost accounting, the cost of all resources incurred by healthcare providers; usually refers to paid resources. In hospital cost accounting, the cost of resources (doctors, nurses, lab techs) that are directly involved in the provision of care; overhead costs are excluded.

Direct Price—See OUT-OF-POCKET PRICE.

Direct Teaching Costs—For hospital care, the costs in a teaching hospital that can be directly traced to educational rather than patient care functions. These include resident and intern salaries.

Discharge—The formal release of a patient from a hospital or physician's care.

Discharge Planning—The process of assessing needs and making sure that arrangements are made outside the hospital to receive the patient upon discharge and ensuring that appropriate continuity of care is provided.

Discount (Time Discount)—A constant applied to future costs and benefits in order to value them as equivalent to costs and benefits occurring in the present period.

Disease Prevention—See PREVENTION.

Disequilibrium—A state in which a market is not in equilibrium (demand and supply are not equal). As a result of a shift in demand or supply, a market will be in disequilibrium until the price and quantity adjust to the new equilibrium levels. A state of disequilibrium can be permanent if there is some barrier (e.g., government price control) that permanently maintains the price at a level above or below that of equilibrium.

Disruptive Innovation—New technology or processes that upset current conditions but in such a way that progress, in terms of better results or lower costs, is the final result.

Distributive Justice—The principles of ethics used to allocate resources that are limited in supply; many different approaches are available, such as egalitarianism, desert-based principle, libertarianism, difference principle, resource-based principle, and welfare-based principle.

Doctor–Patient Relationship—The legal term for the relationship between a patient and a healthcare provider that gives rise to legal obligations.

Doughnut Hole—A gap in Medicare Part D prescription drug coverage.

DRG—See DIAGNOSIS-RELATED GROUPS.

DRG Cost Weight—The weight assigned to each DRG to reflect the DRG's use of resources relative to the cost of the average Medicare patient. The average Medicare patient's cost, when multiplied by the DRG cost weight, gives the price for the DRG.

DRG Creep—A change in the distribution of patients among DRGs without a real change in the distribution of patients treated in the hospital.

Dual Eligible—An individual who qualifies for both Medicare and Medicaid coverage.

Economic Cost—See OPPORTUNITY COST.

Economic Efficiency—The least costly method of producing an output.

Economic Rent—A surplus of total earnings over the amount required to prevent a factor from transferring to another use.

Economic System—The way in which goods and services are produced, distributed, and consumed.

Economies of Scale—Reductions in the operating costs associated with larger-scale operations.

Economies of Scope—Reductions in the operating costs of two or more related services (e.g., home care and hospital care) associated with joint production (e.g., production of both services by the same organization).

Effectiveness—The relationship between an intervention and its health outcome, usually measured in physical units (e.g., life years saved). Some definitions specify that effectiveness is a measure of the ability of an intervention to bring about an outcome under actual practice conditions.

Efficacy—The relationship between an intervention and its health outcome under ideal (usually experimental) clinical conditions.

Efficiency—The relationship between the amount of output and the amount of effort. Technical efficiency is a measure of how close a given combination of resources is to producing a maximum amount of output. Allocative or economic efficiency is a measure of how close a given combination of resources is to yielding maximum consumer satisfaction.

Elasticity of Demand—The quantity of a service demanded in response to the out-of-pocket price of a service or product. Elasticity is calculated by dividing the percentage change in the product demanded by the percentage change in the direct price. The price and quantity in terms of which change is measured can be the original price and quantity (point elasticity) or an average of the original and the new prices and quantities (arc elasticity).

Elasticity of Supply—A measure of the responsiveness of quantity of goods or services supplied to a change in the market price calculated by dividing percentage change in quantity supplied by the percentage change in market price.

Emergency Care—Involves immediate decision making and action to prevent death or any further disability for patients in a health crisis.

Encounter—A single visit to a provider (sometimes used as an output measure).

Endogenous Variable—A variable that is explained within a theory (e.g., price is the endogenous variable in the theory of demand and the theory of supply).

Enrollee—A person covered (receives benefits) under a contract for care.

Entry Barrier—A natural or created impediment to entry into an industry.

Episode of Care—A series of temporally contiguous healthcare services related to treatment of a given spell of illness or provided in response to a specific request by the patient or other relevant entity (Hornbrook, Hurtado, & Johnson, 1985).

Episode of Illness—A single unbroken interval of time during which the patient suffers from a continuous spell of signs and/or symptoms that are perceived as sickness or ill health (Hornbrook et al., 1985).

Equilibrium—A situation in which all forces are in balance so that there is no tendency to change. Consumer equilibrium occurs when the individual consuming unit has acquired a composition of goods that gives the unit its maximum attainable satisfaction (utility) given the constraints (prices, incomes) it faces. Producer or provider equilibrium occurs when the firm is producing the level of output that achieves its objectives (e.g., maximum profits, maximum output). Market or competitive equilibrium occurs when all buyers and sellers simultaneously achieve their maximized positions; demand and supply are therefore in balance at these determined levels of price and quantity.

Equity—Fairness (e.g., in the provision of health care). See also HORIZONTAL EQUITY and VERTICAL EQUITY.

Evidence-Based Medicine—Using current best information in making decisions regarding care of individual patients.

Exogenous Variable—A variable that influences endogenous variables in a theory but is itself determined by factors outside the theory.

Experience Rating—A method of setting health premiums for healthcare coverage. In this method, each insured in the group pays a premium that is based on his or her risk-related characteristics.

Explicit—Specifically stated conditions.

Externalities—Effects, good or bad, that occur to parties not directly involved in the production or consumption of goods or services.

Extra Billing—Billing for an insured health service rendered to an insured person by a medical practitioner in an amount in addition to any amount paid for that service by the provincial or territorial health insurance plan (Canada Health Act, 1985).

Factors of Production—See RESOURCES.

Fee—A charge for a service provided.

Fee-For-Service Payment—Payment for each item or service provided.

Fee Schedule—A list of prices for specific procedures and services. The schedule may be negotiated between provider and payer or set externally.

Final Goods—Goods that are not used as inputs by other firms.

Firm—A self-contained organization that engages in the production or provision of a service or product. The production can occur in more than one facility. See also PLANT.

Fixed Costs—Costs that remain the same despite changes in the volume of output.

Fixed Inputs—Inputs that, within a selected range, do not vary with output. Examples include office space and equipment.

Flat-of-the-Curve Medicine—Medical care that has no effect on health status. The allusion is to the curve relating medical care inputs to health status output. Eventually, if medical care is provided in large enough quantities, its additional effectiveness is hypothesized to be zero (i.e., the output will be constant and the curve will be flat).

Flexible Spending Account (FSA)—An account managed by the employer, allowing employees to set aside pretax funds for medical, dental, legal, and daycare services.

Formulary—A list of pharmaceutical products covered by a health plan.

Fraud—Obtaining goods or services or payment by intentional false statements.

Freedom of Choice—A policy permitting individuals to select their own physician or hospital.

Full Cost—The cost that a provider incurs in producing services. The total cost covers all inputs, direct and indirect, used in the production of the services.

Funding—A payment made to a provider to cover expenses for services rendered. The funding is not necessarily related to the costs incurred for specific patients or services.

Gag Rule—A practice employed by health plans to forbid physicians to tell patients about alternative, more expensive forms of treatment that are not covered or authorized by the plan.

Gaming—Manipulating the system in an illegal or unethical way.

Gaps—Services not covered by insurance.

Gatekeeper—A person responsible for determining services to be provided to an individual and coordinating the provision of appropriate care.

Global Budget—A fixed annual operating grant paid to a provider that is to cover all services (regardless of location) provided to all patients who are treated; it encompasses all sources of payment.

Global Fee—A single fee charged for certain medical services, such as pregnancy and delivery, instead of a fee charged for each service or procedure.

Gross Domestic Product (GDP)—The money amount of all final goods and services (consumer, investment, government) produced within defined geographical boundaries during a defined period of time. A standard measure of relative health expenditures for a given state, province, or country is total health spending divided by GDP.

Gross National Product (GNP)—The money amount of all final goods and services produced by residents of a country during a defined period of time, regardless of where the actual production took place.

Group Model HMO—A health maintenance organization in which the HMO contracts with an independent group practice to provide care for its members. The contractual arrangements are usually on a per capita basis.

Group Practice—A medical practice in which several practitioners share some inputs, such as office staff and space.

Health—A complete state of physical, mental, and social well-being and not merely the absence of disease or illness (Grad, 2002). A state characterized by anatomic integrity; ability to perform personally valued family, work, and community roles; ability to deal with physical, biologic, and social stress; a feeling of well-being; and freedom from the risk of untimely disease (Stokes, Noren, & Shindell, 1982).

Health Care—A range of services and products whose end purpose is the preservation or enhancement of health.

Health Economics—A branch of economics dealing with the provision, delivery, and use of healthcare goods and services.

Health Insurance—Payment for the expected costs of a group resulting from medical utilization based on the expected expenses incurred by the group. Payment can be based on community or experience ratings.

Health Insurance Portability and Accountability Act of 1996 (HIPAA)—Federal legislation whose primary function is to provide continuity of healthcare coverage; it also imposed protection of patient privacy.

Health Insurance Purchasing Cooperative (HIPC)—An insurance organization that acts as a broker between payers of health insurance (households, businesses, governments) and healthcare providers. The HIPC sets standards for healthcare services and seeks competitive bids for these services; consumers can then select from among the competing providers.

Health Maintenance Organization (HMO)—An organization in which a provider or management group takes on the responsibility for providing health services to a specific group of enrollees in exchange for a set annual fee for each enrollee. The HMO can be the provider or it can contract for services with outside providers.

Health Plan—An organization that acts as an insurer for an enrolled group of members (Prospective Payment Assessment Commission, 1993).

Health Promotion—Education and/or other supportive services that assist individuals or groups to adopt healthy behaviors and/or reduce health risks, increase self-care skills, improve management of common minor ailments, use healthcare services effectively, and/or improve understanding of medical procedures and therapeutic regimens (American Hospital Association, 1991).

Health-Related Quality of Life (HRQOL)—A measure of health status that can incorporate physical, emotional, social, and role functioning; pain; and many other factors. It is usually based on the responses of patients to questions in professionally devised instruments.

Health Savings Account (HSA)—A replacement for the medical savings account and available to anyone who has a qualified high-deductible health plan and is not covered by other health insurance. Contributions up to a defined amount are tax deductible, and cash in the account is available to pay for qualified health expenditures.

Health Status—The state of health of an individual or population.

Health Technology—All procedures, devices, equipment, and drugs used in the maintenance, restoration, and promotion of health.

Health Technology Assessment—A comprehensive form of policy research that examines the technical, clinical, economic, and social consequences of the introduction and use of health technology.

Herfindahl Index—A measure of market concentration, computed as the sum of the square of firms' market shares; also called *Herfindahl-Hirschman Index*, or HHI.

High-Deductible Health Plan—Health insurance with a high deductible for which the insured individual is responsible.

Home Care—Care provided in the home for a wide variety of purposes, including health maintenance, preventive care, and substitution for acute care (Hollander & Pallan, 1995). See also HOME SUPPORT.

Home Support—Home- and community-based long-term care services provided by persons other than such professionals as nurses or rehabilitation therapists (Hollander & Pallan, 1995).

Horizontal Equity—Fairness in the treatment of individuals who are at the same level with regard to some scale (e.g., people who are equally wealthy or have the same degree of health).

Horizontal Integration—The combining under one management or ownership of two or more previously independent producers of the same type of service.

Hospice—A combination of services for terminally ill patients and their caregivers that is based on a humanistic philosophy of care.

Human Capital—Capitalized value of productive investments in individuals.

Human Capital Approach—A method of valuing outcomes that is based on lost productivity.

Implicit—A part of, but not specifically stated.

Inappropriate Care—See APPROPRIATENESS OF CARE.

Incentive—A reward for desired behavior.

Incidence—The number of new events occurring in a defined period of time.

Income Effect—The effect of a change in real income on quantity demanded.

Income Elasticity of Demand—A measure of the responsiveness (sensitivity) of quantity demanded to a change in income, calculated by percentage change in quantity demanded divided by percentage change in income.

Increasing Returns—When output increases more in proportion to input as the scale of a firm's production increases.

Incremental Cost—The additional cost resulting from a change in output by one or more than one unit.

Indemnity—A type of insurance contract in which the insurer pays for care received up to a fixed amount per episode of illness.

Independent Practice Association (IPA)—A type of health maintenance organization that contracts with independent physician practices to provide health care for the enrollees. Payment to providers is usually on a fee-for-service basis.

Indifference Curve—A curve showing all combinations of two goods or services that provide an equal amount of satisfaction and between which the consumer is indifferent.

Indigent—An individual who cannot pay for his or her own care.

Indirect Cost—In social cost accounting, the cost of time lost due to illness (i.e., resources that are not directly paid for). In hospital cost accounting, the cost of resources not directly related to patient care.

Indirect Teaching Costs—The additional costs that a teaching hospital incurs in the process of training interns and residents. These costs cannot be measured directly because they are inseparably joined with treatment costs.

Inelastic Demand—For a given percentage change in price, there is a smaller percentage change in quantity demanded.

Inferior Good—Goods or services for which income elasticity is negative; as income increases, quantity demanded of the goods or services decreases.

Informed Consent—Legal permission to provide a treatment or to release information.

Inpatient Care—Care provided to individuals lodged within a healthcare facility.

Inputs—See RESOURCES.

Insurance—A method of paying for specific types of losses that may occur; a contract between one party, the insurer, and another party, the insured.

Intensity of Care—The amount of resources and services embodied in a unit of care (e.g., a day of hospitalization, a hospital stay, or a physician visit).

Intensive Care—Care provided to patients with life-threatening conditions who require intensive treatment and continuous monitoring.

Intermediate Care Facility (ICF)—A facility providing a lower level of nursing care than a skilled nursing facility. Medicare no longer pays for ICF-level care.

Intermediate Product—Outputs that are used as inputs by other producers in another stage of production.

International Classification of Diseases, Injuries, and Causes of Death, Tenth Revision (ICD-10)—A comprehensive disease coding system developed by the World Health Organization.

International Classification of Diseases, Injuries, and Causes of Death, Tenth Revision, Clinical Modification (ICD-10-CM)—A two-part medical information coding system used in abstracting systems and for classifying patients for DRGs. The first part consists of a comprehensive list of diseases with corresponding codes compatible with the World Health Organization's list of disease codes. The second part contains procedure codes that are independent of the disease codes. ICD-10-CM was developed in the United States and based on the World Health Organization system; it is the U.S. coding standard. Some Canadian provinces also use ICD-10-CM diagnosis and procedure codes.

Intervention—A task or set of tasks performed by a health professional with the object of influencing health status by interrupting or changing the course of events in progress.

Inventory—A stock of raw materials, goods in process, and finished goods held by firms to mitigate the effects of short-term fluctuations in production or sales.

Investment—The employment of physical or human capital to create the conditions for further production.

Joint Venture—A business arrangement to share profits, losses, and control in health care, often between a hospital and physicians.

Law of Diminishing Returns—If increasing quantities of a variable factor are applied to a given quantity of fixed factors, the marginal product and average product of the variable factor will eventually decrease.

Leading Health Indicators—A set of 10 key determinants that influence health and are used to measure the health of the nation (U.S. Department of Health and Human Services, 2000).

Length of Stay—The number of days an individual remains in an institution.

Life Expectancy—An estimate of how much longer an individual with a given characteristic may be expected to live; a common measure is life expectancy at birth.

Loading Charge—The portion of an insurance premium that is over and above the amount expected to cover payment for insured services.

Long Run—A period over which all inputs can be increased, including capital stock and specialized labor.

Long-Run Cost Curve—The relation between the cost of production and volume of output or scale of plant for a period during which all inputs, including capital equipment, have sufficient time to vary.

Long-Term Care—Services that address the health, social, and personal care needs of individuals who, for one reason or another, have never developed or have lost the capacity for self-care. These services may be continuous or intermittent, but it is generally presumed that they will be delivered indefinitely.

Malpractice—Loss or injury to a patient resulting from failure of care or skill by a professional, leading to legal liability.

Managed Care—Any system of health service payment or delivery arrangements in which the health plan attempts to control or coordinate the use of health services by its enrolled members in order to contain health expenditures, improve quality, or both. Arrangements often involve a defined delivery system of providers who have some form of contractual arrangements with the plan (Physician Payment Review Commission, 1994).

Managed Care Plan—An organization providing managed care.

Managed Competition—A manner of funneling payments for health services from a collective insurance fund to competing providers (Enthoven, 1993a, 1993b; Reinhardt, 1993).

Mandate—A legal requirement that certain actions be carried out. For example, the requirement that businesses provide health insurance coverage to their employees.

Mandatory Assignment—A requirement for physicians to accept Medicare payment as payment in full for their services.

Marginal Cost (MC)—The change in cost resulting from a change in output by one unit. Because fixed costs do not change with output, marginal cost is related to variable cost only.

Marginal Productivity—The additional output due to the application of one or more units of an input or resource, holding all other inputs constant. Marginal productivity can be increasing, constant, or diminishing.

Marginal Rate of Substitution—In consumption, how much more of one product or service must be provided to compensate for giving up one unit of another product or service, if the level of satisfaction is to remain constant. In production, how much more of one factor of production must be used to compensate for the use of one less unit of another factor of production, if production is to remain constant.

Marginal Revenue (MR)—The additional revenue that a firm obtains from selling one more unit of a service.

Marginal Value Product—The money value of additional output that is produced by one extra unit of an input (e.g., labor).

Market—A network of buyers and sellers whose interaction determines the price and quantity traded of goods and services.

Market Clearing Price—The price at which quantity demanded equals quantity supplied: the equilibrium price.

Market Structure—The organizational characteristics of a market that determine the relationship of sellers to sellers, buyers to buyers, and sellers to buyers.

Medicaid—A federally aided, state-administered program that provides medical assistance to certain low-income people.

Medical Care—A component of health care. A process or activity, guided by medical practitioners, in which certain inputs or factors of production (e.g., physician services, medical instruments, and pharmaceuticals) are combined in varying quantities to yield an output (medical care services) or outcome (health status). The totality of diagnostic efforts and treatment involved in the care of patients.

Medical Devices—An apparatus, instrument, or machine used for diagnosis, treatment, or prevention that does not depend on chemical action on or within the body (distinguished from a drug).

Medical Harm—Physical injury resulting from, or contributed to by, medical care (or the absence of medical care) and requiring additional monitoring, treatment, and hospitalization or resulting in death (Conway, Federico, Stewart, & Campbell, 2011).

Medical Loss Ratio (MLR)—A percentage of the insurance premium that must be paid out to care for patients.

Medically Necessary—A medical service that a health professional has determined to be medically required, or indicated, for the diagnosis or treatment of a patient in a particular instance and not mainly for the convenience of the patient or provider.

Medicare—In the United States, a nationwide, federally administered program that covers hospital care, physician care, some related services, and prescription drugs for eligible persons age 65 and older, persons receiving Social Security disability insurance payments, and persons with end-stage renal disease or Lou Gehrig's disease. In Canada, the health insurance system that is jointly financed by the federal and provincial governments and administered by the provincial governments.

Medicare Advantage (Formerly Medicare+Choice)—A program of benefits for Medicare beneficiaries that provides choice among different types of health plans, including capitation coverage.

Medication Error—A failure in the process of drug administration that violates one of the following: right medication, right dosage, right patient, right time, or right route of administration.

Medigap—A class of insurance policies designed to cover gaps in coverage left by Medicare, such as deductibles, coinsurance, and copayments.

Money Cost—Expenditures incurred (paid out) for a given volume of output.

Monopolistic Competition—A state of monopolistic competition exists in a market if there are many sellers but each is able to achieve a certain degree of customer loyalty and thus has some influence over price.

Monopoly—A state of monopoly exists in a market if there is a single supplier. The supplier will then have control over prices in the market.

Monopsony—A single buyer in a market. The monopsonist generally uses market power to achieve a satisfactory price.

Moral Hazard—The risk to an insurer that its insureds will increase their consumption of insured services because of the reduction in the out-of-pocket price resulting from insurance coverage.

Morbidity—Illness, injury, or other than normal health. The morbidity rate is the rate of illness or injury in a population.

Mortality—Death. The mortality rate is the number of individuals who died divided by those at risk.

Most Responsible Diagnosis—The ICD-10 code identifying the disease or condition considered by the physician to be most responsible for the patient's stay in the institution. In a case in which multiple diseases or conditions may be classified as most responsible, it is the one responsible for

the greatest length of stay (Juurlink et al., 2006). This is the Canadian coding convention. For the U.S. convention, see PRINCIPAL DIAGNOSIS.

Multiproduct Firm—A firm that produces a variety of products with different specifications (e.g., types of medical services).

Natural Monopoly—An industry characterized by sufficiently large economies of scale to supply the entire market demand.

Need—A quantity of services that an expert (doctor, planner, etc.) judges that a patient or group of patients should have in order to achieve a desired level of health status (Boulding, 1966).

Network—An entity providing comprehensive, integrated health services to a defined population of individuals. Historically, a network was associated with a health maintenance organization composed of several different medical groups under contract to provide care to enrollees; currently, it refers to a broader set of arrangements than just HMOs.

Noncompliance—Failure or refusal of a patient to take medications as instructed or follow through on recommended or prescribed therapy.

Normal Good—A good for which income elasticity is positive; the higher the income, the greater the quantity of the goods or services demanded.

Normal Profits—The opportunity cost of capital and the risk taking needed to keep the owners in the industry.

Not For Profit—A not-for-profit organization has as its prime purpose the provision of services to a specified population rather than the earning of profits for shareholders. The term *not-for-profit organization* is being replaced with *tax-exempt organization* to decrease confusion regarding the role of normal profits in the organization and its mislabeling as nonprofit. Every organization must make some profit if it is to survive and grow in the long run.

Nursing Home—An institution providing supervised, personal care for people who are not ill enough to require hospitalization in an acute care or auxiliary hospital but who require assistance with the activities of daily living.

Oligopoly—An industry that contains two or more firms, at least one of which produces a significant portion of the industry's total output.

Open Access Plan—The beneficiary or member of a health plan can go directly to a healthcare specialist without going through a gatekeeper.

Open Enrollment Period—A limited time period during which individuals are given the opportunity to enroll in a health insurance plan without medical screening and without regard to health status.

Opportunity Cost—The value of the alternative use of resources that was highest valued but not selected. With some exceptions (e.g., when resources are overpaid), this equals the market value of all resources used to produce a given volume of output.

Outlier—A patient who has a long length of stay (or a long length of treatment) or generates unusually high costs, compared with other patients with the same diagnosis.

Out of Area—Beyond the geographical service area of a managed care plan, as well as those providers who are not participating in the plan. Services of these providers are usually covered only for emergency or urgent care.

Out of Plan—Either providers or services that are not part of the enrollee's health plan.

Out-of-Pocket Price—The price that is directly paid for healthcare services by the consumer and is not subsequently recovered from an insurer or government. The out-of-pocket price is the burden that falls directly on the consumer as a result of his or her use of medical care.

Outpatient Care—Hospital-provided care that does not involve an overnight stay.

Output—The goods and services that result from the process of production; an activity or process during which a patient is treated or "cared for" by healthcare resources with the object of improving the patient's health.

Pareto Optimality—A situation in which it is not possible to reallocate production or consumption activities to make someone better off without simultaneously making someone else worse off.

Patient—A person who is receiving services from a healthcare provider.

Patient Care—The totality of diagnostic, treatment, and preventive services provided to an individual to meet his or her physical, mental, social, and spiritual needs.

Patient-Centered Care—Care that takes into consideration the patient's preferences, values, lifestyle, family, and friends; care approached from the patient's point of view.

Patient-Centered Medical Home—A team-based model of care led by a personal physician who provides continuous and coordinated care throughout a patient's lifetime to maximize health outcomes.

Patient Days—The number of days that patients are under inpatient hospital or nursing home care during a year.

Patient Empowerment—Enabling individuals to control their own health and healthcare decisions.

Patient Protection and Affordable Care Act—On March 23, 2010, President Obama signed into law the Patient Protection and Affordable Care Act. This law put in place comprehensive health insurance reforms to be rolled out over 4 years and beyond, with most of the changes having taken place by 2014. Challenges have been lodged against the bill, including hearings by the Supreme Court, which has upheld the constitutionality of the law.

Patient Safety—The protection of patients from injury and illness during the provision of healthcare services.

Pay For Performance (P4P)—A model of payment for healthcare services designed to offer incentives to providers to improve quality and reduce costs, either through payment of bonuses for meeting a target or through withholding payments for failure to meet a target.

Peer Review—Review of performance by individuals from the same discipline and with essentially equal qualifications (peers).

Per Capita Payment—A fixed annual payment per person made to a provider or health maintenance organization. The totality of payments is intended to cover the cost of care for all enrollees during the year.

Per Diem Payment—A flat-rate payment to a hospital or other institution for each day the patient is an inpatient in the institution.

Perfect Competition—A market structure in which all firms are price takers and in which there is freedom of entry into and exit from the industry.

Perspective—The viewpoint (of the person or group) with respect to which economic assessment is taken.

Plant—A single facility engaged in production. See also FIRM.

Point Elasticity—A measure of the responsiveness of quantity to price at a particular point on the demand curve.

Point of Diminishing Average Productivity—The level of output at which average product reaches a maximum.

Point of Diminishing Marginal Productivity—The level of output at which marginal product reaches a maximum.

Point-of-Service Plan (POS)—A health maintenance organization plan that allows members to use providers not on the organization's panel at the time (and each time) service is needed. To gain access to such providers, members must pay an added premium or additional out-of-pocket payment.

Population—A group of individuals occupying a specified area at the same time.

Portability—The ability of a beneficiary to move from one employer to another without loss of benefits or having to go through a waiting period for coverage.

Potential Years of Life Lost (PYLL)—The sum of years that a group of individuals would have lived had they not died prematurely.

Preadmission Certification—The prospective review and evaluation of proposed elective hospital admissions using acceptable medical criteria as the standard for determining the appropriateness of the site or level of care and certifying the length of stay required (Scheffler et al., 1991).

Predatory Pricing—A practice by insurers of giving low premiums to a low-risk small group or individual and then raising premiums when the insured file claims; also called *churning the books.*

Preexisting Condition—A physical or mental condition discovered before an individual applies for health insurance, often leading to the insurance company denying coverage for the individual or condition or requiring a waiting period before the condition is covered.

Preferred Provider Organization (PPO)—An arrangement in which a group of health providers agrees to offer services to a defined group of patients at an agreed-upon rate for each service (Ermann, deLissovoy, Gabel, & Rice, 1986).

Premium—The payment made to an insurance company in return for insurance coverage.

Prepaid Group Practice (PGP)—A group practice that charges patients on an annual per capita basis and bears the risk for providing the insured services.

Present On Admission (POA)—A diagnosis, condition, disease, or cause of injury that an individual had at the time of admission to the hospital.

Prevalence—The number of events or cases present in a given population at a given time.

Prevention—Any intervention that reduces the likelihood that a disease or disorder will affect an individual or that interrupts or slows the progress of the disorder. Primary prevention reduces the likelihood that a particular disease or disorder will develop in a person. Secondary prevention interrupts or minimizes the progress of a disease or irreversible damage from a disease by early detection and treatment. Tertiary prevention slows the progress of the disease and reduces the resultant disability through treatment of established diseases (Spitzer, 1990).

Preventive Medicine—That aspect of the physician's practice in which he or she applies, to individual patients, the knowledge and techniques from medical, social, and behavioral science to promote and maintain health and well-being and prevent disease or its progression (Hilleboe, 1971; Last, 1988).

Price—An amount of money paid or received per unit of a service or commodity.

Price Ceiling—A government-imposed maximum permitted price at which a good or service may be sold.

Price Discrimination—The charging of different prices for the same product to different customers made possible by the inability of consumers to resell the product to one another. The charging of different prices is usually due to the existence of different demand conditions for different groups of customers.

Price Fixing—When two or more competitors agree on prices.

Price Floor—A government-imposed minimum permitted price at which goods or services may be sold.

Price Taker—A supplier that has no influence over the price of the goods or services it sells; the supplier can alter its rate of production and sales without significantly influencing the market price of its product.

Primary Care—A type of medical care that emphasizes first-contact care and assumes ongoing responsibility for the patient in health maintenance and therapy for illness. Primary care is comprehensive in scope and includes overall coordination of treatment of the patient's health problems.

Principal—The person in whose interests an agent is contracted to act.

Principal Diagnosis—The diagnosis that, after investigation, is found to have been responsible for the patient's admission to the hospital. This is the U.S. coding convention. For example, if a patient is admitted to the hospital for a minor TURP (transurethral resection of the prostate) procedure and it is discovered that he has carcinoma of the lung, the prostate diagnosis would be the one coded under this convention. For the Canadian convention, see MOST RESPONSIBLE DIAGNOSIS.

Principle of Substitution—The method of production will change if the relative prices of inputs change, with relatively more of the less expensive input and relatively less of the more expensive input being used.

Procedure—An operative or nonoperative intervention or course of action designed to improve the health of an individual.

Producer Surplus—The difference between the total amount that producers receive for all units sold and the total variable cost of producing the goods or services.

Product Differentiation—The existence of similar, but not identical, products sold by a single industry.

Production—The act of combining resources to yield output.

Production Function—A quantitative relationship expressing how outputs vary when the quantity of inputs changes. Also called *production relation*.

Production Possibility Boundary—A curve that shows alternative combinations of goods and services that can be attained if all available resources are used; the boundary between attainable and unattainable output combinations.

Productivity—The ratio of physical inputs to physical outputs. The inputs can be one single input (e.g., labor), with others held constant, or all inputs combined.

Productivity Efficiency—The production of any output at the lowest attainable cost for that level of output.

Products of Ambulatory Care (PAC)—An ambulatory care classification system developed in New York State primarily for the funding of nonsurgical, nonemergency ambulatory care visits, based on body parts and purpose of visit (Tenan et al., 1988).

Products of Ambulatory Surgery (PAS)—An ambulatory surgery classification system developed in New York State for funding ambulatory surgery procedures, based on similar resource-using procedures (Kelly, Fillmore, Tenan, & Miller, 1990).

Profit—Total revenue minus total cost. Accounting profit is defined as total revenue for a period's sales minus costs matched to those sales. Economic profit is total revenue minus economic costs.

Progressive Tax—A tax that takes a higher percentage of income the higher the level of income.

Prospective Payment—Payment to providers based on predetermined rates unrelated to current or past costs of the individual provider.

Provider—A supplier of healthcare services.

Public Health—The combination of science, practical skills, and beliefs that are directed to the maintenance and improvement of the population's health. It is one of the efforts organized by society to protect, promote, and restore the people's health through collective or social actions (Last, 1988).

Quality-Adjusted Life Year (QALY)—A numerical assessment of the proportion of an individual's state of full health experienced over a year. QALY values generally range from 0 (assigned to death) to 1 (full health), although certain states of health can be valued at less than 0. QALY values can be directly derived from individuals' utility measurements or can be based on existing values of health states.

Quality of Care—The degree to which the process of medical care increases the probability of outcomes desired by patients and reduces the probability of undesired outcomes, given the state of medical knowledge (U.S. Congress, 1988).

Quality of Life (QOL)—The degree to which an individual enjoys everything. It has been defined, by a philosopher, as the possession and enjoyment of all the real goods in the right order and proportion. See also HEALTH-RELATED QUALITY OF LIFE and HEALTH STATUS.

Quantity Demanded—The quantity of goods or services that an individual or group is willing to buy at one specific rate during a specified time; a change in quantity demanded refers to a movement along a given demand curve in response to a change in price.

Quantity Exchanged—The identical amount of goods or services that individuals actually purchase and producers actually sell in some time period.

Quantity Supplied—The amount of goods or services a supplier or market is willing to supply at any one price during a specified time; a change in quantity supplied refers to a movement along a given supply curve in response to a change in price.

Rate—The price per unit charged by an institution for its services.

Rate of Return—The ratio of net profits earned by a firm to total invested capital.

Rate Review—Review by a regulatory agency of a budget and financial picture in order to determine the reasonableness of the proposed rate change.

Rate Setting—The setting of institutional prices by a paying or regulatory agency.

Rationing—The process of making choices regarding who will receive scarce resources.

Real Income—Income expressed in terms of the purchasing power of money income; the quantity of goods and services that can be purchased with money income.

Referral—The sending of a patient by one physician (the referring physician) to another physician (or some other service), either for consultation or for care.

Refined Diagnosis-Related Groups (RDRGs)—Also called *refined group numbers* (RGNs). A classification system in which resource-use patterns and secondary diagnoses are used to refine the assignment of patients to severity classes (RDRGs).

Regression Analysis—The quantitative measure of the systematic relationship among two or more variables.

Regressive Tax—A tax that takes a lower percentage of income the higher the level of income.

Regulation—A law or rule imposing government or government-mandated standards and significant economic responsibilities on individuals or organizations outside the government establishment. The process carried out by the government or mandated agencies through such means as setting or approving prices, rates, fares, profits, interest rates, and wages; awarding licenses, certificates, and permits; devising safety rules; setting quality levels; enacting public disclosure of financial information regulations; and enacting prohibitions against price, racial, religious, or sexual discrimination (Khemani & Shapiro, 1993).

Reimbursement—The payment made by an insurer to a provider for specific services provided to an insured patient. Reimbursement is usually associated with payments based on a service-by-service or patient-by-patient basis.

Relative Price—The ratio of the money price of one product or service to the money price of another product or service; a ratio of two absolute prices.

Relative Value—A value placed on a specific unit of service (e.g., a follow-up office visit, a blood test, or an inpatient cholecystectomy) expressed in relation to some standard (e.g., a minute of lab test time or physician care).

Resource Allocation—The distribution of an economy's (or firm's or industry's) scarce resources of land, labor, and capital among alternative uses.

Resource-Based Relative Value Scale (RBRVS)—A resource-weighted service-classification system that aims to set resource weights according to the total relative cost of each service, including "psychological" costs of the provider, time costs, and training costs.

Resource Intensity Weights (RIW)—Canadian relative weightings for inpatient groups. RIWs combine Canadian length-of-stay and U.S. cost-per-day data to form hybrid cost-per-case weights. Separate weights are calculated for "typical" and "atypical" cases.

Resources—The means used in producing services, which can include physical capital (beds and equipment) and human capital (physicians, nurses, etc.). Also called *inputs* and *factors of production*.

Resource Utilization Groups (RUGs)—Clusters of nursing home residents, defined by residents' characteristics, that explain resource use (Fries et al., 1994).

Retrospective Payment—Payment to a provider for services provided based on actual costs incurred by the provider. Because the payment is based on costs incurred, the amount to be paid must be determined after the service has been provided (i.e., retrospectively).

Retrospective Review—A review of claims after the episode of care is concluded and the claim is submitted to the insurer (Scheffler et al., 1991).

Returns to Scale—The relationship between total output and scale of operations, which are measured as proportional increases in all resources. Because all resources are allowed to increase in proportion, this is a long-run relationship.

Revenue—Income earned from the provision of services. Gross revenues equal income earned overall, while net revenues equal income earned minus costs or expenses.

Risk—Uncertainty as to loss; in the case of health care, the loss can be due to the cost of medical treatment or other losses arising from illness. Risk can be objective (relative variations between the difference between actual and probable losses) and subjective (psychological uncertainty relating to the occurrence of an event) (Howarth, 1988). See also RISK AVERSE, RISK NEUTRAL, and RISK TAKER.

Risk Averse—A person is said to be risk averse if losses of a given amount create more disutility than the utility that comes from gains of the same amount (and so losses will tend to be avoided).

Risk Factor—A behavior or condition that, based on evidence or theory, is thought to directly influence the level of a specific health problem.

Risk Neutral—A person is said to be risk neutral if he or she values losses and gains of the same amount equally.

Risk Pooling—The sharing of the costs incurred by members of a population. The payment method can vary but will not be based on the risk of individuals.

Risk Taker—A person is said to be a risk taker if, for that person, the utility of gains is greater than the disutility of losses of equal value. A risk taker is therefore predisposed to gamble.

Safe Harbor—Assurance that a certain specified behavior or action will not result in civil or criminal penalties when done in a specified way.

Safe Harbor Regulation—Describes certain acts or behaviors that will not be illegal under a specific law, even though they might otherwise be illegal.

Safety Net Provider—A provider obligated to provide health care to patients whether or not they are able to pay for the services.

Scarce Good—A good or service for which the quantity demanded is greater than the quantity supplied.

Secondary Care—Specialist-referred care for conditions of a relatively low level of complication and risk. Secondary care can be provided in an office or hospital and can be diagnostic or therapeutic.

Second Surgical Opinion—Patients are sometimes required to get a second or even a third consulting opinion for specified nonemergency surgical procedures (Scheffler et al., 1991).

Selective Contracting—A procedure whereby an insurer can legally exclude providers from its list of participating providers (Melnick & Zwanzinger, 1988).

Self-Insurance—The assumption of risk by an individual or entity by setting aside their own resources instead of purchasing an insurance policy.

Sensitivity Analysis—Determining the extent to which the conclusions or results of a model depend on the model's assumptions.

Severity of Illness—The gravity of a patient's illness.

Severity Score—A mathematical score that expresses the severity of illness of a patient according to a predefined method.

Shortage—An excess of supply over demand at a given price.

Short Run—A period in which all of the inputs cannot be adjusted (increased or reduced). Those inputs that cannot be adjusted are called *fixed* and include capital stock. Short run

also refers to the length of time insufficient for new firms to enter a market or industry.

Short-Run Cost Curve—The relation between cost and volume of production of a plant during a short adjustment period in which only some inputs are variable (and the rest are fixed).

Side Effect—The effect of a drug or treatment that is other than the intended, desired effect.

Sign-Out Case—A patient who leaves the hospital against medical advice.

Single Payer System—A reimbursement system in which there is a single payer or one dominant payer.

Single Product Firm—A production unit that produces a single, homogeneous product.

Sin Tax—A tax on goods, services, or activities that are allegedly harmful, such as taxes on alcohol and tobacco products.

Skilled Nursing Facility (SNF)—A facility that provides skilled nursing care to residents who do not need acute hospital care but who do need inpatient professional nursing care and other social and health needs.

Social Benefit—The contribution that an activity makes to society's welfare.

Social Cost—The cost to all members of society of any activity or service. It can be the sum of private and external costs or of direct and indirect costs. It is also viewed as the value of the best alternative use of the resources available to society as valued by society.

Solo Practice—A single physician medical practice.

Specialization of Labor—The organization of production in which individual workers specialize in the production of particular goods or services (and satisfy their wants and needs by trading) rather than producing everything they consume.

Staff Model HMO—A health maintenance organization whose practitioner staff are employees of the health plan. Usually, the practitioners are paid on a salary rather than a fee-for-service basis.

Standardized Mortality Rate (SMR)—A single mortality rate for a large group of individuals who are in different age and gender categories. The total rate for the entire group is made up of the rates in different age and gender subgroups, which are weighted or averaged according to a given structure of a standard population (e.g., the population of an entire country or the population in a base year).

Stop-Loss Insurance—Insurance purchased to pay a health plan or a group of providers for costs of care for individual patients or a panel of patients over a ceiling amount; designed to protect against catastrophic claims.

Substitutes—Goods or services that compete with one another, such as aspirin and Tylenol. The direct price of one of the substitutes will cause a shift in the demand curve for the other.

Substitution Effect—The shift from one product to another as a result of a price change, after compensating for any increase or reduction in real income that accrues from the price change.

Supplier-Induced Demand—The amount of shift in the demand for services resulting from the suppliers' influence on consumers' tastes (intensity of desire for the services).

Supply—A supply curve. The quantity supplied at each price.

Supply Curve—For a single firm, the quantity the firm is willing to supply of a service at alternative prices of the commodity. For the market, the relationship between the quantity that all firms are willing to supply and alternative prices of the service.

Supply Function—For a single provider, a quantitative relationship between the quantity the supplier is willing to supply and a series of variables that influence the supplier's behavior, such as price, technology, case mix, quality, and input prices. For a market, the quantitative relationship between the quantity that all suppliers in the market are willing to supply and a series of variables that influence all of the suppliers' behavior, including price, technology, case mix, quality, input prices, and the number of suppliers in the market.

Surplus—For a tax-exempt firm, total revenue minus total expense (the counterpart of profit for a investor-owned firm). For a market, the excess of quantity supplied over quantity demanded at a given price.

Tastes—Consumer preferences for goods and services expressed in terms of an index of satisfaction or utility. Taste is a catchall concept for everything other than prices and incomes that affect demand, including health status, age, gender, level of education, and so on.

Technology—See HEALTH TECHNOLOGY.

Technology Assessment—See HEALTH TECHNOLOGY ASSESSMENT.

Tertiary Care—Highly specialized care administered to patients who have complicated conditions or require high-risk pharmaceutical treatments or surgery. Tertiary care is provided in a setting that houses high-technology services, specialists and subspecialists, and intensive care and other highly specialized services.

Third-Party Payment—Payment by a private insurer or government to a medical provider for care given to a patient.

Time Cost—The value of time required to conduct an activity. This variable has two components: value per unit of time and time actually spent in the activity. Value per unit of time is taken as equivalent to lost earnings or the value placed on foregone leisure activities.

Total Costs (TC)—The sum of fixed and variable costs. All of the costs required to produce a specified level of output.

Total Fixed Costs (TFC)—All of the fixed costs required to produce a specified level of output.

Total Product—The total amount of output produced.

Total Variable Costs (TVC)—All of the variable costs required to produce a specified level of output.

Transaction Costs—The costs of reaching an agreement and coordinating activity among participants in a market. These include the costs of searching for potential buyers or sellers and for product quality and cost; negotiating an agreement; monitoring that the agreement conditions are met; and enforcing the terms of the agreement.

Transfer Case—A hospital inpatient who is admitted from or discharged to another institution.

Transfer Payment—A payment made to an individual or institution that does not arise out of current productive activity.

Trim Point—A point, calculated using a statistical formula, applied to all lengths of stays (or cost per case) within a single DRG (or CMG) in order to separate outlier cases from the rest.

Typical Patient—A patient who receives a full, successful course of treatment in a single institution and is discharged when he or she no longer requires acute care services.

Unit Costs—Costs per unit of output, equal to total costs divided by total output.

Utility—An index comparing various levels of an individual's satisfaction with alternative quantities of specified goods, services, or situations under certainty. The index that allows the quantification of differences between the levels is called *cardinal utility* (Pigou, 1920). A ranking of alternative bundles of goods and services under certainty, on the basis of better, equal, or worse, with no indication as to degrees of satisfaction (ordinal utility). A ranking of alternative risky situations on the basis of an individual's own preferences regarding probabilities—von Neumann–Morgenstern utility (Torrance et al., 1996).

Utilization—The actual use of services by consumers (the services must be demanded and supplied).

Utilization Management—A set of techniques used by or on behalf of purchasers of healthcare benefits to manage healthcare costs by influencing patient care decision making through case-by-case assessments of the appropriateness of care prior to provision (Gray & Field, 1989).

Utilization Review (UR)—The examination and evaluation of the efficiency and appropriateness of any healthcare service that has already been provided.

Value-Added—Reflects the position that an activity performed on a given product or service has increased its value.

Value-Added Tax (VAT)—A tax imposed on goods and services at each stage of production.

Value-Based Purchasing—Obtaining the highest quality health care at the most reasonable price; links payment for care to the quality of care and rewards cost-effective practices.

Value-Driven Health Care—A healthcare system in which price and quality are made visible (transparent) so purchasers of care can make choices based on value.

Value Judgment—A pronouncement that states or implies that something is desirable (or undesirable) and is not derived from any technical or objective data but instead from considerations of ultimate value— that is, ethical considerations (Nath, 1969).

Variable Costs—Costs that change in response to changes in output. Variable costs can be expressed as total, average, or marginal.

Variable Inputs—Inputs that can vary in quantity during a specified time period.

Vertical Equity—Fairness in the treatment of individuals who are at different levels with regard to some scale (e.g., people who fall into different income classes).

Vertical Integration—The combining under one management of activities at different stages of the production process.

Virtual Merger—A loosely defined concept in which healthcare organizations agree to cooperate in some areas in which they had previously competed.

Volume—The number of cases (or other service units) provided.

Wants—Consumer tastes or desires.

Wealth—The sum of all of the valuable assets owned minus liabilities.

Willingness-to-Pay Approach—A method of valuing an outcome that is based on the consumer's own preferences.

Windfall Profits—A change in profits that arises out of an unanticipated change in market conditions.

X-Inefficiency—The use of resources at a lower level of productivity than is possible, even if they are allocated efficiently, so that the economy is at a point inside its production possibility curve.

REFERENCES

American Hospital Association. (1991). *AHA guide*. Chicago, IL: Author.

Boulding, K. E. (1966). The concept of need for health services. *Milbank Memorial Fund Quarterly, 44*(4), 202–223.

Burwell, B. O., & Crown, W. H. (1994). *Public financing of long-term care: Federal and state roles*. Washington, DC: Office of the Assistant Secretary for Planning and Evaluation, U.S. Department of Health and Human Services.

Canada Health Act, RSC 1985, c. C-6. Retrieved from www.canlii.org/en/ca/laws/stat/rsc-1985-c-c-6/latest/rsc-1985-c-c-6.html

Centers for Medicare and Medicaid Services. (2015). *Accountable care organizations (ACO)*. Retrieved from www.cms.gov/Medicare/Medicare-Fee-for-Service-Payment/ACO/index .html?redirect=/ACO/

Conway, J., Federico, F., Stewart, K., & Campbell, M. J. (2011). *Respectful management of serious clinical adverse events* (2nd ed., IHI Innovation Series White Paper). Cambridge MA: Institute for Healthcare Improvement.

Due, J. F. (1957). *Government finance: Economics of the public sector*. Homewood, IL: R. D. Irwin.

Enthoven, A. C. (1993a). Achieving effective cost control in comprehensive health care reform: The Jackson Hole "managed care managed competition" approach. *Health PAC Bulletin, 23*(1), 13–15.

Enthoven, A. C. (1993b). The history and principles of managed competition. *Health Affairs, 12*(Suppl 1), 24–48.

Ermann, D., deLissovoy, G., Gabel, J., & Rice, T. (1986). Preferred provider organizations: Issues for employers. *Health Care Management Review, 11*(4), 26–36.

Fetter, R. B. (1992). Hospital payment based on diagnosis-related groups. *Journal of the Society for Health Systems, 3*(4), 4–15.

Fries, B. E., Schneider, D. P., Foley, W. J., Gavazzi, M., Burke, R., & Cornelius, E. (1994). Refining a case-mix measure for nursing homes: Resource utilization groups (RUG-III). *Medical Care, 32*(7), 668–685.

Government of Saskatchewan. (1993). *The Occupational Health and Safety Act, 1993, Chapter 0–1.1*. Saskatchewan, Canada: Queen's Printer.

Grad, F. P. (2002). The preamble of the Constitution of the World Health Organization. *Bulletin of the World Health Organization, 80*(12), 981–984.

Gray, B. H., & Field, M. J. (Eds.). (1989). *Controlling costs and changing patient care? The role of utilization management*. Washington, DC: National Academy Press.

Hilleboe, H. E. (1971). Modern concepts of prevention in community health. *American Journal of Public Health, 61*(5), 1000–1006.

Hollander, M. J., & Pallan, P. (1995). The British Columbia Continuing Care system: Service delivery and resource planning. *Aging Clinical and Experimental Research, 7*(2), 94–109.

Hornbrook, M. C., Hurtado, A. V., & Johnson, R. E. (1985). Health care episodes: Definition, measurement and use. *Medical Care Review, 42*(2), 163–218.

Howarth, C. I. (1988). The relationship between objective risk, subjective risk and behaviour. *Ergonomics, 31*(4), 527–535.

Juurlink, D., Preyra, C., Croxford, R., Chong, A., Austin, P., Tu, J., & Laupacis, A. (2006). *Canadian Institute for Health Information Discharge Abstract Database: A validation study.* Toronto, Canada: Institute for Clinical Evaluative Sciences.

Kelly, W. P., Fillmore, H., Tenan, P. M., & Miller, H. C. (1990). The classification of resource use in ambulatory surgery: The products of ambulatory surgery. *Journal of Ambulatory Care Management, 13*(1), 55–63.

Khemani, R. S., & Shapiro, D. M. (1993). *Glossary of industrial organisation economics and competition law.* Paris, France: Organisation for Economic Co-operation and Development.

Last, J. M. (1988). The future of health in Canada. *Canadian Journal of Public Health, 79*(3), 147–149.

Melnick, G. A., & Zwanziger, J. (1988). Hospital behavior under competition and cost-containment policies: The California experience, 1980 to 1985. *Journal of the American Medical Association, 260*(18), 2669–2675.

Nath, S. K. (1969). *A reappraisal of welfare economics.* London, England: Routledge & Kegan Paul.

Physician Payment Review Commission. (1994). *Annual report to Congress.* Washington, DC: Author.

Pigou, A. C. (1920). *The economics of welfare.* London, England: Macmillan.

Prospective Payment Assessment Commission. (1993). *Report and recommendations to the Congress.* Washington, DC: Author.

Reinhardt, U. E. (1993). Comment on the Jackson Hole initiatives for a twenty-first century American health care system. *Health Economics, 2*(1), 7–14.

Scheffler, R., Sullivan, S. D., & Ko, T. H. (1991). The impact of Blue Cross and Blue Shield plan utilization management programs, 1980–1988. *Inquiry, 28*(3), 263–275.

Spitzer, P. G. (1990). Building a model for the development of better health-care systems. *Health Informatics, 7*(12), 42–44.

Starfield, B., Weiner, J., Mumford, L., & Steinwachs, D. (1991). Ambulatory care groups: A categorization of diagnoses for research and management. *Health Services Research, 26*(1), 53–74.

Stokes, J., III, Noren, J., & Shindell, S. (1982). Definition of terms and concepts applicable to clinical preventive medicine. *Journal of Community Health, 8*(1), 33–41.

Tenan, P. M., Fillmore, H. H., Caress, B., Kelly, W. P., Nelson, H., Graziano, D., & Johnson, S. C. (1988). PACs: Classifying ambulatory care patients and services for clinical and financial management. *Journal of Ambulatory Care Management, 11*(3), 36–53.

Torrance, G. W., Feeny, D. H., Furlong, W. J., Barr, R. D., Zhang, Y., & Wang, Q. (1996). Multiattribute utility function for a comprehensive health status classification system: Health Utilities Index Mark 2. *Medical Care, 34*(7), 702–722.

U.S. Congress, Office of Technology Assessment. (1988). *The quality of medical care: Information for consumers* (OTA-I-I-386). Washington, DC: U.S. Government Printing Office.

U.S. Department of Health and Human Services. (2000). *Healthy People 2010: Understanding and improving health* (2nd ed.). Washington, DC: U.S. Government Printing Office.

Index

Note: Page numbers followed with *f* and *t* refer to figures and tables respectively